UNIX*
— the Book

M.F. <u>Banahan</u>, B.Tech., M.Sc.
and
A. Rutter, B.Tech., M.Sc.

Sigma Technical Press

*UNIX is a registered Trade Mark of Bell Laboratories

ISBN: 0 905104 21 8

Published by:

Sigma Technical Press, 5 Alton Road
Wilmslow, Cheshire, SK9 5DY, UK

Typesetting and copy preparation by H Charlesworth & Co Ltd
using tapes prepared on The UNIX Operating System

Printed and bound by H Charlesworth & Co Ltd, Huddersfield

Distributed by:

John Wiley & Sons Ltd, Baffins Lane
Chichester, Sussex, PO19 1UD, UK

Contents

The authors would like to thank Nigel Martin of University College, London for his contribution of Chapter 7.

Introduction

This is a book about the UNIX operating system and the 'lookalikes' that imitate it.

UNIX was first developed in the early 1970s at Bell Laboratories in the USA. Fed up with battling against cumbersome and awkward operating systems, the originators of UNIX tried to design and build a system that they would enjoy using. Many people would say that the attempt was successful.

Various releases of UNIX were made available to colleges and universities where the software became very popular, enjoying a cult status in some places. The release of UNIX Version 7 in 1978 and System III in 1982 heralded the beginning of the widespread use of UNIX in non-academic applications.

Why the popularity? There are two reasons. First must be the portability of UNIX, the fact that UNIX already runs on so many different makes of computer. Write your programs in a portable language, say COBOL, FORTRAN77 or C (the language UNIX itself is written in), get them working under UNIX and you're confident that they'll work on any other computer running UNIX **without any changes!** From huge IBM mainframes to tiny microprocessors the software environment will be the same: a powerful argument for a standard operating system. From the computer user's point of view this is ideal – learn just one system properly and forget about the others. Not having to spend months learning a new system every time you move from one computer to another is a dream that can only be appreciated if you've ever had to do it the hard way.

The second reason for UNIX's popularity is simply that it's so good! Even without the benefit of portability, when it was only running on PDP-11 computers, in the days when it wasn't a realistic commercial proposition, UNIX was eagerly sought by academic users. UNIX was the first simple, modular, flexible and well-structured operating system that would run on a minicomputer. Users of UNIX have a wide range of software tools at their disposal, tools that can be combined and manipulated to perform such a wide variety of jobs that users of the system can carry out sophisticated tasks without even writing programs. The standard UNIX toolkit has programs ranging in complexity from the simple utility that counts the number of words in a file to the 'compiler compiler' which takes a formal grammar and produces half of a compiler for that language. The tools, the filestore, the input/output system, the very powerful command language (a programming language in its own right) - it's these that combine to make UNIX fun to use and a highly productive environment for the production of software.

This book is written for people who either want to use UNIX or just find out what it is and how it works. The early chapters are for the 'casual' user of UNIX, showing you, in what we hope is a friendly and informative way, how to log in, use the command language, use the editor, write programs and use the software tools. The later chapters are for the serious user of UNIX; they explain in detail what's actually going on when you use the system, and provide a considerable body of useful reference material. We've already found the draft copies very convenient for our own use, especially when there isn't a copy of the system manuals within easy reach.

We don't pretend to replace the UNIX system manuals, what we do try to do is give as much information in as readable and concise a way as is practical. We've been careful to give examples where we think they're needed, and to try wherever possible to explain what we find is hard to read in the manuals themselves. We've tried to complement the 'official' documentation and to provide a handy pocket reference for the beginner who expects to use UNIX a lot in the future.

We've used the Bell Laboratories UNIX Version 7 as our standard throughout. Of the copycat systems available at the moment only a few differ substantially from this standard; if you're thinking of buying a UNIX-like system and are concerned about its compatibility with other systems, we suggest that you ask the supplier concerned to let you have the comments of the European UNIX User Group on the version being offered.

We hope this book helps you to have as much fun as we've had from using UNIX.

Mike Banahan,
Andy Rutter.
University of Bradford.

Chapter 1

In the beginning

1.1. Preamble

This is the first of the introductory chapters. With the four that follow, it forms a step-by-step guide to the use of a UNIX system from a practical point of view. At times, these chapters will have to mention the use of a technique without being in a position to explain fully the significance of what is being done; this is a consequence of the 'practice first, theory later' approach that we feel is the best way of coming to grips with something like UNIX. Some users will be quite happy never to bother with all the reasons for things being the way they are – these users still get a lot of work done – but if you aren't sure what's going on, you're bound to get a surprise sometimes. For this reason we try to explain as much as seems possible at every point.

Each new point builds on the experience gained already and expects an understanding of the previous ones, so you'll find it difficult to appreciate things if you insist on picking and nibbling at these early chapters. We recommend this style of reading:

1. Take the chapters in order.
2. Read each one, then try the exercises.
3. Experiment!

Experimenting is a good way of learning provided that you are in a position to interpret the results. This is when access to someone with experience becomes invaluable, but be sure that they know what they are talking about! Pick your guru carefully, like a horse. Go for one with an alert expression, bright eyes and a quiet voice: if they type with ten fingers it's a good sign. Avoid at all costs the terminal freak; bags under the eyes, a glazed expression and an unwashed appearance are signs to beware of. This breed thinks it knows everything and will tell you so interminably. Even if they do know it all, they generally can't explain anything without reference to even more complicated examples that you won't understand either.

Occasionally you may come across the UNIX 'expert'. Too old and weary for anything of use, these creatures are put out to grass, where they immediately elect themselves to committees and start writing books. If you have one of these, be kind to it, buy it drinks and treat it with respect. On no account ask it for advice, for its language is no longer the same as yours.

1.2. Logging in

Before you can do anything useful with UNIX you have to 'log in' to the system. This means you will need:

a UNIX system
a terminal
a username (sometimes called a 'login' name)

The usernames are allocated by the manager of the computer system or an approved minion. It's not a difficult job to persuade the system to accept a new user, but if **you** are the manager as well as a brand new user with no UNIX experience then you are going to have a lot to learn.

For the moment we'll assume that you have been given a username and that you can find a terminal connected to UNIX. Most terminals nowadays are like television sets and are known as CRTs (Cathode Ray Tubes). In Europe a CRT is known as a VDU, or Visual Display Unit. We shall use the term CRT for the remainder of this chapter.

If you're working on a printing-on-paper terminal then you will have grounds for annoyance when we refer to its screen – please be patient. Having located a terminal and made sure that it's switched on you have to persuade it to say:

Login:

to you. With a bit of luck it'll be in this state already, but there's always the chance that whoever used it last either didn't bother or forgot to log out at the end of their session. If you can't get the 'Login' to appear then you will need to find another terminal or get somebody who knows the system to come and work some magic†.

In reply to 'Login' you type your username and press the 'return' key. Some terminals call it 'new line'. If you've got one of those, sell it. In all

---

†If you're really on your own then read through this chapter to pick up some ideas. By the end you will know enough about the system to try to pummel the terminal into letting you log in unless something is broken.

normal conditions UNIX won't act on anything you type until you have pressed the 'return' key, which indicates to the system that a line has just been completed. Occasionally beginners forget this and type in a line then sit back, proudly, waiting for results that they will never see. They missed the 'return' key. You won't, will you?

If you get the username right, then the system will either ask for your password or let you in straight away. Should it be awkward and demand a password then you will probably have been given the password along with your username. Type it in followed by 'return'; don't be surprised that it doesn't get printed back to you, this is to stop evil people peering over your shoulder and stealing it.

On the other hand you might have got your username wrong. Then you get the friendly message

    Login incorrect.
    Login:

and you can try again. If a couple of repeated attempts meet with failure then something is obviously going wrong. At this point you might find it helps to know that UNIX prefers to work in lower case and might not take kindly to a username typed in capitals, also that usernames don't usually have any spaces in them. Our system has lots of users with usernames like 'abc123'. Some of the users think that 'abc 123' would mean the same thing, but they're wrong.

Successfully logging in is followed by the system's message of the day and perhaps a couple of other things. Have a look at them, they might be important. Here is a typical login on our machine.

    Login: mike
    Password:
    WARNING: System closing down at 13:00 for approx one hour
             whilst the disc packs are being cleaned.
    You have mail.
    $

The 'You have mail.' message can safely be forgotten for the moment, but if it's nearly 13:00 then you could get slung off soon so this means you should check the time. You can see that the password wasn't printed (echoed is the term) when the user logged in.

After the messages you get the *prompt*. The prompt means you can type in commands, on our system the prompt is a '$' sign but other systems may use other prompts. If your system comes up with something really annoying like 'Ready' or 'ok', don't worry, you'll soon find out how

3

to change it. In any case they all mean the same thing: you are being invited to type in commands. One of the simplest of these is **echo**.

1.3. A simple command

Echo types back to you whatever you typed in. Try typing this in at a terminal – it will encourage you if you're feeling lost and need some comfort:

echo hi there

Don't forget the return key! The system will reply:

hi there

Sweet, isn't it?

You have just given a command that is typical of the way UNIX is used. The command was typed on a single line (typical) and consisted of the 'command' **echo** followed by the 'arguments' 'hi' and 'there'. The arguments were separated by spaces†, again typical. We will be using the terms 'command' and 'argument' a lot from now on, so this is a good time to think about them. Except in rare cases UNIX commands are always given on a single line and consist of a command name followed by a list of arguments. The list of arguments may be of zero length in some cases – like the case when there aren't any. The command and the arguments are separated from each other by spaces unlike a lot of other systems which use either commas or, worse, a combination of both. Re-read this paragraph and make sure you understand it, then look at the three examples below. In each case the command is **echo**; the first example having no arguments, the second has one and the third has three.

echo
echo 1argument
echo with 3 arguments

One consequence of the fact that arguments are separated by spaces is that spaces themselves cannot be included in an argument; they would automatically split it up. This is quite unacceptable and isn't actually true. Throughout UNIX the rule is 'of course you can', rather than 'not on your life', so a restriction like that is immediately given the heave-ho. You want spaces in your arguments? Well, it's easy but this isn't the place to explain how to do it, you'll have to wait a little while yet. A warning about

†The 'tab' character is treated just like a space when it's on a command line.

4

arguments is in order, however. Not all of the characters in an argument are passed on to the command without some jiggery pokery being done. It'll be fine if you stick to letters and digits for the present, but don't try anything else unless you are told to. Certain characters will cause results you don't expect!

1.4. The Shell

We really must dispel any misunderstandings about what you have just done. You were **not,** in any shape or form, 'talking to UNIX'. Trying to talk to UNIX is about as profitable as talking to the clouds and a good deal more difficult since at least clouds are visible and identifiable. We defy you to open up the processor cabinet and point to 'the UNIX' in there.

What actually happened, although quite simple, is fundamental to the philosophy of UNIX. Everything done in a UNIX system is carried out by quite ordinary programs, each running in the same way as any other. Some are privileged, it's true, the thing that logs you in (called **login)** has special powers, but the majority are very ordinary. When you log in **login** checks that your username and password are in order and after one or two acrobatics it simply starts a program called 'the shell' on your behalf.

The shell reads from your terminal and interprets what you type in. Usually you are typing commands, with arguments, and the shell arranges for those commands to be carried out and passes the arguments to them. **How** it does this is explained later, what matters is **what** it does. The shell, not UNIX, is interpreting your instructions. The shell, not UNIX, is initiating those commands. The commands are separate programs which run under the supervision of UNIX; they eventually terminate and then the shell gives you another prompt. **Echo** is a very simple program, written in the language 'C', which prints its arguments and terminates.

This approach to the command interpreter and the commands is a very flexible one and is rare. UNIX is one of very few operating systems which is capable of allowing users to write their own shells (the shell is just an ordinary user program) to provide any form of command language they like. It's quite possible that on your system there are several different types of shell in use for different classes of user, allowing access to different sets of commands.

1.5. The Manual

There are lots of commands available to the users logged in to UNIX. Section one of the UNIX Programmer's Manual lists most of them, together with rather terse explanations of their purpose and use. Most beginners find the style of the manual rather obscure, although experienced users tend to prefer it. If you have a copy, look up the entry in section 1 for **echo**. Alternatively, you may find that the manual is available on-line on your system. If it is then you can try the **man**†command to print the page you want. Try

    man 1 echo

and see if you get the page for **echo**. If it turns out that you do have the manual available like this, you'll want to know more about the **man** command. Get it to type its own page with

    man man

    Interpreting manual pages isn't difficult but you need to know what some of the special notation means. Each manual page is headed by the name of the command it describes, so **echo** has the heading

    ECHO(1)

meaning that the command name is **echo** and this is the entry in section one of the manual. Then comes the name of the command and a very brief explanation of what it does. The SYNOPSIS part is important; it tells you how to give the command. The synopsis for **echo** is

    echo [−n] [arg] ...

showing that to give the command you type

    echo

followed by an optional argument of '−n' and further optional arguments. In the synopsis anything enclosed in square brackets is optional and doesn't have to be supplied if you don't want it. The row of dots '...' means any number of the thing on the left: in this case it means any number of (optional) arguments. If you have got a copy, look at the manual's description of **echo** and try to interpret in the light of our description. Try the command with and without the '−n' to see what that does.

    Other information provided in a manual page will be a description of the command and how to use it, any files the command uses or maintains, any error messages it is likely to produce (diagnostics) and

---

†The commands to print the manual may or may not be available depending on your system. The name of the command may not be **man** either; try **help**.

6

finally, any known 'bugs' in the command. Whenever you see examples of a command being used, compare our use of it with it's description in the manual. This will help you to learn how to read the manual.

In several places in this book we'll refer to a command in this way

echo(1)

which will mean 'the command called **echo** which is described in section one of the manual'.

1.6. The Terminal

The terminal is your only means of communicating with the system; it's what you use to issue your commands, to inspect the results and to ponder the relics of dead programs. The terminal is the eyes and ears of your dialogue with the operating system; you need to know it well.

What about your typing? You might be one of those lucky people who never make mistakes, that select band who sit at a terminal all day long with their fingers flying over the keys and never once touching the wrong ones. You might, alternatively, be a normal human being – the sort who finds that carving inscriptions on stone looks easy by comparison with typing stuff in to a computer. UNIX has a place for you.

Unfortunately one of the most variable features of UNIX systems is the way that they elect to handle their terminals. For example, Standard UNIX doesn't treat CRTs and teletypes separately; they're all treated like teletypes. It's most annoying to watch output zooming off the top of a CRT screen at high speed when you wanted to read it, but of course on a printing terminal you get a permanent record and nothing is lost. Another niggling point is the way 'rubout' gets handled. Making mis-typed characters disappear is not particularly difficult on most CRTs – you just backspace and overtype the wrong one – but Standard UNIX thinks that backspace is a valid character and certainly doesn't rub anything out with it, so if you try it what goes in to the computer is different from what you see on the screen!

Most sites with access to the source code (the original programs) of UNIX have made changes to the terminal handling parts, most commercial suppliers of UNIX have stuck to the original standard, but how long that will last isn't clear. What results is a mildly confusing situation where the key that rubs out mistakes on one system is likely to be used to interrupt a running program on another. Fortunately most users adapt very quickly and little confusion exists.

7

There are four important 'special keys' that you, as user, will need to know about — here are their names and functions:

ERASE — rub out the last character typed.
CANCEL — cancel this entire line of input.
INTERRUPT — see later.
EOT — simulate end-of-file from a terminal; used when you log out.

The 'CANCEL' key is called 'KILL' in standard UNIX documentation, but the name has been known to be confused with the **kill** command. For this reason we've decided to rename it in the hope that we'll reduce, not increase, any confusion. The Standard UNIX versions of these characters are:

ERASE — #
CANCEL — @
INTERRUPT — the 'rubout' or 'delete' key.
EOT — control-D

To type control-D you have to press the 'control' key and then type 'd' whilst still holding down 'control'; it's just like the 'shift' key.

The choice of # for ERASE and @ for CANCEL is most odd. It's the result of a decision made so long ago that it counts as prehistory in UNIX terms, but has lingered until present times; some users seem to like it. We must admit that we don't care for it but this may be due to the fact that our system is modified and doesn't use the standard arrangement; perhaps we're biased in favour of what we are used to.

To use UNIX successfully you will need to find out what your local arrangements are. Hunt for them in your system manuals or ask a handy guru, write them down and memorise them. They're most likely to be found under tty(4), i.e. the heading of 'tty', section 4 of the manual.

The **echo** command is very useful to try out the action of ERASE, and to a lesser degree, CANCEL. Try typing

echo hello fred < ER > < ER > < ER > < ER > sailor

where < ER > means pressing your system's key for ERASE. Then press return: you should get

hello sailor

typed back to you. Do you see why? Try it with CANCEL, too.

The INTERRUPT key is used for a function common to most computer systems, even though the way it carries out that job is unusual. For the moment you can treat it as being the 'break in' key; you use it to stop the currently running command and get the shell's prompt back. Imagine that you have started compiling a huge program – it will take half an hour or so to do this (say) – when you realise that there is still a bug in it and you want to abandon the compilation. That's when you press INTERRUPT.

The last of the four keys, EOT, is used to tell a command that you've finished typing to it. Typing EOT to the prompt causes your shell to terminate and results in the 'Login:' message appearing. What it actually does is to simulate an end-of-file on your terminal which is detected by the shell; the shell then deliberately goes away. EOT is a good thing to try if you can't persuade a terminal to come up with the login message; INTERRUPT followed by EOT usually gets some sort of response even if it's only fury from the previous user whose two-hour simulation program you just wrecked. Don't be concerned if you aren't sure what end-of-file means, we'll have more to say about it later.

By now you know how to

    log in
    issue a simple command
    correct typing errors
    interrupt programs
    log out

If you're feeling happy with all this then you can go on to the next section, but we would recommend some practice with it first. In particular, logging in and out are worth trying several times. You will need enough confidence to be able to recognise that something has gone wrong if you make a mistake when you change your password.

1.7. Your Password

UNIX is the same as most multi-user operating systems as far as usernames and passwords are concerned. Usernames are used to identify individual users to the system and are tied in with the ideas of privilege and protection – which users have access to which files, which users may use which commands. Since (as you will learn) UNIX commands are themselves stored in files†, on a UNIX system the whole question of who has permission to do what is settled by the filestore and you will have wait to find out how that works.

Obviously, there's no point in having a system to protect users from

---

†Files are introduced in chapter 2.

9

one another if they just need to know each other's names and can impersonate their victims. To prevent this, each user has a secret password which they have to provide when they try to log in. Get it wrong and they don't get logged in. UNIX allows users to change their passwords to suit themselves; popular passwords tend to be the names of personal idols, sweethearts, telephone numbers and that sort of thing. Unhappily these are easy to guess and are the first things tried by people determined to work out what your password is. The choice of your password is up to you and will be determined by your circumstances. If you're the only user of a system then you may decide to do without passwords at all, an installation with a group of people working on one project (who trust each other) may have one password for the lot of them, our university installation is subject to determined assault on its security by scheming undergraduates and as a result has some highly unusual passwords.

If security is a matter for concern, here are some tips:

    choose unusual passwords
    include digits and control codes
    NEVER let anyone watch you log in
    change your password regularly
    look out for signs of intrusion

Why these rules? It's simple. An unusual password is unlikely to be guessed during casual attempts to breach your defences. Digits and control codes in a password make it highly unusual and also help to stop people from working out what you are typing if they watch while you log in. Letting people watch while you log in is dangerous insofar as they then stand a good chance of finding out the first few characters of your password. It helps them enormously if they are going to try the brute force method of password cracking, which involves trying all possible passwords. Even if somebody does find out what your password is, probably after spending a lot of time and effort on the problem, they will have to start all over again as soon as you change it. A bonus is that if they know the password is changed regularly, they might not bother in the first place, since by the time they have succeeded they could well have calculated yesterday's password which is useless to them.

How can you tell if somebody has discovered your password? UNIX systems usually keep a log of who has logged in and when, so you can look at that from time to time and see if you appear on it when you weren't (as far as you know) anywhere near a terminal. Keeping an eye on the access and modification dates of your files may give pointers to any funny business too, although it's probably too late by then.

There are some really dread methods employed by ace password crackers, who tend to look upon this as a sort of intellectual challenge: the security system was built for them to break it. Some of these are so hard to combat that their names are mentioned only in locked rooms at dead of night, and the secrets are passed amongst the initiates like some sort of pagan ritual. We have no intention whatsoever of giving any hints about these techniques, which are bad enough in the hands of the odd few who manage to think them up for themselves without there being any need for us to spread the bad news. This is in accordance with the well known military principle of security: the longer the enemy spends working out how to attack you, the less time is left to do it. We would only pause to point out that it isn't just UNIX which is vulnerable to this sort of attack; all operating systems using a username/password combination are equally at risk. There is an interesting paper on the subject which you will discover if you look hard enough.

On to changing your password then. The paragraphs before have probably frightened you and this is no bad state to be in just now. Decide what you want your password to be and **make sure you can remember it**. Forget it and you have found the path to scorn and derision. The number of lamebrains who manage to forget their password is a perpetual source of amazement to those of us who have to go and put it right for them.

The command to change your password is called **passwd**. It's an unusual command, unusual because it interacts with the user. Most UNIX commands prefer not to ask questions of the user because it would make their inclusion in 'scriptfiles' more awkward. The reasons will become apparent when you read about such things. It's more usual to give any variable parameters to commands through their arguments and only rarely interact with them through the terminal. Naturally there are some programs which are highly interactive in the way they do business, the editor is one example but it's an exception.

To invoke **passwd** login and type:

    passwd

This will result in **passwd** asking for your old password; it's checking to see if you really are who it thinks you are, in case some joker tries to change your password while you leave a terminal still logged-in. If you get that right it will ask for the new password and not echo it. You can't be sure that your typing was error-free because it doesn't echo on the screen, so you're asked to type it again. If both attempts agree **passwd** will change your password to whatever you typed in. **Passwd** tries to make you pick a password which obeys the simplest of the security rules mentioned earlier, but allows you to insist if you really want one which it doesn't like, the rules it uses are explained in its entry in section one of the manual. Here's an example of it in use; remember that the passwords the user types in are not printed back.

```
$ passwd mike
Changing password for mike
Old password:
New password:
Retype new password:
$
```

1.8. Questions

1) What are the ERASE, CANCEL, INTERRUPT and EOT keys at your site?
2) What is the difference between commands and arguments?
3) How do you separate arguments from commands and one another?
4) You have issued a command which seems to have got stuck in a loop and is producing huge quantities of output that you do not want. How do you stop it?
5) What is the shell? How does it differ from a program that you might have written yourself?
6) How do you log out of the system? Why bother?

Chapter 2

Files and Simple Commands

Now that you can successfully "log in" to UNIX, you may wish to do something useful.

2.1. Files

A file is a storage bin for information.

Many UNIX commands have the capability to create, read and/or write files of information. This information may be a program source, an executable program, a letter for text processing, payroll data, and so on. Obviously the executable program is meaningless gibberish when read by a language compiler, and you will be hard put to find a computer to execute the payroll data. Many computer systems enforce this distinction between files of information, some even differentiate between sources for different languages (eg FORTRAN and Pascal). UNIX is not so short-sighted; a file, no matter what information it contains, consists of a randomly addressable collection of characters (bytes).

UNIX imposes no restrictions on access methods, what data can be stored in a file, or what format that data should take. The significance of the contents depends entirely on the program reading the file. No naming conventions are enforced, except that most language compilers produce fixed name output files by default.

2.1.1. What's in a Name?

A filename may consist of up to 14 characters (letters, digits or otherwise). Even control characters may be used, although common sense says that you should stick to ones that actually print. Also, some characters may have special meanings, so for the moment just use names consisting of letters and digits.

2.2. The Filestore and Directories

The UNIX filestore appears as a hierarchical tree structure, each node of which comprises a file (there's a picture on the next page). Many of these nodes will have branches leading to other nodes on the tree. In this case, the node is a special type of file known as a directory; it is still, however, a file and may be read in exactly the same fashion as a file you create yourself.

As a user of UNIX you will have something called a 'home directory', the name 'home directory' is used because this is where you are placed after you login to UNIX. When you create a new file (we will explain exactly how later) the new file is made in your own directory. The only relationship between your new file and any other file of the same name that might exist in someone else's directory is that they are both different members of the same tree structure.

You may also create subdirectories of your home directory containing more files and possibly further directories. In this way you can group associated files together in one directory. User home directories generally appear as entries in the directory 'usr', which itself is an entry in the root directory '/'.

The full name of any file residing in the filestore specifies the path to be taken when searching the tree from the root directory. This full name is called the 'pathname†' of the file. UNIX pathnames consist of a number of components separated by a '/'. Each component, except the last, names a directory in which the next component resides. Thus the pathname

/bin/echo

specifies a file in the directory 'bin' which is a subdirectory of the root directory '/'. Within this directory is a file named 'echo' which is the executable version of the command **echo**. Pathnames not beginning with '/' are interpreted as starting in the current directory.

2.3. Listing Directories

Perhaps the most important thing you can do to a directory is list its contents. The ability to save files is not much use if you can't see what is there.

The **ls** command lists the contents of a particular directory, which is

---

†The UNIX filestore, its mechanism and construction is revealed in chapter 5.

14

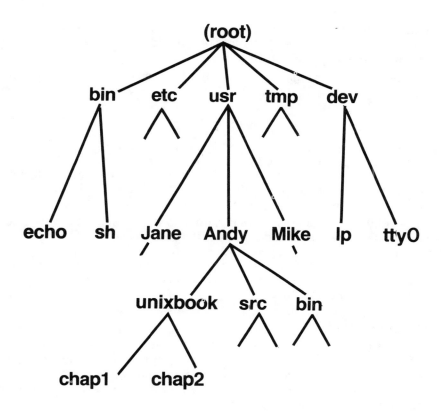

Figure 1 — Picture of filestore tree structure

the same thing as saying that it lists the names of the files which can be found in that directory (it lists the names, not the contents of those files). If you type

    ls

without a directory name as an argument then the contents of your current directory will be listed in alphabetical order. Some UNIX systems know **ls** by the names **dir** or **list**.

If this is your first login then using the **ls** command will result in the following display

    $ ls
    $

Nothing was printed, why? The logical answer is that your home directory is empty because you have not yet created any files†. This is, however, not quite strictly true as all directories, when created, are given two entries which are not normally listed by **ls**. The names of these are '.' and '..', often referred to as dot and double dot (or dot dot).

The entry '.' corresponds to the directory itself; this is the file read by **ls** when no name argument is given, as in the example above. The entry '..' refers to one level back up the tree structure toward the root of the filestore; so, '..' is the directory in which the current directory (the one we're looking at) appears as an entry. In the case of your home directory '..' will be the directory '/usr'.

To put this simply, '.' is the name of the current directory, and '..' is the name of its parent.

One of the most useful ideas used with UNIX commands is the *flag* argument, which specifies an optional capability of the command to be invoked. Flags may be combined to select a combination of options. By convention these flag arguments begin with the character '−'. **Ls** is no exception; amongst the flags it accepts are '−l' (long listing format) and '−a' (list all entries). Thus

    ls −al

in the same directory as before might produce something like

    drwxr−xr−x   2 andy   32 Dec 25 14:34 .
    drwxr−xr−x   3 bin   1168 Dec 25 14:38 ..

---

†You may find that several files were created for you when your login name was generated. Your local documentation should tell you what these files are for.

What appeared at first to be an empty directory we now discover has the two entries '.' and '..'. The date and time shown are those of the last change to these files. The 32 and 1168 are the number of characters in the files, while 'andy' and 'bin' are the owners of these files.

The 'rwxr−xr−x' tells us who has access permission on the files (more of this later), and the preceding 'd' signifies that they are directories. The numbers 2 and 3 appearing after the permissions refer to the number of 'links' to this file. UNIX allows a file to be known by many different names in different directories. These are what are called 'links'; don't worry too much about them at the moment.

2.4. Creating and Changing Directories

We said earlier that your share of the filestore consists of a home directory plus one or more subdirectories. The home directory is created by the system manager when he sets up your user name; but what are subdirectories?

It's often convenient to arrange files so that all the files related to one another are in a separate directory. The manuscript for this book was printed using the UNIX text formatting tools; all the source text was kept in a directory called 'unixbook'. This was created using

    mkdir unixbook

and after loging in to our home directory we can move to the directory 'unixbook' by typing

    cd unixbook

To get back into our home directory from 'unixbook' we type

    cd ..

because the entry '..' is a branch backwards to one directory level higher.

The command **mkdir** uses a *system call* to create the subdirectory,† entries '.' and '..' are then formed. You may create as many directories as you wish, but please be sensible about it. There will usually be a limit on the amount of filestore space allocated to individual users; directories use up this space as well as ordinary files.

The command **cd** allows you to wander around the filestore tree; it is

---

†System calls are UNIX's method of communication between user programs and the operating system.

one of the few commands that does not cause the execution of a program. The shell interprets **cd** directly and uses a system call to change its current directory to the directory given in the pathname. This is a very useful feature if you want to avoid typing full pathnames all the time. Examining figure 1, you can see that user 'jane' might access Andy's file 'chap1' using one of the following pathnames

/usr/andy/unixbook/chap1

or

../andy/unixbook/chap1

The first pathname is an absolute reference from the filestore root whilst the second is specified relative to Jane's home directory, '/usr/jane'. Either version takes time to type and would become tiresome if Jane wished to look at several files in that directory. The alternative method is to first change directory to '/usr/andy/unixbook' and then issue commands involving files contained therein (the command **cat** is explained later in the chapter).

```
$ cd /usr/andy/unixbook
$ ls −l chap1
$ cat chap2
```

You may change directory to anywhere on the filestore, providing a) you know the pathname to that directory (either full path or relative to your current position), AND b) that the filestore protection (see next section) will allow you.

If at any time you get lost on the filestore, **pwd** will tell you. The name stands for "**p**rint **w**orking **d**irectory"; **pwd** prints the complete pathname from the root to your current directory. For example, if we have just changed directory to 'unixbook' then issuing the **pwd** command would print:

/usr/andy/unixbook

2.5. Protecting your Privacy (Filestore Protection)

A good filestore system must (amongst other things) allow sharing of files between co-operating users but protect files against access by unauthorised users†.

†Reference [1], p76, 81-83

UNIX filestore protection can be broken down into the ability to read, write and/or execute a file. This protection is very important to say the least; you might get a bit upset if other people were able to erase any of your files! There are also certain system files which must be read-only — the password file for example.

UNIX provides three categories of user to whom permission to read, write and/or execute a file may be given. These categories are *user* (owner of the file), *group* (people in the same group as the owner) and *other* (everybody else). The owner of a file will be the one who created it originally, unless the ownership has been subsequently changed.

Group ownership of files is intended to aid users working together on a project by allowing them controlled access to each other's files. Members of a group will have a common group name as well as their individual login names. Users are not restricted to one group: they can be members of many groups, and whenever it suits them they can change their 'current group' to any one they have permission for. The ' − g' flag to **ls** will show the group ownership of files. Thus

        ls − lg /usr/andy/unixbook

might produce

− rw − r − − − − −	1 staff	1237	Dec	20	12:04	chapter2
− rw − r − − − − −	1 staff	56043	Dec	30	09:47	chapter5
− rw − r − − − − −	1 staff	196	Jan	4	14:32	index

showing that Andy was a member of the group 'staff' when he created these files; any other member of that group is allowed to read them.

Let's examine permissions in more detail by inspecting the "ls −l" printout for a fictitious file

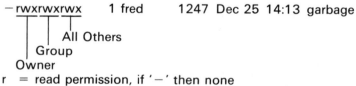

This entry shows a file called 'garbage'; it is owned by user 'fred' and has read/write/execute permission for everybody. The next example is again an ordinary file owned by 'fred'; this time only the owner has both read and write permission. Members of his group and all others have only read permission

```
$ ls −l more__garbage
−rw−r−−r−−     1 fred      684 Jan 4 11:30 more_garbage
```

Directory permissions have slightly different meanings from those for ordinary files (the '−d' flag tells **ls** to list the directory itself rather than the entries.)

```
$ ls −ld unixbook
drwxr−xr−−    2 andy      32 Nov 10 16:03 unixbook
$ ls −lgd unixbook
drwxr−xr−−    2 staff     32 Nov 10 16:03 unixbook
```

d = this is a directory, if '−' then ordinary file
r = directory contents may be listed
w = directory entries may be created or removed
x = directory entries may be accessed or the directory may be the subject of a **cd** command

Thus in the example shown above, members of group 'staff' may list the contents of this directory and access files within it. Anybody else may only list the directory contents (entries).

You may change the protection modes (permissions) on any file you own using the **chmod** command

chmod mode file ... ...

The mode is specified using either an octal number corresponding to the new mode, or a symbolic description. We will look at the symbolic form here and leave further investigation of modes until later. The symbolic expression of a protection mode takes the following general form:

[ugoa][+ − =][rwxstugo]

where:
  [ugoa]
          u : user (owner)
          g : group
          o : others
          a : all

  [+ − =]
          + : add permissions
          − : delete permissions
          = : directly replace permissions

20

[rwxstugo]
        r   : read
        w   : write
        x   : execute
        s   : set owner or group id (see chap 5)
        t   : save text (see chap 5)
        ugo : permission to be taken from the present mode

Any character, or combination of characters, may be chosen from between the square brackets. This conforms to the notation used in the UNIX manuals.

Let's see that in practice; taking our previous fictitous file 'garbage', which if you remember had its permissions set like this

    − rwxrwxrwx   1 fred   1247 Dec 25 14:13 garbage

The simplest way to protect your files from removal by other people is to prevent anyone from writing on them (*'write protect'* them). This is not completely foolproof, but will go a long way to prevent accidental removal. In order to fully protect a file, its parent directory must also be write protected. If you look back to the meaning of directory protection modes you will see that the ability to remove a file depends entirely on whether or not you can remove its directory entry, NOT on your permission to write to the file. Directory entries are the only tie between filenames and the actual data on disc; remove the entry and as far as you are concerned the file has disappeared (forever)!

To remove write permission for the group and others on file 'garbage' you type

        chmod go − w garbage

and to see the result

        ls − l garbage

which should produce something like

    − rwxr − xr − x   1 fred   1247 Feb 10 20:41 garbage

Look back to the table of symbolic expressions to see why "go − w" means 'remove write permission for group and others'.

The following example changes the permission for 'other' to nothing at all because nothing follows the ' = ' sign

        $ chmod o = garbage
        $ ls − l garbage
        − rwxr − x − − −   1 fred   1247 Feb 10 20:51 garbage
        $

21

Be VERY careful when changing permissions on directories, especially your home directory; don't forget the ability to **cd** to a directory depends upon the execute permission. Remove user execute permission and hey presto! you won't be able to log in next time you try.

2.6. Standard Input/Output and Redirection

You met the command **echo** earlier; any arguments are typed back to you onto the terminal. In UNIX terminology, **echo** is writing to the 'standard output'; the terminal keyboard is called the 'standard input'.

Most UNIX commands write to the standard output (print on the terminal), some also take their input from the keyboard (read from the standard input). One feature of the shell is the ability to redirect this input/output to or from a file.

Output from a command can be sent to a file by following the command line with the character '>' plus the name of a file where output is to go. If the file does not exist already then it is created for you. Try typing

echo Mary had a little lamb > poem

What is printed on the terminal? Nothing --we hope. The file 'poem' has just been created with 23 characters consisting of "Mary had a little lamb" followed by a line feed. It is universal in UNIX that the end of a line is denoted by a line feed character (newline).

If 'poem' had existed already then its original contents would have been thrown away. You cannot yet look at the contents of this file. Don't panic, all will be revealed. Now try

echo > junk

This time there were no arguments to **echo,** and so logically the file 'junk' will be empty. You can verify this using the "ls −l" command, which should produce something like

```
-rw-rw-rw-    1 andy     0 Dec 29 15:26 junk
-rw-rw-rw-    1 andy    23 Dec 29 15:20 poem
```

File 'junk' has indeed got a character count of zero, which shows that for a file to exist it needn't have any contents.

Information can be added to the end of a file in the same way, but this time using the characters '>>' plus a filename. Again the file is created if it did not exist already. To add a second line to the poem, type

echo Its fleece was white as snow >> poem

22

At this point you might like to see what's in the file you've been playing with. The command **cat** is commonly used to print the contents of files. (Its name arises from the ability to take many filename arguments and concatenate them.) Thus to merge several files, one after the other, into one

        cat f1 f2 f3 f4 > bigfile

and to look at the contents of 'poem' type the command "cat poem", thus

        $ cat poem
        Mary had a little lamb
        Its fleece was white as snow
        $

The redirection of standard input is just like redirection of output, but using the character '<' plus the name of the file to be read. The input to a command, after redirection, is taken from the specified file rather than from the terminal keyboard.

    For example, the command **mail** expects one argument specifying the name of a user to whom mail is to be sent. After typing the command "mail *username* " you type the message to be sent and terminate it with the EOT key for your system. There is no way of altering the message once you have started to type.

    Instead create a file called 'message' with the contents "Hello there, nice to see you again", and then type the following command (Don't forget to replace *your — username* with your actual login name).

        mail *your — username* < message

This causes **mail** to read text from the file 'message' rather than your terminal. Using **mail** in this fashion allows you to get the text of the message correct before you send it. To send mail to another user replace *your — username* with their UNIX login name.

    Now log out and log back in again — you should get the "You have mail." message. To receive your mail type

        mail

with no argument. The system will reply with something like

        From *your — username* Wed Dec 30 15:11:30 1981
        Hello there, nice to see you again
        Save?

The screen cursor stops immediately after the question mark whilst **mail**

23

waits for you to type either yes or no. If you type yes the message will be saved for later perusal in a file called 'mbox'; "no" would be a good reply for the present. This is a perfectly valid use of the **mail** command; by sending mail to yourself you can implement a simple but effective diary or reminder system.

2.7. Removing Files and Directories

You're probably wondering by now how to get rid of all the redundant files left hanging about by the examples carried out so far. The command **rm** exists for just this purpose; typing

> rm junk message

will remove the directory entries for files 'junk' and 'message'.

The corresponding command to remove a directory is **rmdir;** of course the directory will refuse to go away unless it's empty apart from the entries '.' and '..'. Always remove files and directories as soon as you no longer need them; the system manager will remain a life-long friend if you keep your filestore usage to a minimum.

2.8. Moving Files About

We learned above how to create and append to a file using the shell facility for redirection. Apart from the ability to remove a file there remain two important operations; copying and renaming. The command **cp** copies one file to another, leaving the original untouched. Typing

> cp poem new — poem

creates an identical copy of 'poem' in the file 'new — poem'. BEWARE: if 'new — poem' exists already then any contents will disappear. You may verify that they are the same by looking at the directory using **ls** or by using the **diff** command on the two files. The terminal screen should look like this

```
$ ls  − l
− rw − rw − rw −      1 andy       52 Dec 31  11:03 new − poem
− rw − rw − rw −      1 andy       52 Dec 29  15:20 poem
$ diff poem new − poem
$
```

Ls has shown that both files are the same length, the command **diff** compares the two files and reports any differences, remaining quiet if the

24

files are identical. Using diff makes the **ls** unnecessary.

The general format of **cp** is

cp file1 file2

If 'file2' is a directory then the target file is created in that directory with the same name as 'file1'.

Renaming files is accomplished with the **mv** command

mv file1 file2

which causes 'file1' to be renamed as 'file2'. The original name disappears. Section 1 of your local manual will give a full explanation of the behaviour of **mv**.

2.9. Pipes and Filters

Using yet another sleight of hand of the shell, the standard output of one command may be connected to the standard input of another. This is known as a pipeline and is achieved by writing the pipe operator '|' between two commands. Pipes are an extremely important feature of UNIX and are being widely copied in other operating systems.

Suppose you wish to print your data files 'dat1', 'dat2', 'dat3' and 'dat4' so that all the information is run together. One method would be to collect the data in one file first and then print that

cat dat1 dat2 dat3 dat4 > tempfile
pr − h Test- Data tempfile
rm tempfile

The command **pr** produces a printed listing of one or more files. It accepts various flags specifying how the output is to be formatted. The flag ' − h' means that pr is to treat the next argument (in this case 'Test-Data') as a header to be used for each page. If you want to find out more about **pr** then look up the entry in section 1 of your manual.

Clearly the method above is more work than necessary; what we want to do is to take the output of **cat** and connect it to the input of **pr** using a pipe.

cat dat1 dat2 dat3 dat4 | pr − h Test- Data

Cat reads the 4 files and produces one stream of text which is sent through a pipe to the standard input of **pr**. As you will find later the command above can be made shorter still.

25

Pipes may also be used to construct specials commands which are not directly available from a single UNIX command. If you type

    ls | wc −l

a count of the number of files in the current directory will be printed. The command **wc** normally counts lines, words and characters in the file(s) whose name(s) appear as arguments, or if no filenames are specified, in the standard input. In the above example the flag '−l' instructs **wc** to count only the lines; try it for yourself. Other flags are '−w' and '−c' which may be combined, so

    wc −lc afile

will count just lines and characters in 'afile'. To see **wc** in action we shall use it on our two previous files 'poem' and 'new−poem'

```
$ wc poem new−poem
        2      11        52 poem
        2      11        52 new−poem
        4      22       104 total
$
```

The first column reports the number of lines, the second the number of words and the third the number of characters.

Many UNIX commands operate in the same fashion as **cat, pr** and **wc**; they read their standard input if no arguments are given, modify or use the information, and then write to the standard output. When used in this way the commands are known as 'filters'; they can be combined in pipelines to build commands of arbitrary complexity. There is usually a system-imposed limit on the number of elements you may have in a pipeline, although we would be very surprised if you can think of a valid situation where this limit is reached.

We have mentioned once or twice the mysterious 'shell', which is in fact sh(1). Just as the terminal is your eyes and ears, the shell is your interface with the operating system. It is a user command, no different from **ls, echo, pr** or even a program you might write yourself. You have already learnt how the shell can interpret your commands, redirect input/output and create pipelines. It has other capabilities too: more than one command may be run from a command line by separating the commands with ';'. The shell recognises the semicolon and breaks the line into separate commands to be run sequentially. Thus

    command 1   ;   command 2

will run both commands before returning with a prompt.

2.10. Running Commands in the Background

Normally the shell waits patiently for a command to terminate. However, if you are doing somthing time-consuming, such as sorting a long file, and you don't want to wait around for the results before starting something else you can say

sort longfile &

The '&' (ampersand) placed at the end of a command line causes the shell not to wait for the command to terminate. Further commands may then be typed. Of course to keep the output of **sort** from interfering with what you're doing on the terminal, it would have been better to have typed

sort longfile > sort.output &

to redirect its output away from the terminal.

When a command is started with an '&' the shell replies with a number called the process number, which uniquely identifies that command. This number may be used later to stop it, as the INTERRUPT key will now no longer work on these 'background' commands. If you do want to terminate the command you type

kill *process – number*

The command **kill** sends a special signal† to the specified process – so it dies. A multi-command line may also be run in the background by surrounding the commands with parentheses

(cmd1 ; cmd2 ; ... ; cmdn) &

or you can start a background pipeline with

cmd1 | cmd2 &

So far so good – by now you should know

What a file is and how it relates to the filestore
What file protection is available and how to change it
How to list a directory
How to create, remove, copy, rename and list a file
How to redirect terminal input/output to and from files
How to combine simple commands in a pipeline
How to run commands in the background

†Signals are dealt with later. You may also like to read kill(1) and ps(1) in your manual.

27

Command Summary

cat	:	concatenate and print
cd	:	change directory
chmod	:	change file protection
cp	:	copy files
diff	:	differential file comparator
echo	:	echo arguments
kill	:	terminate a process
ls	:	list contents of a directory
mail	:	send mail to users
man	:	run off a section of the UNIX manual
mkdir	:	make a directory
mv	:	move or rename a file
pr	:	print a file
pwd	:	print working directory
rm	:	remove a file
rmdir	:	remove a directory
sort	:	sort or merge files
wc	:	word and line count

Before reading any further, we suggest that beginners to UNIX stop at this point. The material which follows IS important, but we doubt if it will be understood by newcomers, who will probably prefer to read about the editor and perhaps 'C', then gain some experience with the system. You'll almost certainly be put off using UNIX if you try to digest any more at this stage – but you'll find it extremely useful later.

Shell Programming

2.11. Filename Generation and Pattern Matching

Most commands expect the names of files as arguments, which may either be a simple name, such as the name of a file in your current directory, or the full pathname of a file anywhere in the filestore. Filenames consist of a sequence of alphanumeric characters and maybe one or more '.'s: in fact any character, except of course '/', may appear in a filename. Non-alphanumerics should be avoided as many of them have a special meaning to the shell. They are called *metacharacters*. You've already met some of these '&', '>', '<', etc.

One exception is '.', which is not a metacharacter. It is often used where related files share a common part of the filename. The part of the name following the dot is used to indicate what the particular file contains. For example, the files

    prog prog.c prog.lst prog.o prog.out prog.s

might all be related: the names share a root portion to show this relationship. The file 'prog.c' might be the source for a C program, the file 'prog.o' the corresponding object version, the file 'prog' executable, and so on. This convention has been adopted by certain UNIX utilities; it hasn't been imposed by the operating system.

The shell provides a simple mechanism for filename generation and expansion. Pathnames (relative or absolute) may be written using special characters to replace part or all of the name. Other systems call these characters *wild-card* specifications. Expressions involving shell metacharacters are known as *metanotation*. The word

    prog*

matches all the files shown above, indeed the above line of names would have been produced by the command

    echo prog*

if they existed in the current directory. The word 'prog*' is expanded by the shell before the command is executed. Any names which match are sorted alphabetically and passed on to the command as separate arguments.

The character '*' matches any sequence (including none) of characters in a filename. '*' by itself will match every file in the current directory.

The character '?' matches any single character in a filename. Thus ls ? ?? ???

will list all those files in the current directory with one, two and three character names. Also, a sequence of characters between '[' and ']' will match any single character from the set. The name

prog.[cos]

will match

prog.c prog.o prog.s

from the example above. The important point to remember here is that any expansion is performed by the shell **before** the execution of a command; all names matching the pattern are supplied to the command as separate arguments. If **no** filenames match a particular metanotation then the word is passed on without any expansion, **complete with metacharacters.**

The metacharacters we have just been using for filename generation (and those used for redirection of input/output) pose a problem in that we cannot use them directly as part of a word. One solution is to enclose the entire word in single quotation marks; if you wish to echo the character '*' then

echo '*'

must be used. Another method is to insert the symbol '\' (yet another metacharacter) just before the metacharacter that needs its special meaning removing. To use '\' within a filename two must be used, thus

ls −l xyyz\\f\|*

invokes **ls** on filename xyyz\f|*. If you are perverse enough to use such names, then you deserve all you get.

This is definitely not the end of the shell's pattern matching facilities: a complete description of them appears in appendix C. Practice the ones you have learnt so far before moving on.

2.12. Shell Variables

The shell provides string variables, names of which may be chosen by the user and given values. For example, the command

mark = /usr/andy/bin

assigns the value '/usr/andy/bin' to the string variable 'mark'. The value of a variable may be substituted into a command line by preceding its name with a dollar

    mv afile $mark

will move the file 'afile' from the current directory to the directory '/usr/andy/bin'. A more general notation for substitution is

    ${var__name}

which should be used when the variable name is followed by further characters. For example

    b = /tmp/andy −
    ls −l myfile > ${b}ls

will direct the output of **ls** to the file '/tmp/andy − ls', whereas

    ls −l> $bls

would cause the value of variable 'bls' to be substituted: this would be blank if there had been no previous assignment to 'bls'.

    Some variable names have a special meaning to the shell.

    $PATH

is a list of directories to be searched when the shell attempts to execute a command. If you don't explicitly set 'PATH' then the current directory, '/bin', and '/usr/bin' are searched by default. This is how commands like **echo, ls** and **cat** are found. To set PATH a list of directory names are typed, separated by colons, eg

    PATH = :/usr/andy/bin:/usr/mike/bin:/bin:/usr/bin

specifies that the current directory (the null string before the first :), '/usr/andy/bin', '/usr/mike/bin', '/bin' and '/usr/bin' are to be searched, in that order. In this way users can have their own private commands that are accessible independently of the current directory. If the command name contains a '/' then the '$PATH' string is not used; a single attempt is made to find the command.

    When the shell is ready to accept a command line it will issue a prompt. By default this prompt is '$ ', but it may be changed by assigning a value to the string variable 'PS1'.

    PS1 = 'hello   '

sets the prompt to the string 'hello   ': it is usually a good idea to have at least one space following the prompt string. In certain circumstances commands may be spread over several lines. The shell gives the special prompt '>' when you're in the middle of one of these. This second prompt may be changed by typing

    PS2 = 'again   '

You may examine the state of the shell variables at any time using the command **set**, for example

    $ set
    IFS =
    PATH = :/usr/andy/bin:/bin:/usr/bin:/usr/games
    PS1 = $
    PS2 = >
    TERM = 920c
    $

The variable 'TERM' shows what type of terminal is in use. This information is exported† to commands so that they may determine the terminal characteristics. (Screen editors are an example of commands which need this facility.)

   Other string variables with special meanings are

    $? $#
    $$ $!
    $ − $HOME
    $MAIL $IFS

they should be avoided in general use. For an explanation of their interpretation see appendix C.

2.13. Shell Procedure – Command Files

   Just as you can cause a program like **sort** to take input from a file rather than the terminal, you can tell the shell to read a file to get commands. For example, suppose you wish to find out the date and who's on the system every time you log in. The command **date** writes the current date and time to its standard output

    $ date
    Fri Jan 14 16:51:56 GMT 1982
    $

---

†A system call is used to convey such information to the executed program. The collection of variables exported by the shell is called the *environment*. See chapter 8 and section 2 of your manual for details.

and the command **who** lists the name, terminal name, and login time for each user currently logged in to the system

```
$ who
jackie   ttyr   Jan 14  16:13
andy     ttyG   Jan 14  09:12
mike     ttym   Jan 14  12:35
$
```

One way of obtaining your required information is to type the above commands after you login. A much simpler method, however, would be to use the shell's capability of reading commands from a file. First you create a file containing the necessary commands, (we shall call it 'startup'). The command line

```
echo 'date ; who' > startup
```

puts the single line "date ; who" into a file called 'startup'. (The primes (') were needed around the argument to **echo** to prevent the semicolon from splitting the line into "echo date" followed by the command **who**). Such a file containing commands is called a *shell procedure* or *scriptfile* (we will use both terms interchangeably). Then you run it with either

```
sh < startup      or      sh startup
```

Both of these cause the shell to run with the file 'startup' as input: the effect is as if you had typed the contents of 'startup' on the terminal.

An even better solution would be if the shell could automatically execute the desired commands after you login. This is done by moving 'startup' to a file named '.profile't in your home directory. The shell will read and execute commands from this file when you login before taking input from the terminal.

The command line we used earlier

```
cat dat1 dat2 dat3 dat4 | pr −h Test-Data
```

may be implemented as a scriptfile with a further simplification. Create a file named 'prdata' containing

```
cat dat? | pr −h Test-Data
```

which can be executed by typing 'sh prdata'. The word "dat?" is expanded to match any files whose names begin with the characters 'dat'

---

†The name '.profile' is used by the standard UNIX shell. Other names may be in use at your installation: look at sh(1) for details.

and have a single character following. If this command file is to be used regularly then it would be a good idea to eliminate the need to type "sh". This is achieved by changing the protection mode of the file to include execution permission

    chmod +x prdata

Now the scriptfile is invoked just by typing its name as though it were an executable command. The shell can tell that the file is not really an executable program and reads the contents instead.

2.13.1. Shell Procedure Arguments

Arguments may be supplied to a shell procedure in exactly the same way as a normally executable program. They are referred to from within the file using special parameters (known as *positional parameters*). The character '$' is another shell metacharacter which is used to refer to a command argument: '$1' refers to the first supplied argument; '$2' the second; and so on up to '$9'. The name of the command itself is available as '$0'.

If the file 'where' contains

    who | grep $1

and has execute permission then

    where andy

will print out a single line showing which terminal user 'andy' is logged onto; if Andy is not logged in then nothing will be printed.

The command **grep** searches text for the occurence of expressions (in the simplest case just strings). In this example **grep** is operating as a filter, reading the standard input and printing all lines containing the string "andy".

When the scriptfile above is interpreted by the shell the positional parameter '$1' is replaced with the word 'andy'. If we assume that Andy is still logged in then the terminal screen should look like this

    $ where andy
    andy   ttyG Jan 14 09:12
    $

Grep is capable of substantially more than this: see grep(1).

As well as providing names for the positional parameters, the number of arguments in the call is available as $#. Create a file called 'howmany' containing the line

> echo $#

and then execute (don't forget to change the permission) the command with a few arguments: the number of arguments you typed should be printed.

> $ howmany these are just examples
> 4
> $

Try this for yourself. If it didn't work can you explain why? Don't forget that '$' is a shell metacharacter with all the usual pitfalls.

The special parameter $* is used to substitute all the supplied arguments, except the name of the command '$0'. A typical use of this is when the same operation is to be performed on all the arguments; for example, a command file containing

> sort − nr $*

will sort the contents of all the supplied filenames into reverse numerical order. The advantage of using $* rather than the individual parameters ('$1', '$2', etc) is that more than 9 arguments can be handled.

A line starting with ':' as the first character will be completely ignored by the shell. This is useful for introducing comments into your command files, for example

> : the command 'where'
> : a single line is printed showing the terminal
> : if the username cannot be found then nothing is printed
> :
> who | grep $1

2.14. Shell Programming: Control-of-Flow

A frequent use of shell procedures is to loop through the arguments, executing commands conditionally once for each. The shell provides control-of-flow constructs such as **for, case, if** − **else** − **fi** and **while** to deal effectively with this application. The commands may be used either from within shell procedure files, or typed directly at the terminal. In the latter case the shell prompt will change to $PS2 after the first line has been typed.

Many UNIX utilities return an *exit-status* or value that may be used to determine control-flow. The **test** command, for example, was written solely for use by shell programs; it provides no output other than an exit status.

    test −f file

returns zero exit status (true) if 'file' exists and non-zero exit status (false) otherwise. Here are some of the more frequently used arguments: for a complete specification see test(1).

    test   s   : true if the argument 's' is not the null string
    test − f file : true if 'file' exists
    test − r file : true if 'file' is readable
    test − w file : true if 'file' is writable
    test − d file : true if 'file' is a directory

2.14.1. For

The general **for** loop notation is

    for name [**in** word-list]
    do command-list
    done

Each time a **for** command is executed, the shell variable 'name' is set to the next word in the word-list. The word-list is optional and if omitted the loop is executed once for each positional parameter (supplied argument): that is

    for I

is equivalent to

    for I in $*

Execution ends when there are no more words in the list. The command-list is a sequence of one or more simple UNIX commands separated or terminated by a newline or semicolon.

    For A in alpha beta gamma
    do echo $A
    done

when executed will print

    alpha
    beta
    gamma

36

Suppose you wish to search all C source files in the current directory for the occurrence of particular function names. A command file which performs this task is

```
for i
do grep $i *.c
done
```

Thereafter, if the command file were called 'findref'

```
findref 'hash(' 'insert(' 'symbol('
```

will print all the lines in files, whose names end with '.c', that contain references to functions 'hash()', 'insert()' and 'symbol()'. The quotation marks are necessary in order to remove the special meaning of '('.

2.14.2. Case

The **case** notation provides a multi-way branch facility similar to that available in most modern structured programming languages. The general form of the **case** command is

```
case word in
     pattern) command-list;;
 ...
esac
```

The command-list associated with the **first** pattern that matches 'word' is executed and the execution of the **case** completed. The pattern matching method is the same as that for filename generation. Since the metacharacter '*' matches anything it may be used for the default case. The command

```
for A in alpha beta gamma
do case $A in
    alpha)   B = a;;
    beta)    B = b;;
    gamma)   B = g;;
    esac
echo $B
done
```

when executed will print

```
a
b
g
```

Try typing it now: the shell prompt should change to PS2 (usually ">")
after the first line.

A good use of the **case** command is to distinguish between different
arguments. The following is a prototype for a **compile** command that
will invoke the appropriate language compiler or assembler

```
:        initialise flag to nothing
flag =

:        repeat for each argument
for a in $*
do case $a in

:        concatenate the flags with a separating space
- [ocSO]) flag = $flag' '$a';;
- *) echo 'unknown flag $a';;

:        compile each source file then reset flag
*.c) cc $flag $a; flag = ;;
*.s) as $flag $a; flag = ;;
*.f) f77 $flag $a; flag = ;;

:        complain if a bad argument given
*) echo 'unexpected argument $a';;
esac
done
```

Note that ';;' is used to terminate each command, and **esac** (**case** spelt
backwards) terminates the whole statement.

2.14.3. If-Else-Fi

This construction may be used as a general conditional branch, having
the form

```
if command-list
then command-list
[ else command-list ]
fi
```

The command-list following **if** is executed and if the last command in the
list returns a zero status (true), the command-list following **then** is
executed. The **else** part is optional: if it is present then the corresponding
command-list is executed for a non-zero (false) return from the **if**
command-list. Try the following example

```
for A in *
do if test −d $A
    then echo $A: is a directory
    else echo −n $A: is a file and
        if test −w $A
        then echo writeable
        else if test −r $A
            then echo readable
            else echo neither readable nor writeable
            fi
        fi
    fi
done
```

Line 1 causes the program to loop setting the shell variable 'A' consecutively to each filename in the current directory. The first **if** command tests the file to see if it is a directory itself and if so a message is printed at the third line.

Subsequent lines of the program are only executed if the first test fails (ie '$A' refers to an ordinary file). The **if** command on line 5 will become true if the file specified by '$A' is writeable (ie has write permission for the user running the program). The **echo** command at line 8 is executed if the file is readable, otherwise line 9 is executed.

2.14.4. While and Until

While is used to form loops. Each time round the loop, the **while** command first executes the command-list associated with itself, then if the last command in the list returns a non-zero status the **do** command-list is executed. Otherwise the loop terminates.

> **while** command-list
> **do** command-list
> **done**

The following extract from a command file waits until a particular file disappears before proceeding with further actions. The presence of this file could be used to implement a simple semaphore† system between cooperating processes.

---

†The concept of semaphores was introduced by Dijkstra (1965) as a technique for inter-process communication. A semaphore may be thought of as a flag which is set or reset to control access to common objects. Simple systems use the presence of a file to indicated that the semaphore is set (locked); however, this is not a true semaphore. Reference [1], p16-23 and reference [2].

```
while test −f lockfile
do sleep 30
    echo waiting for semaphore
done
: create the semaphore file
echo > lockfile
: further commands
```

If **while** is replaced by **until** the loop termination condition is reversed. The determining test is made in the command-list associated with the command **until**.

```
until command-list
do command-list
done
```

Two further UNIX commands exist solely for use with control-of-flow constructs. These are **true** which always returns a true (zero) exit status, and **false** which always returns false (non-zero). Both

```
while true
do echo hello andy
done
```

and

```
until false
do echo hello mike
done
```

will execute until the processor breaks down! (Well, at least until you press the INTERRUPT key.)

2.15. Summary

You should now understand the basic principles of file creation and manipulation; some time spent practising with them now will save you hours later. This chapter has only touched briefly on the capabilities of the shell. However, this is enough to get you going on the system. Once you have gained confidence then the more advanced features may be explored.

As an example of shell programming we include a version of the **man** command which is used to print sections of the UNIX manual. If you have already used **man** you may be forgiven for thinking that it is an executable program. The version in use on your system will probably be very similar. To have a look type

40

```
cat /bin/man        or        cat /usr/bin/man
```

It should be there, unless someone has moved it.

A version of the man command

```
cd /usr/man
: 'colon is the comment command'
: 'default nroff ($N), section 1 ($s)'
N=n
s=1

for i
do case $i in
    [1−9]*)    s=$i;;
    −t)        N=t;;
    −n)        N=n;;
    −*)        echo unknown flag \'$i\';;
     *) if test  −f man$s/$i.$s
        then    ${N}roff man0/${N}aa man$s/$i.$s
        else
                : look through all manual sections
                found=no
                for j in 1 2 3 4 5 6 7 8 9
                do if test  −f man$j/$i.$j
                    then man $j $i
                            found=yes
                    fi
                done
                case $found in
                    no) echo "$i: manual page not found"
                esac
           fi
    esac
done
```

2.16. Questions

1) How many characters may you have in a filename ?
2) What is your home directory ?
3) How many directories and files can you have at any one time ?
4) How can you tell a directory name from an ordinary filename ?
5) What levels of file protection does UNIX provide ?

6) What is a group ?
7) What is the standard input and where is output from a command normally placed ?
8) What are metacharacters and what are their functions in filename generation ?
9) How do you connect the output of one command to the input of another without going through an intermediate file ? Do the commands have to modified in any way to achieve this ?

Chapter 3

A book of verses underneath the tree, a jug of wine, a loaf of bread, the editor and thee.

(apologies to Fitzgerald)

Forget the food and booze, the party comes later. Pick up the editor on your way.

3.1. Some random thoughts

If you are anything like the ordinary UNIX programmmer, the editor is the program that will absorb most of your time and attention. It and the shell are the two main programs used under UNIX; you need to be completely familiar with them because you will use them so much, using the shell to execute the commands written with the aid of the editor.

There's a peculiar psychology at work when you come to think about editors. Programmers using interactive systems probably spend more of their working lives using an editor than any other piece of software. Writing programs, preparing documentation and test data, tabulating results are all done with the editor. One might expect that under the circumstances an equivalent degree of thought would be put into the design and production of good editors, but it isn't. Contrast the endless wrangles about which is the best language – BASIC vs Pascal, is FORTRAN usable – with the deafening silence on the subject of editors. OK, if you look hard in the literature there are a few references to the subject, but nothing to compare with the 'respectable' fields such as language design. International committees sit spending large sums of other people's money while they standardise this language and that extension. In the meantime hundreds of programmers the world over are churning out text editors that do nothing new and which are incompatible with anything that has been done before.

UNIX is a well designed, usable, operating system but it can't protect users from ill-conceived attempts to produce 'enhancements'. As if nothing had been learnt from the sorry histories of BASIC and FOR-TRAN, some suppliers feel duty bound to include their own souped-up editor with the UNIX systems they sell. Are they really doing you a favour?

If you feel that you **must** use the flashy editor supplied with your particular system, give some very careful thought to portability; both its and yours. Even if UNIX were not such a good operating system it would still become popular because it is so portable. Who cares about the hardware? The operating software is what counts. If you start using non-standard software and don't have a copy of the source code of it then you could be in big trouble when it comes to moving from one piece of hardware to another. Users who only know a non-portable editor (by portable we mean one which **has** been ported, not one the vendors say **could** be), are at a big disadvantage straight away.

3.2. The UNIX Editor

There is one editor **'ed'**, which comes with Standard UNIX. Whether it is a good editor or not is irrelevant as long as it is usable and portable. The second attribute isn't in doubt – get UNIX and you get ed – so all you need now is experience using it. The reasons for sticking to ed should be obvious by now!

It would be difficult to improve on the UNIX system documentation on ed in the space we have available, so if you can, take a long look at it [3] [4]. As well as the written documents you might be lucky enough to have the 'learn' system working on your machine. To get 'learn' to talk about the editor, type

    learn editor

and follow the instructions. If you haven't got 'learn' the shell will tell you.

Most sites running UNIX give copies of the ed documentation to anyone who needs it; as we said before, the editor gets so much use that this is a worthwhile expenditure. For those who aren't so lucky and for people who want their own personal reference material on ed, we supply the following:

    an introduction to using ed
    a reference to the detailed features of ed

and as a result probably please nobody. If you are a first-time user of ed then the reference section may not be very easy to understand; persevere!

3.3. Using the Editor Ed.

Ed is a text editor; an interactive program whose job is to allow its users to manipulate text in a file; to move text, change it, add to it or delete it. As for what a file of 'text' is – well, ed expects a file to contain printable characters and a few sundries such as tab, space and newline. To some extent ed is a line oriented editor, most of its commands applying to one or more lines of text rather than treating the file as a shapeless whole: this is exactly what most users want. Rather than giving a whole load of theory, let's take a look at how to use ed.

3.4. Starting Ed.

Ed is invoked by typing 'ed' to the shell's prompt. You can give an argument if you like; most people do. The argument is the name of the file to be edited, this file doesn't have to exist before the ed command is given.

Make sure that there isn't a file called 'fred' in your directory by giving the command

> rm fred

and type

> ed fred

to the prompt. This gets ed started and tells it you want to edit 'fred' whether or not fred exists. Since fred doesn't exist, ed will let you know by printing a '?' to you. So far the screen will look like this:

> $ ed fred
> ? fred

The query (?) is ed's response to everything it doesn't expect. This isn't exactly helpful, but once you are used to ed's moods you can usually work out where or why ed is complaining. This time it's because 'fred' didn't exist.

All you can do now is to add things to the file. It didn't exist to start with so it must be empty; what else could you do but add to it?

3.5. The append command

Adding stuff is done by **appending** it to the current contents of the file; you tell the editor you want to add things by typing **a** to it. This sequence

```
a
They hit the bank of the Rio Grande
At the height of the blazing noon;
To slake their thirst and do their worst
They sought Red Kate's saloon.
```

will add the text between the 'a' and the '.' to the file. Ed doesn't give a prompt of any description, so the text shown above is exactly what you would see on the screen if you try the example. The period '.' by itself means that you have finished appending text. Write the text out to 'fred' and quit the editor with this sequence

```
w
q
```

After the **w** command, which means **write** the output file, ed will tell you how many characters it wrote. The screen will look like this:

```
w
143
q
$
```

the $ is your prompt from the shell, showing that ed has finished. To find out if fred really contains what it ought to, look inside it with **cat;** the command

```
cat fred
```

will print the contents of 'fred' on your terminal.

The file 'fred' exists now and at last has got some text in it, so we can try some fancy things. Start editing it again: the screen will look like this:

```
$ ed fred
143
```

This time ed doesn't query the command – fred exists – and ed copies fred into somewhere secret, telling you how many characters were copied. This number will of course be the same one you got in response to the **w** command before. Any editing you do is done on the secret copy and only gets copied back onto your own version of fred when you tell ed to write the file with **w**. This is handy – if you really mess up the edit, you can quit by typing **q** to ed and not affect the file you were editing.

At any time during the edit you can issue the **w** command to write out to fred what ed thinks the current version of the text looks like. It's a good idea to do it occasionally during a long editing session anyhow as a protection against system failures. There's no excuse for spending five hours editing a file only to lose all the changes just because an engineer dropped a mug of tea inside the processor. If you don't want to overwrite fred then you can give a filename to the write command:

    w anyfile

will write the current text to 'anyfile', overwriting it if it already existed, creating it if it didn't.

The **q** command simply means **quit**. If you have changed the text in any way and try to quit without writing it out, ed will start to argue with you:

    q
    are you sure? (y)

is what ed says. If you do want to quit without writing (see above on 'mess up'), then replying **y** will do what you want. A similar effect is caused by typing the EOT character instead of an ed command; ed will die quietly in this case and not argue. Users who come from a system where the editor automatically writes out the text at the end of an editing session are often a bit surprised by ed's methods, but pleased the first time they're prevented from messing up an important file.

Back to the example – ed has read in the contents of fred and is just itching to do something to it. Let's see what was read: you use the **p** command (print) to inspect the current line;

    p

should cause ed to say

    They sought Red Kate's saloon.

so, from the top, your screen will show this:

    $ ed fred
    143
    p
    They sought Red Kate's saloon.

This points out the important information that after reading a file, ed positions itself **at the last line in the file.** An append command will now add text after the last line.

The **p** command can be used to look at more than just the current line. Try the commands '2p' and '1p' to see what happens; the second line and the first line will be printed respectively. You can also give a range of line numbers to **p**;

    1,4p

will print lines 1 through to 4 inclusive; in our case the whole file so far.

In fact, it's common to give two line numbers to several of the commands which ed accepts. Putting either one or two *addresses* in front of a command tells ed which line or lines the command applies to. To see how this is done, look at the examples below which also introduce two new commands you haven't seen before: **r** and **d**. The **r** command stands for 'read'. It works like **w** which writes text out – **r** reads it in. The **d** command (delete) deletes lines of text. Once a line has been deleted there's no easy way to get it back, so use **d** with care. Here are the examples; they are only examples and certainly wouldn't make sense as a sequence so look at them one at a time.

    1p
    1,4p
    5r fred
    1,6w temp
    2d
    1,2d
    3a

What do they mean? Here's the same commands with explanations:

1p	– print line 1
1,4p	– print lines 1 – 4
5r fred	– read the file 'fred', place the text after line 5 in the current file
1,6w temp	– write out lines 1 – 6 to the file 'temp'
2d	– delete line 2
1,2d	– delete lines 1 – 2
3a	– append text after line 3

3.6. Some special addresses.

The addresses shown above were all the numbers of lines; this is reasonable since an address **is** a line number. Using numeric line numbers isn't always convenient and ed helps a little on this one. Quite often you want to do things to the last line of a file and don't need the bother of finding out just what its line number is. Ed allows you to use the symbol '$' to indicate the number of the last line, so to print all the lines in a file you can say:

```
1,$p
```

and ed will list the whole lot. If you get fed up watching this (long files can be boring), the INTERRUPT key will break in and stop it. Of course there's no need to have a special symbol for the first line since it is obviously number one.

The current line is one of interest too. It's the one that gets used if you don't give any addresses to commands like p, a, d and so on; it has the special symbol '.' (pronounced 'dot'). It gets most of its use in commands like these

```
.-6,.+6p
.-1
.+1
```

These are commands to print all the lines from 6 before dot to 6 after it, then the one before it and finally the one after it. The last two didn't have the **p** command specified – ed assumes you mean to print a line if you just give an address. Using those commands one after the other might give you a surprise: **some commands move dot** and p is one of them. Dot is set to the address of the last line printed by a **p** command, so

```
5p
```

will both print line 5 and set dot to 5. If you ever need to know the value of dot then the command

```
.=
```

will cause ed to print it.

The most common ed commands are to print either the next line or the previous one; the commands to do this might be

```
.+1
.-1
```

but there's a shorter way. Simply typing 'return' (a blank line), will move dot to the next line and print it; for the reverse case, typing a single ' — ' followed by 'return'

```
—
```

goes back one line and prints it. Oddly enough, the standard version of ed has no easy way of printing a few lines before and after dot, leaving dot unaffected (some editors call this a 'window'). This is a shame because it's something users want to do a lot and there are some modified versions of ed around which allow it. Whilst this is undoubtedly an 'improvement', we refer you to our opening remarks concerning portability for our opinion of the change.

3.7. Summary so far.

You know how to edit a file, applying the commands a, w, q, p, r and d, along with the idea of line addresses. A final command in this family is the **i** command (insert) – this is similar to the **a** command, but inserts text before the addressed line instead of after it.

        5i
        hello
        .

is pretty much the same as

        4a
        hello
        .

Try it, and see what happens to dot. After that, experiment with all the ed commands until you feel confident with them. Remember that you can check the effect of your commands by using

        1,$p

to print the contents of the file you are editing. Ed won't change anything that matters unless you give the **w** command to re-write the file.

You might also like to know that you can tack a **p** onto the end of most commands to print the 'result'. For example,

        dp

deletes the current line and then prints whatever dot is set to. It's common practice, too, to stick a **p** on at the end of a *substitute* command, to find out what happened.

3.8. The Substitute command

The substitute command is one of the most important commands you will use. It's used to change text by substituting one piece for another. Think back to those first four lines of text used to illustrate the append command. If you've been trying the examples as we go then with a bit of luck you will still have a file containing them. Position ed at the first line which is:

> They hit the bank of the Rio Grande

and try this

> s/bank/banks/

It will appear to do nothing – ed doesn't automatically print the lines it changes. To see what happened, print the line using the **p** command – it will now read

> They hit the banks of the Rio Grande

the word 'bank' in the original has been changed to 'banks'.

The general form of the substitute command is this:

> line1,line2s/for this/this/

which changes 'for this' to 'this' on all lines numbered line1 through to line2. Dot is set to the number of the last line changed. Beware! Only the **first** occurrence of 'for this' is changed on any one line; to change all occurrences you will need the 'global' qualifier tacked onto the end of the command like this:

> 1,4s/th/xxx/g

which will change every occurence of 'th' to 'xxx' on lines 1 – 4. Try it and see what happens. Then change everything back.

If you only give one line number to the command then only that line is affected. It is also quite alright to turn something into nothing:

> s/xyz//

will turn 'xyz' into nothing, which is the same as deleting it.

All the examples of the substitute command so far have used the '/' character as if it was something special and somehow reserved for use by the command. It isn't, so smart alecs who want to know how to change a '/' to something else will have no trouble. Any character except space or tab can be used to replace it; the next two lines are equivalent in their effect:

> s/xx/yy/
> saxxayya

they both replace 'xx' with 'yy'.

BUT before getting carried away by the excitement of it all, you need to know that ed uses the characters

∧ . $ [* \ &

for nefarious purposes and you could get a surprise if you involve them in your experiments. Do without them for the moment.

3.9. Context Searching

If you've never used an editor like ed before it will be hard for you to work out which are the important commands and which you needn't bother too much about. One thing is for sure though – only the terminally bewildered would miss context searching off their list of things you need to know. What is it?

It depends on your application, to some degree, whether or not line numbers are convenient to use. Sometimes they are, sometimes they aren't. The problem is that they change as you add or delete lines, so a line-numbered listing soon goes out of date. In circumstances like these it's easiest to forget line numbers and refer to a line by what it contains, not where it is.

Believe it or not, this example is interpreted as a line number by the editor and is the first example of a simple context search:

/abc/

It's the number of the first line to be found which contains 'abc', looking from the line after the one we are currently on (dot); the search continues past the end of the file by starting at the top again if a line isn't found which **does** contain 'abc'. In short the whole file gets searched – every line is looked at once. If you want the search to go backwards rather than forwards you say this:

?abc?

These 'context' line numbers can be used anywhere you would use ordinary numerical ones. In this example

/a/,/b/s/123/456/

a search is made forwards to find the first line containing 'a'. On that line, and all others up to and including the next line to contain a 'b', if the line contains the string '123', it will be changed to '456'.

Quite often you'll use context searching to look through a file until you locate a **particular** line containing the pattern used for the context search†. You may find that neither the first, nor the second, or even the

---

†A detailed explanation of 'patterns' comes later.

fifth occurrence is the one you want, and you keep repeating the search until you find the line you want. At best it's tedious to have to type things like this Welsh place-name [5]

Llanrhaedr-yng-Nghinmeirch

repeatedly until you are in the right place. Fortunately for the Welsh, perhaps more so for the rest of us, ed remembers the last pattern used and lets us refer to it by this shorthand:

//

which means that

/Deadeye Dick/
//
//

will perform the search for 'Deadeye Dick' three times. (If it only occurs once in the file, then the searches will find the same occurrence three times). The pattern is remembered for use by **s** as well.

/Deadeye Dick/s//Mexico Pete/
//s///

will try to find a line containing 'Deadeye Dick': if it does, then the 'Deadeye Dick' is changed into 'Mexico Pete'. A further search is made for 'Deadeye Dick' and if that one succeeds the string is deleted. Make sure you understand why.

3.10. The Change Command

The change command, **c** is used to change one or more lines into something else. You use it by specifying the lines to be changed and then providing the new text as if you were using an **a** or **i** command. Here's an example which changes line 7 of a file into the lines 'aaa', 'bbb', 'ccc'.

7c
aaa
bbb
ccc

To change several lines, give two line numbers: '3,7c' in the example above would have replaced lines 3 through to 7 of the file by the text given. If no line number is specified, dot is assumed.

The **c** command isn't strictly necessary because it could be done with a combination of delete and insert or append. It's easier to use though, and is less confusing when you try it on the last line of a file, when instead of delete followed by insert you would need to use delete then append.

3.11. The Move Command

The move command is used to shift stuff from one part of a file to another. It always needs one line number, telling it where to put the stuff, and in general it looks like this

first-line,last-line m after-this-line

Here's lines 7,8,9,10,11 and 12 being uprooted and stuck on at the end of the file

7,12m$

If you only give one line number in front of the **m** then only one line is moved and as usual if you don't give any line numbers the command assumes you want to refer to dot. Here's the current line being squeezed in between lines 5 and 6

m5

M always moves lines to the position **after** the line number you give it – 'm5' takes the current line and puts it after line 5. After a move, dot is the address of the last line moved. Try it.

3.12. The special characters

Remember those special characters we warned you about? Here's where you find out what they do. Let's look at them again

∧ . $ [* \ &

The first five are used in 'pattern matching'. They allow you to give patterns of characters to the **s** command and context searches; they're not unlike the shell metacharacters – though if you're like us you probably didn't understand them the first time you met them either!

The backslash is only special because the others exist, they become un-special if you put a backslash in front of them. A backslash in front of an ordinary character has no effect at all. You use it this way: to change the special characters '*\$' to 'abc' in a line, the command is

54

```
s/\*\\\$/abc/
```

where each special character (including the backslash) is preceded by a backslash. If the other special characters didn't exist then you wouldn't need the backslash either and it would become ordinary itself. If you don't understand why it's needed, try the previous example without it and see what happens.

Here are the special characters and their meanings.

3.12.1. Carat (∧)

In a pattern this matches the non-existent 'zeroth' character on a line, the one before the first one. You use it to make sure that you only match a pattern at the start of a line. In the following examples, the first one finds the next line that contains 'first' **anywhere** in the line, the second finds the next line after that which **starts** with 'second'.

```
/first/
/∧second/
```

3.12.2. Dollar ($)

Dollar does two jobs for ed. As a line number, it represents the line at the end of the file; in a pattern it means 'the character after the last one' in a line. It's the opposite of carat, and allows you to find the **end** of a line.

```
s/$/end/
```

will stick the string 'end' immediately after the last character on a line. Using it with carat you can specify a line containing exactly the pattern you give and nothing else.

```
/∧just this$/
```

is a context search for a line containing **only** the words 'just this'.

3.12.3. Dot (.)

Dot gets worked hard, like dollar. When it's used as a line number it means the current line; in a pattern it matches exactly one character, but any one character.

```
/a.b/
will match
aab
abb
a.b
acb
```

and so on.

/ ∧ ..$/

will find the next line to contain exactly two characters, no matter what they are.

3.12.4. Star (∗)

Star can be thought of as the complement of dot. It is always preceded by another character; together they mean 'any number of the preceding character' (including none).

/x∗/
/.∗/

mean respectively 'any number of the letter x' and 'any number of anything'. The any number includes zero and has been known to cause consternation in beginners; '/abc∗/' will match all of the following

    ab
    abc
    abcc
    abccc
    abcccc

etc. Ed will find the longest match that it can in cases like these − it will match the 'abcccc' rather than stop looking when it finds the 'ab' part of that string. That means that 's/abc∗/123/' will change 'abcccc' to '123', not '123cccc'.

3.12.5. Open brace ([)

This is used to form a more selective single character match than dot, and always in conjunction with ']' (which is not a special character unless an open brace occurs before it). In these examples

/[abc]/
/[aef]/
/[abc][123]/

the patterns matched are

    any of a b or c
    any of a e or f
    any of a b or c followed by any of 1 2 or 3

A consecutive run of characters can be abbreviated, so '[1234]' can be replaced by '[1–4]' and '[abcdefg]' by '[a–g]'.

To get the closing brace included as one of the characters in this sort of pattern, you can put it next to the opening brace;

[]123]
matches
] 1 2 or 3

A carat in the first position in this sort of pattern reverses its meaning: then it matches any character **not** in the list.

[∧1–4]
matches anything except
1 2 3 or 4

3.12.6. Ampersand (&).

Ampersand is only a special character when it's used in the right hand side of substitutions, then it is a shorthand for the thing that was mentioned on the left hand side.

s/this/& and that/

turns 'this' into 'this and that'.

/∧hello$/s//& & &/
a
what's all this then?
.

finds a line containing only 'hello' and makes it read 'hello hello hello', then appends the line 'what's all this then?'.

It's easy to forget this special meaning of ampersand (of course backslash turns it off) and programmers using the language 'C' often get into trouble converting a logical 'or' (||) into an 'and' (&&).

s/||/&&/

results in '||||'.

s/||/\&\&/

is what was needed.

3.13. G and V – the global commands

The end is nigh. These are the last of the ed commands we'll be dealing with in this chapter, before it takes over the whole book.

The **g** command is what you use when you want to apply some commands to all the lines in a file which contain a particular pattern. Here it is finding all the lines containing 'Eskimo' and printing them.

    g/Eskimo/p

What it did there was to search the whole file for lines containing the pattern 'Eskimo': they are remembered. After the search, dot is set to each remembered line in turn and the commands given to **g** (p in the case above) are executed. If this involves changing the line numbers, don't worry. Ed sets dot to the lines it matched with the **g**, not any funny ones you didn't expect. The general form of the command is this

    g/pattern/then do these commands

The pattern is formed in the ways we've talked about before. The 'then do -these commands' can be any commands except another **g**, although the 'other' sort of **g**, the one you put at the end of a substitute command **is** allowed. The command could be used like this:

    g/abc/s/def/ghi/

which looks at every line in the file, if any contain 'abc' their line number is remembered. After the search, each line remembered has the first occurrence of 'def' (if there is one) changed to 'ghi'; a **g** at the end of the command would change every occurence of 'def' to 'ghi' on each remembered line.

There's also the obscurely named **v** command, which is just like **g** but only works on lines that **don't** match the pattern. Here it finds and prints every line that doesn't have a full stop in it. The character '.' is special and needs a backslash in front of it.

    v/\./p

It's quite common to want several commands after a **v** or **g**; we can change every line containing 'BOLD' into lines reading

    not
    so
    bold

– like this:

/

```
g/BOLD/\
c\
not\
so\
bold\
.
```

Each line in the command list is terminated by a backslash – this says that the command hasn't finished yet.

To prevent **g** or **v** searching the whole file, you can give them a range of line numbers to work on.

```
1,4g/a/p
```

In this case the **g** only looks at lines 1 – 4. What does the command do?

3.14. Conclusions

Well that's it as far as we are concerned. If you've learnt and understood all of that you'll be pretty competent with ed. There's more to learn even so, don't get cocky yet. Appendix B contains a summary of the ed commands including some you haven't met here, read it once now and then again after you have been using ed for a while – you might be surprised how much extra you learn. Brian Kernighan's paper 'Advanced Editing on UNIX'[4] is worth reading too. There are some remarkable things in it, but they highlight an important feature of interactive editors – you use them as you go. It's a waste of time getting clever if you need ten minutes to work out how to use the fancy tricks when the job could have been done with the simple stuff in two. Especially if you get the fancy stuff wrong and have to abandon the edit.

Getting clever with an editor is only worth the effort if the job is done repeatedly; if you're writing a 'program' with ed commands as the language and ed the interpreter. (This is done sometimes to rearrange the output of programs or prepared data which comes in the wrong format. It's the ed equivalent of a shell scriptfile.) It is not a common thing to do. Most users get by quite well enough on the simplest of ed commands, using only a, i, w, s, d and p; together with very simple pattern matching.

Chapter 4

C

4.1. Introduction

This is not an easy chapter to write. To miss out on C in a book about Unix is unthinkable, but to cover the language properly in a single chapter is impossible. We will, therefore, please nobody. Accepting that fact we propose not to let it worry us too much.

This chapter tries to present the minimum amount of tutorial material that we feel will be useful as an informal reference for part-time users of C. It is certainly no substitute for the proper references (they are listed at the end of the chapter); neither does it pretend to teach anything other than the bare essentials.

The order of presentation in this chapter is deliberate; it is meant to be different from other texts on the subject in an attempt to prevent a terminal case of boredom in anybody reading them all at once!

4.2. Preliminary Notes

To a large number of Unix programmers, C and Unix are inseparable. By speaking of one, they think that they have implied the other, which is hardly surprising. The operating system is written almost entirely in C and the amount of work put into making Unix portable means that C is one of the most truly portable languages you can write in; especially if you stick to Unix as the target operating system. A C program written on one Unix system ought to run on another one with no changes at all unless you do try hard to make it unportable. Even if you do, there is a program (called lint(1)) to check what you've done and look for blunders.

This is not to say that we intend to hold C up as the best programming language in the world or any nonsense like that. As long as there are fools around there will be ill-informed argument between them about the 'best' language and we have no intention of being drawn into **that** wrangle.

It's about as profitable (and useful) as trying to decide which is the best colour, or what makes a pretty sheep. The fact that C was used to write Unix by two very able people who had other languages to choose from, and that so many of the most highly competent software authors like it so much says more about C than any argument ever will.

4.3. In the beginning

Let's not mess about any more — we have little enough space anyway — but plunge in straight away. Using the editor, create a file called hi.c and put this text in it.

```
main(){          printf("hello sailor\n"); }
```

Then compile it with the command

```
cc hi.c
```

If there were no errors you'll just get the shell prompt back. To execute the compiled program (which is always called 'a.out' by the compiler) simply give its name:

```
a.out
```

The entire compilation and run will look like this:

```
$ cc hi.c
$ a.out
hello sailor
$
```

If you want to keep the compiled program you will have to rename it before you compile any others; the command **mv** can be used to do the job.

You have just compiled a program consisting of a *function* containing a single executable statement. All C programs have at least one function in them (otherwise they wouldn't be programs); there must also be a function called **main** since this is where the program will be started. Yours is not an exception. In your program, the function **main** calls another function, **printf,** with the argument "hello sailor\n".

Unlike the **writeln** of Pascal, or FORTRAN's **write,** C hasn't got any input-output built in to the language. The function **printf** is widely used for producing output in C programs, but is simply a routine somebody wrote for convenience and put into a **library** of handy functions. By mentioning it in your program, you automatically asked for **printf** to be included from the library. C has absolutely no built-in functions at all. Fortunately we can guarantee that in a Unix system certain library functions will be present and **printf** is one of them.

4.4. Strings

The argument to printf was a *string:* strings are a collection of characters with quote (' " ') marks around them. In C, a string is treated as an array of characters with a null (zero) character tacked on at the end to allow the end to be detected. Certain hard-to-get characters have a special notation which is a backslash followed by an ordinary character; here is a list of them:

\t	the tab character
\r	carriage return
\n	newline
\b	backspace
\\	backslash
\"	quote marks
\f	form feed

C programs are usually a collection of functions – like FORTRAN – with no concept of the local functions you can find in Pascal and the ALGOLs. The order of the functions is unimportant, unlike those other languages (but you must have one called main!). Here's another program that does the same job as the first one, but the function **main** now calls the function **speak** to do the dirty work, and does it twice.

```
main(){
        speak();
        speak();
}
speak(){
        printf("hello sailor\n");
}
```

The order of the two functions could have been reversed; it wouldn't matter. Try the example and see.

4.5. Data types

Of course to do any worthwhile jobs you need to be able to manipulate data, generally speaking numbers or characters. C provides quite a selection of data types and facilities for structuring data. All we will be using for the moment are the types **char, int** and **double;** they represent characters, integers and double-precision floating point numbers respectively.

4.6. Variables and comment

Variables must all be declared before they are used; if they are declared outside function bodies then they are **global** and available for use from all functions. **Local** variables are declared at the beginning of a function and are only usable inside it, so the same name may be used in several functions without confusion. Here is a program to print a table of numbers from 1 to 10, along with their squares. It contains **comments:** in C anything between the opening brackets /* and the closing brackets */ is a comment. Comments can be put anywhere that a space or newline may.

```
main(){
            /* a program to print numbers and squares */
            int i,isquared; /* declare the variables */
            for(i = 1; i < = 10; i = i+1){ /* a loop */
                isquared = i*i;
                printf("%d %d\n",i,isquared);
            }/* end of the loop */
}
```

The example deserves a lot of explanation.

Immediately after the start of the main function is the declaration of the variables it uses, two integers called i and isquared. Several variables can be declared on one line in this way, by separating their names with commas. The names must begin with a letter or underscore and may consist of the letters a-z, A-Z, the digits 0-9 and the underscore __. The length of the names you may use depends on your particular system, so find out. Making them too long means that only the first so-many will actually matter, the rest being ignored. Six is almost always safe.

The next part of the program is a loop controlled by a **for** statement. What it does is threefold. First, the variable i is set to 1; then, while i is less than or equal to 10, the body of the loop is carried out; at the end of each iteration of the loop 1 is added to i. Notice carefully the position of the semicolons in the statement.

To make the loop do something less usual, say go from 100 down to 10 in steps of 5 the statement would look like this:

```
for(i = 100; i> = 10; i = i−5){
```

which should cause little or no surprise.

By now you may be wondering about the curly brackets this program has sprouted. They are used to group statements together, making several 'look like' one (amongst other jobs); they do the same sort of thing that 'begin' and 'end' do in other languages. In our example, the first { and last } mark the beginning and end of the main function. The other pair are used to group the statements inside the loop. If there had only been one statement to be controlled by the loop, the brackets would be unnecessary.

In fact, the two statements inside the loop **are unnecessary** –arguments to a function like printf may be expressions. The actual arguments were

a string	"%d %d\n"
a variable	i
a variable	isquared

but isquared can be replaced by the expression i∗i. Here's the amended program.

```
main(){
        int i;
        for(i = 1; i < = 10; i = i+1)
                printf("%d %d\n",i,i∗i);
}
```

Printf is a library function and is **not** part of C, but it's so widely used that a small amount of explanation is needed here. It gets more detailed treatment in the coverage of library functions in chapter 9. Printf is used to format and print various things on the standard output of your program (usually the terminal unless you've redirected it). The first argument to printf is a string (strictly a **character pointer**) which printf prints, character by character. A '%' character is a warning to printf that it may be called upon to format and print one of the other arguments. In the example above, the %d means to print in decimal, %f would mean a floating point number. Each of these format specifications encountered causes printf to look one argument further through its argument list and print it. Printf is very useful – we use only a little of its power here.

4.7. Increment and decrement

By now, our example program is almost in the form that an experienced C programmer would have written. The final change is to replace the assignment i = i + 1 with a shorthand form. By the way, you should have noticed that in C the symbol for assignment is a single = sign, not := . Adding one to something is so common that C has a special notation for it: i + + . Subtracting one could similarly be done with i − − . Here's the final version of this program.

```
main(){
        int i;
        for(i=1; i <= 10; i++)
                printf("%d %d\n",i,i*i);
}
```

Try it.

The **increment** and **decrement** operators just mentioned can be used two ways. In the assignment

```
a = i++;
```

the variable a is set to the original value of i; i is then incremented. The alternative form is

```
a = ++i;
```

where i is incremented first and then a is set equal to the new value of i. The decrement (subtract one) operation works the same way. When they are not involved in a larger expression

```
++i and i++
```

are equivalent, just as

```
−−i and i−−
```

are. The last part of our **for** statement could have had either version of **increment** with exactly the same effect.

4.8. Control of flow

C provides a powerful kit of parts to let you control the flow of your programs. They all test *logical* whose values are either zero or nonzero. C treats zero as if it had the truth value false; nonzero is considered true.

In the sections which follow you will see a lot of use of the term *statement*. Exactly what a statement is needs careful definition; you will find the definitions in the references. The major problem (as beginners see it) is where semicolons are needed and how to use the curly brackets. We prefer not to give an informal guide which would only tell half the story and end up misleading you; instead we will give examples of programs which work and leave you to draw your own conclusions. If you do have any doubts then the only real solution is to look up what the language definition says, unfortunately parts of it make James Joyce read like Enid Blyton.

4.8.1. The for statement

You've seen this already, here it is again

for(expression1; expression2; expression3) statement

The effect is first of all (and once only) to evaluate expression1. Then, while expression2 is nonzero, the statement part is executed, followed by the evaluation of expression3. The normal use of all this is to use expression1 to initialise a loop counter, expression2 to decide when the loop should finish and expression3 to update the loop counter; as in earlier examples. If one or both of the first and third expressions are missing then it just means that nothing is evaluated at that point. A missing expression2 is treated as a permanently true condition and the loop goes on for ever unless special steps are taken to jump out of it. Try this infinite loop for size (but make sure you know about the INTERRUPT key, chapter1).

```
main(){
        int i;
        for(i = 1; /* no second expression */; i++)
                printf("i= %d\n",i);
}
```

The semicolons are important inside the **for** statement; compare the one above with this loop-for-ever fragment

for(;;)

4.8.2. The while statement

The **while** statement is the same as a **for** with no first and last expression. Its form is this:

while(expression)
        statement

While the expression is nonzero the statement part is executed. A **for** statement can be re-written as a **while;** the following two bits of program are identical in effect† (though rather useless).

---

†Actually, they aren't quite identical. A **continue** inside a **for** loop will cause the expression3 part to be evaluated. The same thing inside a **while** will jump straight to the test of the controlling expression.

```
for(i = 1; i < = 10; i + +){
        a = a + i;
        b = a*a;
} /* same thing with a while instead */
i = 1;
while(i < = 10){
        a = a + i;
        b = a*a;
        i + +;
}
```

Of course the **while** statement checks to see if the loop should ever be executed. In some rather rare cases it's nice to be able to force at least one execution of the loop – the next statement we cover allows you to do it.

4.8.3. The do statement

To force at least one execution of a loop controlled by a **while** statement, the **do** statement is used in conjunction with a **while**.

```
do
        statement
while(expression);
```

Take careful note of the semicolon. Here is another program fragment which uses a **do** statement.

```
j = 5;
do{
        a = a + i;
        i = i*2;
}while(– –j);   /* terminate when (– –j) reaches zero */
```

Or one without curly brackets (only a simple statement inside)

```
i = 7;
do
        a = a + i;
while(– –i);   /* terminate when (– –i) reaches zero */
```

4.8.4. Continue and Break

There are two statements that allow you to take special action inside loops. **Continue** is used to skip to the end of a loop and avoid any statements that were still due to be executed. **Break** causes you to leave

67

the loop immediately. You can't really use them at all until you know about the **if** statement – an unconditional **break** or **continue** inside a loop is no good to anyone. Look for examples of their use later on.

4.8.5. The if statement

This statement must be familiar to everybody using modern procedural languages. In C it looks like this.

```
if(expression)
        statement
else
        statement
```

As usual the **else** part is optional – if you do have it, it refers to the first **else** -less **if** before it, again this is the usual thing. Examples are probably best.

```
if(a < b)              /* if a less than b then      */
        b = 0;         /* set b to zero              */
if(a > b){             /* if a more than b then      */
        i++;           /* add one to i               */
        b = 0;         /* set b to zero              */
}else
        c++;           /* otherwise add 1 to c       */
if(a+b < c)
        if(a > c)
                b++;
        else           /* this else goes with 4th if */
                c++;
else{                  /* this with the 3rd if       */
        a = c;
        b = 0;
}
```

Now a real program: this prints the sequence 12345789 (no 6) and illustrates a poor way of using the **continue** statement. Normally you would change the sense of the test for equality and dispense with the **continue** statement. Unfortunately a good illustration of **continue** would be rather hard at this stage.

68

```
main(){
        int i;
        for(i =1; i < = 10; i+ +){
                if(i = = 6) /* test equality */
                        continue;
                printf("%d",i);
        }
}
```

The **continue** is executed when i is equal to 6 (that's what the = = does) and causes a jump to the end of the loop, thus skipping the printf. Curly brackets are needed as there is more than one statement inside the loop. Since an **if-else** pair are considered to be one statement, the next example does the same job but without extra curly brackets.

```
main(){
        int i;
        for(i = 1; i < = 10; i+ +)
                if(i = = 6)
                        continue;
                else
                        printf("%d",i);
}
```

Replacing the **continue** with **break** would have stopped the loop then and there by jumping out of it completely.

4.8.6. The switch statement

What most languages would call a **case** statement, C is perverse in calling a **switch** (not unreasonably – it isn't exactly a **case** statement). It's used to perform a multi-way selection depending on the value of some expression. For example, to find out if an expression results in an odd number between $1 - 10$, an even one in the same range, or is out of range, you can do this:

```
switch(a+b){
        case 0:
        case 2:
        case 4:
        case 6:
        case 8:
        case 10:
                printf("Even\n");
                break;
```

```
case 1:
case 3:
case 5:
case 7:
case 9:
            printf("Odd\n");
            break;
default:
            printf("Out of range\n");
}
```

The result of the expression in the brackets (they **must** be there) following the **switch** is used to select one of the **case** values. Control is then transferred to the statements following the selected **case**. Execution will continue to proceed normally from that point and if you don't want to end up executing all the following cases as well, you will need to use a **break** statement; the example shows this. The **break** causes the program to leave the **switch** statement entirely. Execution continues at the statement after the closing } bracket.

If the example contained no **break** statements, the "Odd" and "Out of range messages" would be printed as well as the correct one when the statement resulted in an even number between 0 and 10. What would in-range odd numbers do?

The **case** values in any one **switch** must all be different; having two lines reading

    case 1:

in the previous example would be illegal. So would any value in place of the 1 which wasn't an integer constant. The **default** prefix indicates that the statements following it are to be selected if the **switch** expression results in a value that isn't defined by one of the **case** prefixes. If none of the values match and there isn't a **default** prefix present, none of the statements in the **switch** is executed.

4.9. Expressions

Conveniently ignored until now, we can't put them off any longer.

4.9.1. Relational expressions

E.g. a < b. These actually have a value (if you want it): 0 if the expression is false, 1 if it is true. The relational operators are

```
<       less than
>       greater than
< =     less than or equal
> =     greater than or equal
```

They have precedence over (are worked out before) the equality operators

```
= =     equal to
! =     not equal to
```

If you need examples of them, look at the control of flow stuff above.

4.9.2. Bitwise operators

C allows you to treat integer values as arrays of bits. You can perform the following operations on these quantities:

```
&       and
|       or
∧       exclusive or
< <     shift left
> >     shift right
~       ones complement
```

examples of these in use are

```
a = b & 7;      /* select low 3 bits */
a = b | 7;      /* set low 3 bits to 1 */
a = b ∧ 1;      /* flip lowest bit */
a = ~b;         /* ones complement */
a = b< <3;      /* shift left 3 places */
a = b> >3;      /* shift right ditto */
```

Be careful of the right shift; what happens to the most significant bit depends on your hardware and you may have to perform an **and** or an **or** after it to get the result you wanted†‡.

---

†Some compilers give -1 instead of +1. The definition we're working to is the one given in references [6] and [7].

‡ Reference [6], p45.

71

4.9.3. Logical connectives

To form interesting logical expressions you can use the logical **and** (&&), the or (||) and the not (!). **And** gives a result of 1 if both its operands are nonzero, a result of 0 if not. **Or** is like **and** but, surprise surprise, gives a result of 1 if either of its operands are nonzero. **Not** turns a nonzero into zero, zero into 1. Watch out for funny results when you use the editor to edit these expressions, the ampersand (&) is a special character. Here are some examples of the logical connectives.

```
if(a<b && b<c)      /* if a<b AND b<c */
if(a<b || b<c)      /* if a<b OR b<c */
if(!b)              /* if not b (true if b zero) */
```

The **not** operator is often used to test the state of a flag; imagine a variable called 'off' which is true when something is off and false when something is on. Code which reads 'if not off' – if(!off) – makes sense in the right applications.

4.10. Assignments

4.10.1. Assignments themselves

These sound like the sort of thing a gigolo should have – but they have assignations. Assignments are less fun but they're the best you can do with a computer, unless you're very inventive. The simplest form is the straightforward assignment:

```
var = expression;
```

where a variable is set to the value of some expression. The expression can be made up of arbitrary combinations of legal values and operations on them; the relational expressions, bitwise operators and logical connectives could all be involved since they all produce numerical results.

We've neglected arithmetic operators until now on the assumption that you would understand what they meant without having it explained. Just in case you didn't, or would like to make sure, here's a list of them

```
+    /* addition */
-    /* subtraction */
*    /* multiplication */
/    /* division */
%    /* remainder */
```

72

The remainder operator is possibly new to you. It's used in the same way as division but gives the remainder instead of the quotient; it isn't a lot of use with non-integer variables.

x % y

gives the remainder when x is divided by y. A few legal assignments are shown here by way of example.

```
a = b;
a = b + c;
a = (b + c)/d;
a = e > f;
a = (e > f && c < d) + 1;
a = a < < 3;
```

It's quite reasonable to assign the result of a relational expression to a variable; after all, it's only a number.

The last example is interesting. It shifts the variable 'a' left by three places then assigns the result back to a. C has a special form of assignment operator for cases where the left hand side of an assignment is repeated on the right. We can re-write

a = a < < 3;

as

a < < = 3;

which may not look like an improvement. Where it scores is when the left hand part is itself a complicated expression, perhaps involving some nasty array subscripts which you stand a good chance of getting wrong if you have to write them out twice. Another place where this is a convenient notation is in cases like:

a + = 2;   /* add 2 to a */

which reads much better than the other version once you've got used to seeing it. ALGOL-68 users will be used to the idea. The list of legal assignment operators which work like this is:

+ =   − =   * =   / =   % =   < < =   > > =   & =   ∧ = | =

Using these assignment operators instead of the longer forms has two important side-effects. First, the left hand side is only evaluated once; this is important since it may contain array subscripts or pointers which have increment or decrement operators associated with them. Evaluating these twice would not do what you wanted. Secondly, it is a very useful clue to the compiler to help it generate more efficient code.

73

4.10.2. Value of assignments

Assignments actually have a value and may themselves be used in expressions. Their value is the value of whatever is assigned. This is sometimes extremely useful, helping programmers to write concise, lucid programs that are a joy to read. It is equally extremely easy to abuse the feature and write highly unreadable programs. When we use it later, we'll try to point out where we think it's a valuable thing to do.

```
/*
 * an example of assignments with values.
 * This piece of code
 * and the next
 * have the same effect
 */

a = (b = c+d)/(e = f+g);

/* next piece */

b = c+d;
e = f+g;
a = b/e;

/* we prefer the second example */
```

4.10.3. Constants

Constants are written in much the same way as most other languages. Integer constants are written as 1,2,3 etc; floating point ones as 1.0,2.0,3.0 or 1e6 as scientific notation. There is a special class of character constants written as 'a', giving an integer whose value is that of the internal representation for the letter a. You may sometimes bump into octal constants (base eight); they look just like ordinary integers but start with a zero: 011 is equivalent to 9 decimal. There's a character version too; '\011' is another way of representing the ASCII tab character (look it up). You will see character constants in use in the 'ovp' program in appendix F.

4.11. Data Structures

C provides some very good data structuring facilities, which become indispensable once you've got used to having them. We shall look at two of these, **arrays** and **structures**.

4.11.1. Arrays

Every programmer using a modern high level language must have come across arrays. In C the declaration

    int xyz[100];

declares an array called xyz with 100 integer elements, accessible as xyz[0], xyz[1], up to xyz[99]. The range of the indices, from zero up to one less than the size of the array, is a prime cause of mistakes amongst novice C programmers. The reason for this unusual numbering scheme becomes obvious if you bother to look deep into what an array actually is, from C's point of view. For the moment you'll just have to get used to it, and be very careful because currently available C compilers don't bother to check your array accesses.

Multidimensional arrays are treated as arrays of arrays and are declared that way:

    int xyz[3][4][5];

declares 3 arrays of 4 arrays of 5 integers. (This fine distinction rarely matters unless you try clever tricks with pointers (next section but one), since accessing arrays by subscripts makes it irrelevant). If xyz had been declared as above then the expression

    xyz[1][2][3] + = 2; /* add two to the array element */

is both legal and much preferable to

    xyz[1][2][3] = xyz[1][2][3]+2;

since it is both easier to write and more obvious about what it does.

4.11.2. Structures

Arrays aren't always the ideal solution to your particular problem. Often there are more desirable ways of ordering your data, as in Pascal's **record** structure, although refugees from FORTRAN may not realise what they are missing. C has **structures** to offer in this area, as well as **unions** which are broadly equivalent to **records** and **variant records** in Pascal. We aren't going to discuss unions in this chapter.

The declaration

    struct xyz{
            int   aaa;
            char   bbb;
            double ccc;
    }abc;

declares a **structure** variable called abc; the structure contains 3 **members** which are an integer called aaa, a character called bbb and a floating point number called ccc. The members of the structure can be accessed individually as abc.aaa, abc.bbb and abc.ccc.

The xyz in the declaration is known as the *tag* and gives a name to this sort of structure for later use; assuming that the previous declaration had already been made then

    struct xyz s1,s2,s3;

will declare three new structures (s1,s2,s3) identical to the already declared abc. Of course you can have arrays of structures, structures containing arrays and so on.

If you know anything about the use of records or structures – call them what you will – you're bound to be asking yourself about *pointers*. C most certainly does have pointers, in fact they are probably one of its most obvious features. It would be hard to find a C program which didn't use them; they're almost essential. Let's see what they look like.

4.12. Pointers

This is going to be hard work if you've never used pointers before: explaining them is never easy, illustrating their use is difficult too, at least to do it simply is. Please persevere – pointers are widely used in C programs and it's a poor programmer who hasn't got the ability to use them.

In C pointers are declared by saying what sort of object they point to.

    int obj,*p;

declares two things – an integer called **obj** and a pointer called **p**. The pointer is not called *p, the * shows that it **is** a pointer, the **int** part of the declaration says that **p** will be used to point to integers.

Before you can use a pointer you've got to make sure that it **points to something.** Let's make it point to that integer called obj, using the & operator which means 'the address of' when it's used in this context.

    p = &obj;

The assignment assigns the *address* of obj to the pointer p; from now on p is pointing to obj. To refer to the thing a pointer points to, the notation is *p, where p is the pointer. For example,

    p = &obj;
    *p = 2;

is exactly the same as

    obj = 2;

until the value of p is changed, making it point somewhere else.

4.12.1. Using pointers

Trying to teach someone how to use pointers simply by writing about them is likely to be as fruitful as trying to teach them to ride a bike the same way. Examples will help, but there isn't room for enough here; our best suggestion is to refer you to the other texts and any example programs you can get your hands on.

A few points might help you understand any examples you do see. Pointers can help make programs more efficient, especially for sequential access to arrays or structures. Copying one array into another is a common enough operation:

```
int a[100],b[100],i;
for(i=0; i<100; i++)
        a[i] = b[i];
```

can be re-written as

```
int a[100],b[100],*ap,*bp;
ap = a; bp =b;
while(ap < &a[100])
        *ap++ = *bp++;
```

In the second example the assignments ap = a and bp = b are interesting. You might have expected to see the address of the first element of each array being assigned instead. In fact you did. The name of an array is identical to taking the address of its first element, so **a** and **&a[0]** are equivalent. After initialising the pointers, a loop is executed until one of the pointers falls outside the array it points to (&a[100] is not part of a). Both pointers are automatically incremented.

Why doesn't *ap++ increment what ap points to? Because the increment operator binds more tightly than indirection. (*ap)++ would increment the thing ap points to, but of course the **while** loop would never terminate then, as well as the whole assignment becoming meaningless.

Now admittedly the pointer version doesn't look like an improvement on the other one. Nonetheless, it stands a good chance of being more efficient, particularly if the objects pointed to are large (like **double** variables). It would be even better where the objects pointed to were large structures **but** some C compilers will not permit assignment of one structure to another, although the current Unix Version 7 compiler does. If you've got one of the older ones, you'll have to do it member-by-member.

This introduces another point (pun). Pointers are especially useful for handling structures; they make it very easy to build linked lists and trees of these things. Remember back to that structure tagged **xyz**. Let's declare another one of them, and a pointer to it, like this:

```
struct xyz anothr,*sp;
/* initialise the pointer */
sp = &anothr;
```

Now we can access individual members of the structure that the pointer points to. Each member can be referred to by the use of the 'pointed to' operator, ' −'. An example of this would be

p − >member

where **p** is the pointer and **member** is the name of the member you want. The resulting quantity has the same *type* that the member was declared to have: p − >aaa refers to the *integer* member of **anothr,** p − >bbb to the *character* and p − >ccc to the *double* member. The −> operator binds very tightly indeed.

Like the example accessing an array of integers, an array of structures could be accessed using the **increment** operator. C makes sure that adding 1 to a pointer causes it to point to the next object in an array, provided that the pointer was declared to point to that sort of object. C doesn't check that the pointer is pointing to anything sensible, it's up to you to make sure. C will let you index an array by anything, no matter what you declared the array to be; the same lack of restriction extends to pointers.

We can illustrate one use of pointers by looking at a singly-linked list. An array of 100 structures is declared, each structure containing a **double** variable and a pointer to one of these structures. A loop is used to a) set the number part to 1.0, 2.0, etc. and b) set the pointer part to point to the next member of the list. The list is then traversed by following the pointers and the number contained in each structure is printed.

```
/* the array of structures */
struct list__ele{
        double num__part;
        struct list__ele *point__part;
}list[100];
```

78

```
main(){
        int i;
        struct list_ele *lp;
        /* initialise */
        for(i=0; i<100; i++){
                list[i].num_part = i+1;
                list[i].point_part = &list[i+1];
        }
        /* mark end of list */
        list[99].point_part = 0;
        /* traverse list */
        for(lp=list; lp!=0; lp=lp->point_part)
                printf("%f\n",lp->num_part);
}
```

Let's explain the hard bits. The initialisation is reasonably simple provided you remember that array indices start at 0 and go upwards. The pointer at the end of the list is set to 0; this is perfectly legal and very useful. C guarantees that a pointer whose value is 0 is not pointing to anything, which makes the value convenient to indicate a 'null' pointer.

Traversing the list is done by setting the pointer 'lp' to point to the first element. While lp is non-zero, the number part of the structure it points to is printed, then lp is set to the value of the pointer part; that makes it point to the next member in the list. This traversal is, therefore, insensitive to the position of all but the first member of the list.

Make very sure that you understand this example. The time spent working out what happens will be well repaid if you have to use C to write important programs. What happens if the line

```
list[99].point_part = 0;
```

is replaced by

```
list[99].point_part = list;
```

and why?

4.13. Functions

And about time too.

4.13.1. Declaring functions

You declare a function by giving its type, its name and its **arguments**; then its **local variables**. Next comes the executable part of the function and finally the return, either by falling through the last curly bracket or by explicitly saying **return**. Here's an example of a function which returns the sum of its arguments.

```
int sum(arg1,arg2)
        int arg1,arg2;{
        int total;
        total  =  arg1 + arg2;
        return(total);
}
```

The function is declared as **int sum** which means it's a function returning an integer. In fact the **int** isn't needed because C will assume it unless you say otherwise. The two *arguments*, **arg1** and **arg2**, are also declared to be integers. Once again the declaration is unnecessary because of C's assumption that it's dealing with integers unless told otherwise. There is also one local variable called **total** which **does** have to be declared to be integer.

The function calculates the sum of the arguments and returns it. Here it is again, but in a complete program. The unneccessary declarations have been dropped.

```
main(){
        int i,j;
        for(i  =  1; i<100; i++)
                for(j  =  1; j<100; j++)
                        printf("%d + %d  =  %d\n",i,j,sum(i,j));
}
sum(a,b){
        int total;
        total  =  a+b;
        return(total);
}
```

The variable **total** isn't needed either and the body of the function could have been just

```
return(a+b);
```

if you really bothered to write it in the first place.

The **return** statement doesn't have to have an argument. By itself

```
return;
```

causes a return from the function, but with an unpredictable value. This is perfectly alright if you don't want a value; presumably because the

80

function is being used as what Pascal would term a *procedure*; something without a value. In C the two function calls

    sum(x,y);

and

    a = sum(x,y);

are both quite legal – the first call of **sum** returns a value which is ignored.

Local variables aren't guaranteed to contain any specific value when a function is entered and they certainly won't retain their values between one call of the function and another. You must always assign a value to a local variable before using it. Global variables are different: They're available throughout the program and are set to zero when the program is started **unless** they've been specifically initialised to something else. The example program at the end of this chapter shows how to initialise a global variable.

C assumes, unless you warn the compiler, that a function returns an integer. If anything else is returned, the functions calling it will get confused **unless you tell them.** The best way of doing this is to declare all the unusual functions at the head of the program. Here we do just that, calculating the values of the square root of $\sin(x) + \sin(x)*\cos(x)$ for various values between 0 and 2*pi.

```
#define TWOPI (3.141592*2)
extern double sin(),cos(),sqrt();
double func();
main(){
        double i;
        for(i=0; i<TWOPI; i += 0.1)
            printf("i=%f, f=%f\n",i,func(i));
}
double func(x)
        double x;{
            return(sqrt(sin(x) + sin(x)*cos(x)));
}
```

The first line isn't actually part of C. It's used by the *preprocessor* which the **cc** command invokes before compiling a program. The preprocessor recognises the #define and makes a note of what was defined, in this case **TWOPI**. Wherever that string is found in the text of the program it's replaced with the rest of the line where **TWOPI** was defined. This facility is widely used to make programs readable and easier to maintain – if all the constants are defined in this way, only one line has to be changed to update them throughout.

The line

> extern double sin(),cos(),sqrt();

says that the program will be referring to three functions which return double-precision values, called **sin, cos** and **sqrt** respectively. The **extern** bit means that they aren't actually part of the current file but are to be found somewhere else. In fact they're in a library. Contrast this with the declaration of **func** which **is** found in this file. Declaring the functions here, at the beginning of the file, prevents any later use from expecting integer results. The rest of the program should now make sense!

4.13.2. Arguments to C programs

When a program is started by Unix it can be given arguments. You've done this already with things like **ls** and of course **cc**. These arguments appear as arguments to **main** and are available inside that routine. The proper declarations for them are:

```
main(argc,argv)
        int argc; char **argv;{
```

which says that **argc** is an integer and **argv** is a pointer to a character pointer. When the program is started, **argc** contains the count of the arguments and **argv** is set to point to an array of strings, the arguments themselves. Here's a program which echoes its arguments back to you.

```
main(argc,argv)
        int argc; char **argv;{ /* see notes above */
        int i;
        char **cpp;
        cpp = argv;                    /* take a copy of argv */
        for(i = 0; i<argc; i++ ) /* for every argument */
                                       /* print the argument */
                                       /* and step on to next */
                printf("%s\n",*cpp++ );
}
```

The %s tells printf to expect a string. Think hard about why this program works, then try it. You've just rewritten the system utility **echo.**

Well it's almost **echo** except that when you try it, you'll get a surprise. The first thing it prints is its name (a.out unless you've changed it) because, by agreement, the first argument to a program is always its name. Some programs actually rely on that fact to decide what they should be doing – a sort of hidden flag.

82

4.13.3. What's in an argument

When a function is called, its arguments are available for use inside the function as if they were variables. If the function changes their values, the corresponding change is **not** seen by the part of the program which provided the arguments (the 'caller'). This is because the compiler takes a copy of all the arguments to a function and passes it the copies, not the originals. How, then, do you write functions that change things in their caller? It can be done by passing pointers rather than the objects themselves. Try this and see why it works:

```
main(){
        int i;
        i = 10;
        zero(&i); /* pass the address of i */
                  /* i.e. a pointer to i. */
                  /* and print the resulting value */
        printf("i = %d\n",i);
}
zero(arg) int *arg;{
        /* write zero into wherever arg points */
        *arg = 0;
}
```

The function **zero** is passed a pointer to an integer and puts 0 into whatever the pointer points to.

4.14. The Standard I/O

Quite a lot of effort has been put into making C programs portable. Much of it has been directed at trying to provide a consistent and portable I/O interface – the Standard I/O package. To save our fingers (we have to type this ourselves) we are going to call it the SIO from now on. To get the SIO into your program you need to have the preprocessor control line

#include <stdio.h>

near to the front and with the '#' in the first column. The control line makes the preprocessor read a file containing all the necessary declarations and definitions for the SIO; it passes them on to the compiler which means you needn't bother about what's in there.

The entire package is much too large to describe in this chapter.

Kernighan and Ritchie [6] do a good job on it and it's given the full treatment in chapter 9; the most we can manage here is some short examples.

4.14.1. Reading and Writing

Your program will normally have three files open when it starts; they are passed on to it by the shell and are known as the *standard input*, the *standard output* and the *standard error* To use these from the SIO, as indeed any file, you need something called a *file pointer*. They are true pointers, used by the SIO routines to point to internal structures whose form is none of our business.

The SIO declares three of these pointers for us; they are called **stdin, stdout** and **stderr** which shouldn't leave you in much doubt about what they are used for. We'll look at i/o on these standard files first before going on to see how to get file pointers for other files.

To read a character you use the function **getc**.

        c = getc(stdin)

will read one character from the standard input and put it into the variable c. The same function can be used with any valid file pointer you have got. If you try to read past the end of a file, the special value EOF is returned; again EOF is defined for you in the SIO. The values returned by **getc** are integers, not characters, because in addition to providing all legal character values the function must also return the value EOF.

Writing to a file is just as easy.

        putc(charac,stdout)

writes the character **charac** on the standard output. Once more you can use any valid file pointer – perhaps **stderr**. Be careful, though, using character pointers with **putc**. There is a strong likelihood that **putc** will be something called a *macro* (macros are another feature of the preprocessor). When the macro is handled by the preprocessor it may make several references to **charac,** which is no problem if charac is a **simple character variable.** If, on the other hand, it's a pointer with an **increment** operator attached, the pointer may be incremented several times. We have to recommend that you should avoid the use of increment/decrement operators within calls to the SIO functions.

The use of character i/o is easily shown in this example which copies the standard input to the standard output a character at a time. It also counts the characters and reports how many were copied by printing a message on the standard error file.

```
#include <stdio.h>
main(){
        int c;
        int count;
        /* read characters up to end-of-file */
        while((c = getc(stdin)) != EOF){
                count++; /* if not EOF then count it */
                putc(c,stdout); /* and print it */
        }
        /* then say how many characters were read */
        fprintf(stderr,"%d characters read\n",count);
}
```

Notice how the **while** tests the result of an assignment. This is a very common use of assignment statements – putting them inside conditional statements and testing the result – so you would do well to remember it. There's also a call of **fprintf** which is a close relative of the **printf** we've already met. The only difference is that **fprintf** expects a file pointer as its first argument and prints on that file. **Printf** only prints on the standard output.

Compile and run it with its input redirected from its own source code. Here's how we did it – the source code file is called zz1.c.

```
$ cc zz1.c
$ a.out < zz1.c
    ( it prints its own source code)
165 characters read
$
```

4.14.2. Opening and closing files

It's all very well playing with the standard input and output files but there's a limit to what you can do with them. The big boys and girls will want (gasp) to open and close their own files. First they will need some file pointers.

The SIO predeclares a type called **FILE** so you can declare your own file pointers and be sure they are the right sort of thing. Having declared one you need to get it pointing to a file structure in the depths of the SIO routines; happily there's a function provided which will do it. To open a file, you call the function **fopen,** giving it the name of the file you want and a **mode** taken from one of "r", "w" or "a"; they mean read, write and append respectively. The name you give it is the UNIX pathname of the file you want. **Fopen** returns either a valid file pointer or the predeclared value NULL; you should always check to make sure the file was opened successfully. Here's a program which opens a file called 'fred' and copies it into one called 'bill'.

```
#include <stdio.h>
main(){
        FILE *fp,*bp; /* two file pointers */
        int c;
                        /* set up fp          */
        if((fp = fopen("fred","r")) == NULL){
                fprintf(stderr,"Can't open fred\n");
                exit(-1); /* instant death */
        }
                        /* set up bp          */
        if((bp = fopen("bill","w")) == NULL){
                fprintf(stderr,"Can't open bill\n");
                exit(-1);
        }
        while((c = getc(fp)) != EOF)
                putc(c,bp);
}
```

The **exit** function will always terminate a program immediately; we guarantee that it will never return from a call. The argument passed to exit is returned to, and sometimes used by, the program which invoked the current one. You should always pass back a value which indicates whether or not the program was able to run correctly; this is normally a zero. Any other value is taken to mean that a problem cropped up, so we've chosen −1.

The read, write and append modes of **fopen** are self explanatory to a large degree. Read is obvious – you get a file you can read from. Write creates the file if it didn't exist; throwing away any previous contents if the file did already exist. Append is like write but leaves the previous contents intact.

4.15. The end!

Well, that wraps it up. We haven't covered a third of what we wanted but there just isn't room. Lots of people will be annoyed by our choice of what we put in and what we left out; to them we say "write your own book" and we wish you well.

You've met quite a lot of the language now, but it's practice that you need to learn it properly. Do experiment, devour the listings of as many real programs as you can, read the other books and enjoy yourself. As a final example we present a short and slightly ugly system utility written by Banahan during a boring Boxing day. It's called ovp; it reads either the standard input or from named files and writes on the standard output. What it reads it writes, converting characters which are underlined into characters which are repeatedly overstruck. It has been in use at Bradford for some time and doesn't contain any bugs that we know about. The text of ovp is in appendix F.

Ovp uses *register* variables, we didn't mention them earlier. They are the same as any other but they don't have an address; you can't use a pointer to point to them. Declaring register variables is a hint (only a hint) to the compiler that they will be heavily used and it might be a good idea to use a hardware register to hold them. Declaring register variables where they aren't needed can have the opposite effect to the one you wanted; you might mislead the compiler into using registers to hold variables when they could be more efficiently used elsewhere.

Chapter 5

The UNIX Filestore

The UNIX filestore is organised in a hierarchical fashion, forming a tree structure of directories and files. Every file store (usually an individual disc pack) is a self-contained unit consisting of a root directory and a number of files, some of which may themselves be directories.

5.1. Directories

Directories are treated in exactly the same way as other files, but with one exception, UNIX won't allow anybody to write directly into them. Allowing all and sundry to write in directories would be very silly, giving users the ability to destroy the structure of the filesystem even if only by accident.

It's the directories where the names of files are to be found, each entry in a directory being one name for a given file. Each user has a 'home directory' where you are placed upon login; you may also create subdirectories to contain files which it's convenient to group together. UNIX maintains several directories for its own use; one of these is the 'root' directory. Any file in the system can be found by tracing a path from the root through a chain of directories until the desired file is found. Other system directories contain all the files provided for general use; commands generally reside in '/bin' and libraries in '/lib'.

Each entry in a directory consists of two parts; a name of up to fourteen characters and a pointer, called a 'link' The link points to something called an 'i-node', which is really (as far as the operating system is concerned) the important part of a file. The i-node is where all of the information about a file is stored; a file's length, date of creation, ownership, modes and all the other important details are kept here. Thus a file doesn't exist within a particular directory, the directory entry merely consists of its name and a pointer to the information actually describing the file, see figure 1.

Each directory always has at least two entries; the name '.' in a directory is a link to the directory itself. Thus a program (such as **ls**) may read the current directory without knowing its pathname. The command

   ls

is equivalent to

   ls .

The name '..' refers to the parent of the directory in which '..' appears; put simply '..' is a link back up the tree structure toward the root. Look at Chapter 2, figure 1 if you're confused by this.

5.2. Pathnames

UNIX calls the route to a file through the directory hierarchy a 'pathname', which is a sequence of directory names separated by '/' and ending in a filename. If the sequence begins with '/' then the pathname is absolute and the search commences at the root directory; for example

   /dir1/dir2/dir3/filename

would cause UNIX to look in the root directory for 'dir1'. Then it looks in 'dir1' for 'dir2', in 'dir2' for 'dir3' and finally in 'dir3' for 'filename'. Pathnames not starting with '/' cause UNIX to begin the search in the user's current directory; it's not uncommon for processes to change their current directory to some convenient place in order to reduce the length of any pathnames they want to use.

5.3. I-nodes

Each file on the system has exactly one i-node. The number of the i-node appears in the directory entry for filenames which refer to this file; so there's no imposed one-to-one correspondence between filenames and actual files of data. Two or more directories may have entries with the same i-node number; the directory entries then refer to the same file, and are said to be **links** to it. In this way it's possible for a single file (a single i-node) to be known by several different pathnames; a path name is simply a way of associating a name with an i-node, so one i-node can have lots of different names.

I-nodes are the system's description of files, directory entries allow a user to refer to a particular file by name. The i-node contains information such as

File type : regular / directory / special
Owner
Group
Protection information
Number of links
Date of creation
Date of most recent access and modification
Pointers to the data blocks

Figure 2 shows a directory containing four entries: 'fred', 'jane', 'bill' and 'coo'. Files 1 and 3 have one entry each in the directory, 'fred' and 'coo' repectively. File 2 has two entries 'jane' and 'bill' which are therefore synonyms for file 2. File 1 and file 3 could also be directories, each in turn linking to further files. Multiple links to one file need not be in the same directory, they may be almost anywhere on the filestore. The only restriction is that they must all be on the same logical device. The synonyms can result from the use of the **ln** command. If you'd like to try this sequence

      echo hello > jane
      ln jane bill

you'll create the situation described above for 'jane' and 'bill'.

Figure 3 shows a small filestore constructed in the way we've described. A typical UNIX installation will consist of more than one physical storage device; we will see later how these separate filestores may be combined into one large logical filestore spread over the physical devices.

5.4. File System Structure

Figure 4 shows an overall picture of the layout of one physical file system. UNIX treats any file system as a sequence of 512 character blocks numbered 0, 1, 2, ... The first block is reserved for a bootstrap if necessary. (A bootstrap is used during the start-up of UNIX and usually contains a stand-alone program that can load and execute a file).

The second block (block 1) is the file system 'superblock'; it contains all information necessary for using the filestore. The superblock includes the file system size, 'fsize' (number of blocks); the number of blocks reserved for i-nodes, 'isize'; and a pointer to the head of the list of free blocks. For a complete description of the format see File System(V) in your local manual.

Blocks from isize + 2 to fsize are set aside for data storage; unused

Directory

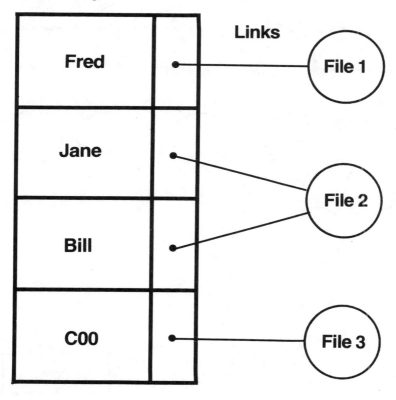

Figure 2 — A Directory

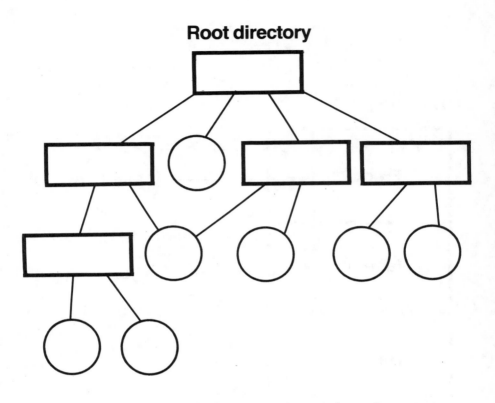

Root directory

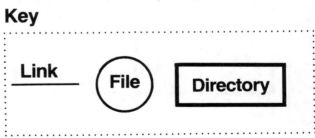
Figure 3 — A small filestore

blocks are chained together to form a 'free list'. Also mixed in with the data blocks are indirect blocks which are full of block numbers. I-nodes contain only a limited number of data block pointers; some of them are used to reference an indirect block which contains pointers to further data blocks. If fsize is less than the number of blocks available from the disc pack then the remaining space may be used for memory swapping.

When UNIX tries to open a file it first goes to the directory in which the filename resides to find the i-node number. It then reads the i-node to determine its type and to check permissions. If the file was either regular or a directory then the first block pointer is used to find the beginning of the data.

5.5. Special Files

You will remember from the description of an i-node that there are essentially three types of file. We have looked at the first two; regular files and directories. The third case constitutes the most unusual feature of UNIX, and corresponds to external devices - terminals, line printer, tape drives, disc drives, main memory, even the memory occupied by the kernel of the operating system. Of course, active discs and the memory special files are protected from indiscriminate access.

Special file i-nodes contain a reference to the operating system handler for the particular device. These special files may be accessed just as if they were ordinary files, taking into account device restrictions. It is obviously meaningless to write to a paper tape reader, or read from a line printer.

By convention, special files reside in the directory '/dev', but this is not enforced by the operating system. Thus

    cat plotfile > /dev/gp

will result in 'plotfile' being sent to the graph plotter, and

    pr −4 /dev/mt0

will read data from tape drive 0 printing it out in four columns.

This file/physical device equivalence is an essential feature of UNIX. In fact any source or sink of data is treated in exactly the same fashion; all are identical for the purposes of I/O.

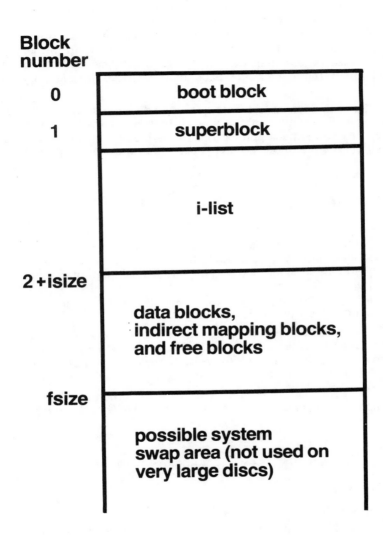

Figure 4 — Physical File System Layout

5.6. Protection

Permissions and changing them were looked at in chapter 2; but we will return to the subject briefly to explain how the protection information is stored in an i-node.

One word (16 bits) of storage is used, with each individual bit corresponding to a different permission:

Bit pattern (octal)

04000	set user id on execution (suid)
02000	set group id on execution (sgid)
01000	save text after execution − sticky bit ???
00400	owner read permission
00200	owner write permission
00100	owner execute permission
00070	group read/write/execute permissions
00007	all others read/write/execute permissions

This bit pattern is used in the alternative method of using the **chmod** command; the file protection mode is specified by a logical OR of the desired modes. An example terminal session followed by an explanation will illustrate this:

```
$ ls −l mycmd
−rw−rw−rw− 1 andy    4529 Jan 28 14:37 mycmd
$ chmod 755 mycmd
$ ls −l mycmd
−rwxr−xr−x 1 andy    4529 Jan 28 14:38 mycmd
$
```

The '−rw−rw−rw−' printed by **ls** shows the permission bit pattern for file 'mycmd'. Each character in the sequence corresponds to a bit in the i-node protection information. If a particular bit is ON then the appropriate character is printed, a '−' is interpreted to mean that bit is OFF.

The first character in the pattern will be a 'd' if the file is a directory itself, in any case users are not allowed to change the directory bit so this is for information only. The following 9 characters are split into 3 groups of 3: the first three correspond to the permissions for the owner of the file (in this case 'andy'); the middle three are the permissions for everybody in the same group as the owner; and the last three characters are the permissions for everybody else (other). The characters 'rwx' are interpreted as read permission, write permission and execute permission.

The original permissions on file 'mycmd' were '−rw−rw−rw−' which corresponded to a bit pattern (assuming 16 bits) of

95

```
1000000110110110    : binary
100666              : octal
```

the first '1' shows that 'mycmd' is just an ordinary file. After execution of the **chmod** command the permissions were changed to ' − rwxr − xr − x', giving a bit pattern of

```
1000000111101101    : binary
100755              : octal
```

We have already met the owner/group/others read/write/execute permissions; the remainder deserve some explanation here.

As you know, execution of a command causes the creation of a new process. Each active process has an effective user and group id used in determining its access permissions, normally these are set to those of the invoker. However, commands with set id (user (04000), group (02000), or both) in their permissions have the effective user (and/or group) set to that of the owner of the file rather than the invoker. **Ls** shows the set id bits as an 's' in the execute bit position of the appropriate group of 3 (either user or group). For example

```
$ chmod 4711 mycmd
$ ls −l mycmd
−rws− −x− −x 1 andy       4529 Jan 28 14:45 mycmd
```

which gives a bit pattern of

```
1001000111001001    : binary
104711              : octal
```

Commands with the 'save text' bit set, once invoked, are saved in the system swap space even if they are not currently executing. This is done for commonly used commands (like **ed, cat, ls**) in order to reduce the time to find, read, and execute them, this is because UNIX no longer has to read a file from a disc into memory one disc block at a time. Instead, the whole file can be read in one piece by the memory swapping system and started almost immediately. This can be a considerable asset in the case of commonly used commands, but has the disadvantage of requiring space in the system swap area, which is usually limited. It's up to you to decide whether or not you want to do it; only 'root' (see below) is allowed to set the save text bit.

There's one special user of the system who has privileged powers beyond those of an ordinary user. The login name is 'root', but the user is described as the 'super-user'. There are two ways of becoming the 'super-user'; one is to login as the user called 'root', the other to invoke **su** from the shell. In both cases you must give the the correct password – which we hope is a closely guarded secret. Once you are the super-user the shell prompt changes to

#

to remind you of your awesome power. No file protections affect the super-user, who can read or write anybody's files, and do all sorts of things ordinary users can't.

Some system commands require the power of the super-user to run; one of these is **passwd** which allows users to change their passwords. The password file, '/etc/passwd' is owned by 'root' and has only read permission for everybody else. The command **/bin/passwd** is also owned by 'root' but has the 'set-uid' permission assigned so that whoever runs it can modify the password file; the effective user id of the command **passwd** is therefore 'root'. When an ordinary user runs the command it is as if they temporarily become 'root'.

5.7. Multi-Volume File Systems

Although the root of a file system always resides on the same physical device, it's not necessary that the entire filestore be confined to this device. A properly structured volume (usually a disk or tape) can be 'mounted' onto any directory in the current file system. The effect of mounting a filestore volume onto a file is to transform all references to that directory into a reference to the root directory of the mounted file system. After the mount there's virtually no distinction between files on the removable volume and those on the permanent file system. Filestores may be mounted and unmounted while UNIX is running, and without any interruption to the service.

For reasons of efficiency and security, it's advisable, if possible, to have an entire file system of scratch space and use this as the '/tmp' directory. Efficiency, because the '/tmp directory' is heavily used by compilers and the loader, an extra moving head disc used here will help speed things up. Security, for the same reason, if the system does crash then its files which are still open that tend to leave the system corrupted. If the heaviest use is on an unimportant disc, its loss through corruption is less of a problem. If 'rk0' is this scratch volume than the command to mount it on directory '/tmp' is

/etc/mount /dev/rk0 /tmp

Note that the command **mount** resides in '/etc' and not '/bin'. The

97

corresponding command to unmount the file system is

/etc/umount /dev/rk0

Our installation maintains the 'root' directory, '/bin', '/etc', '/lib', plus a few others on one disc pack. The user file store, '/usr', consists of a separate disc pack, containing user files; this is mounted on directory '/usr' by the system initialisation sequence (when bootstrapping). Our '/tmp' directory is provided by a small fixed head disc which has its file system reconstructed before mounting. This has the advantage of removing any temporary files which were left hanging about when the system was last closed down. The technique of mounting and unmounting filestore volumes is also mentioned in chapter 10.

5.8. File Size and Locking

A file is able to grow almost without bound; standard UNIX has no file size limits, although many lookalike versions have some sort of limitation incorporated. If your system has no file size limits (look in your local documentation) then any file can be expanded using write(2) system calls until it exhausts the available space on the device. At this point the write call will fail and the operator's console will start receiving messages like 'out of space on dev X/X'. The only remedy for the situation is to remove the offending file as soon as possible. If the huge file is left then the system is likely to grind to a halt very quickly, particularly if the file is on the root filestore volume.

Notably absent from standard UNIX is the concept of file locking†, which is essential for serious database work. Admittedly, a comprehensive protection scheme may be implemented by cooperating processes; nevertheless, the indivisible nature of an operating system implemented lock is needed if UNIX is to become widely accepted by the commercial community. Some lookalikes already incorporate this feature, your local documentation should tell you if you have it.

---

†A file locking mechanism would allow one process access to a particular file to the exclusion of everybody else. In effect other processes wishing to access the file are made to wait until the first process has indicated that it has finished. Files which are currently open for reading must not be opened for writing, and files which are currently open for writing must not be opened in any mode. Reference [1], p86-88.

5.9. Questions

1) What is a pathname ?
2) What is the basic structure of the UNIX filestore ?
3) What is an i-node and how are they modified for different types of files ?
4) What is meant by the term 'special file' ?
5) How do you have to modify a program in order to read or write one of these special files ?

Chapter 6

Software Tools

6.1. What is a Software Tool?

One of the strengths of the UNIX operating system is the way that the system makes it so easy to use, combine and even write software tools. What are these curiously named things?

The simplest definition of a software tool is just 'a program'. Every program that manages to produce a result of some sort, no matter what the result actually is, can be thought of as being a tool; a tool which you use to produce that result. Now a program which only produces one result makes a tool of extremely limited use – not useless, only limited - and isn't what most people would think of as a 'real' tool. As with any other trade, the business of computing is made easier when you've got a decent toolkit, full of **flexible** tools. It's the flexible tools which are the important ones; once you've got those (and a decent 'workbench' to use them on) you can start producing your masterpieces.

Broadly speaking, there are two sorts of tool used in a UNIX system. There are the tools which do a specific job in a general sense; examples of these are the language compilers which will compile any program written in the right language and produce something which can be executed. These first sort of tools are rather rigid in their application, because (say) the C compiler won't compile a BASIC program; you wouldn't expect it to, either.

The second sort of tool is the flexible one. These tools are usually an order of magnitude less complicated than the first sort, and are intended to do a wide range of similar tasks. These tools usually have a number of optional 'flags' which their invoker supplies when the tool is used, and the tool modifies it's behaviour depending on which flags (or combination of flags) were supplied. Most of these tools have an important feature about them: they manipulate **text**, material which is readable by humans. The second important feature of the general-purpose tools is that they are usable as 'filters'.

6.2. Filters

We've already mentioned filters, but they're so important that we make no apology for bringing the subject up again. All of the general purpose software tools can be used in two ways. You can give them a list of arguments, some of which will be flags telling them how to behave, the rest of the arguments being a list of files; the tool will read those files and produce output that depends on what the tool was told to do and what was in those files. The output from a general purpose tool should always be to the standard output file.

Using the tools in the other way you don't give them a list of files. Instead they read their standard input file and take their input from there. It's this use of the standard input and standard output files which makes the idea of a 'filter' possible.

When a tool is used as a filter, it reads its standard input, manipulates and processes the information it reads, then writes the result to its standard output – it's a very simple idea. The power of filters isn't fully usable unless you can use 'pipes' to connect one to the other; this is where UNIX scores over almost every other operating system we have met. By taking a number of standard tools 'off the shelf', stringing them together using pipes and giving them the right flags, you can build up a structure which performs some highly complex operations on the input data. In many cases you'll find some combination of tools to do the job you want without you having to spend hours writing a complex and probably unreliable special purpose program.

6.3. The toolkit

In this chapter we give examples of the use of some of the most popular tools. There's no point in covering every utility (we haven't got the space anyway), so we will try to highlight the techniques of using tools and, on the way, give a few of the 'tricks of the trade' we've learnt during our association with UNIX.

6.4. Pr

Pr is a text formatter – nothing to do with 'word processing' this, pr is used to print text on your CRT or on a printer. Incidentally, we'd be worried about a system which hadn't got a printer; it isn't easy to do much in the way of useful work without one.

In common with most of the tools, **pr** responds to a number of flags, in this case telling it how to format the stuff it's printing. Without any flags (the 'default' case), **pr** reads the files you told it to, copying them to its standard output with a date, a title and some blank lines at the top of each page and a number of blank lines at the bottom of each page. The output expects to be sent to a line printer; each page will be 66 lines long, **pr** breaking up the input text to suit. If you invoke **pr** without any arguments at all, or only give it flag arguments, it will read its standard input to find the text and is therefore a filter.

A problem with filters is their willingness to read their standard input, this often catches beginners out. If you just give the command

        pr

the system will appear to go to sleep. What's happened? In fact the answer is easy: you've started **pr** with no arguments, so it's working as a filter; reading its standard input (your terminal), and copying what it reads to its standard output (your terminal), with the header and trailer we've already spoken about. The last thing you would want it to do is to provide a prompt, because that would involve it in writing the prompt on its standard output, making the output data useless for either input to a further filter or sending to a printer.

Try it out, typing something as input to the filter and terminating the text with the EOT key. Don't type EOT twice – the first will simulate end-of-file on input to the filter and make it tidy up then exit, the second will be seen by your shell and log you out! Here's an example:

        $ pr
        Have you seen the giant pistons on the mighty C.P.R. ?
        With the driving force of a thousand horse –you know what
        pistons are.
        <EOT>
        Apr 8 11:30 1982   Page 1

        Have you seen the giant pistons on the mighty C.P.R. ?
        With the driving force of a thousand horse – you know what
        pistons are.

The last line of the example above will be followed by enough blank lines to make the whole page of output 66 lines long.

To use **pr** in its other form, not as a filter, you would give it a list of files to be printed. Here's the example from chapter 2 slightly modified.

        pr – h Test- Data tempfile1 tempfile2

The '−h Test-Data' tells **pr** to print 'Test-Data' as a heading at the top of each page. We're going to look hard at the various flags this command will accept, so if you've got any sense you'll take a copy of the pr(1) page of the manual and compare it with our description. You'll learn quite a lot about how to read the manual if you do.

An important feature of **pr** is the way that flags can be given **between** the list of filenames. These flags apply to all further operations performed from the time when **pr** actually looks at them. This command

pr −h heading1 file1 −h heading2 file2 file3

causes file1 to be printed with the heading 'heading1', file2 and file3 are printed with the heading 'heading2'.

Pr will provide multi-column output. This is one of the most common uses we have for the command, helping to save a lot of printer paper (times are hard, trees are precious), especially if the circumstances are right. Imagine, if you will, a program whose output is a long list of words or numbers, one to a line and each only five or six characters long. Sending it to a printer using the standard 132-column paper results in a shocking waste. An example could be the use of **ls** to list the contents of a directory with several hundred entries; the output will be a single column with no line longer than fourteen characters.

By using **pr** to put this output into several columns across the page, you can reduce the amount of wasted paper by up to a factor of eight. Here's the command:

ls dirxxx | pr −8 −w132 | lpr

the output from the command 'ls dirxxx' was piped into **pr**. **Pr** is told to print it in eight columns (the '−8' flag), and that the output page is 132 characters wide ('−w132'). Finally, the output of **pr** is queued for your printer by **lpr**.

If you try the previous example in a directory with only a few entries, the output will only appear in one column; **pr** fills each column completely before it starts filling another. To get more than one column out there must be at least one column's worth of input. You can of course tell **pr** that the output page is to be shorter than 66 lines long:

ls | pr −3 −w80 −l15

will list your current directory in a form suitable for a CRT. The flags tell **pr** that it is to list in three columns, that the screen is 80 characters wide, and that the page is 15 lines long. Issuing that command in a directory with more than five entries will result in output with more than one column.

103

The '−l15' says that the page is 15 lines long, but the header and trailer account for 10 of them, leaving only 5 for the columns of information.

If the header and trailer are a nuisance, you can turn them off with the '−t' flag, so the previous example minus the header and trailer would be:

ls | pr −3 −t −w80 −l5

we suggest that you try them both, but do it in a directory with more than 5 files so you can see that it really does work.

Multi-column output will normally be separated by a 'sensible' amount of space, but this is also under your control − you can force the columns to be separated by a single character of your choosing.

ls | pr −3 −w80 −l15 −s,

will separate the columns by a comma instead.

The last two flags we'll leave for you to interpret. You shouldn't find it hard to work out what '+7' will do (look at the manual) and to realise that '−m' is no use at all when you're using **pr** as a filter. You might also like to ponder the fact that '+7' starts with a '+', not a '−' showing that the interpretation of flags rests with the command, not the operating sytem. The convention that flags should start with a '−' is adopted by agreement, not compulsion.

6.5. Command names

Let's pause briefly to ponder the subject of the names of commands. Several critics have spoken against the standard names of UNIX commands and some look-alike systems have chosen to re-name them. Whilst the naming of some commands is undoubtedly dubious, we'd like to add our own two pennyworth

In fact the name of a command is irrelevant, it's what it **does** that's important. It's a big mistake to confuse the name with the properties of the thing it refers to; calling a cabbage a turnip won't alter the fact that it's green, got leaves and tastes awful; it's a member of the brassicae no matter what names you call it. The mistake would lie in having two things called a turnip, having the same label for more that one referent helps nobody, resulting in confusion. The label (the name) becomes 'overloaded'. An example of an overloaded label is 'list'. In English† it already means

†Reference [8].

a catalogue of names, words etc.
to make such a catalogue
to incline to one side
a border or edging
to desire or choose
to listen to

each of the meanings having to be guessed from the context the word is found in. Now, who are you doing a favour by introducing a new meaning? Yet several voices have been heard suggesting that **cat** or **ls** should be re-named 'list' because it would 'help' beginners.

Well, it's up to the individual to mangle his or her own language, so for the record here are our thoughts.

Command names should be short – three, four or five characters long. Most computer users are poor typists and the probability of them typing a ten-character name without an error is vanishingly small. Single character names shouldn't be used; it's too easy to type them by accident, for the same reason the names of 'dangerous' commands should be relatively long.

Names which are pronounceable become popular. **Pr** is easy ('peear'), **ls** isn't quite so easy but still only two syllables, **pwd** is a real jaw-cracker. It's very important to make sure that pronounceable command names bear no resemblance to any commonly used word in your native language; 'meaningful' names are a complete waste of time, confusing more people than they help. If it takes one or more pages in the manual to explain a command, do you really think that it does any good to overload a word which already has meanings of its own?

A fine example of the right way to name commands is **grep**; short, pronounceable, no previous meaning and rapidly absorbed into the day-to-day conversation of UNIX programmers. Phrases like "Oh, grep for it" and "No trace with grep" are full of meaning to those in the know. Outsiders are, of course, totally baffled by it which is right and proper. There's nothing worse than listening to experts talking jargon and thinking that you understood them just because they used words you'd heard before, when in fact the words were bent far from their original meaning. Listen to a good politician for five minutes and you'll discover **exactly** what we mean.

6.6. Grep and friends

Three very useful tools, **grep, fgrep** and **egrep,** are used to find patterns of characters within files. The patterns are called 'regular expressions' in the documentation, a term which apparently meant something to the people who wrote it†. These regular expressions are in fact our old friends the 'patterns' which are recognised by **ed** and some other utilities.

For example, in a file of text called 'file', the command

    grep .abc file

will find and print every line containing the sequence 'abc' preceded by one other character. It would find 'aabc', 'xabc', '.abc' etc. etc.

    grep ' ∧ xyz' file

will find every line in 'file' starting with 'xyz'; the list of possible combinations is endless — these tools can also be used as filters.

It wouldn't be unreasonable to say that the three varities of **grep** are indispensable, cropping up all over the place — often in scriptfiles. How about this one-liner?

    grep $1 tel − dir

Put that in a file called 'phone', set execute permission on it and then maintain a personal telephone directory in 'tel − dir' with entries like

    mike 0274 733466 x8522
    andy 0274 733466 x8515

and the command 'phone mike' will print every line in the file where the characters 'mike' appear. Equally well, it'll tell you who a particular number belongs to in exactly the same way.

The different varieties of **grep** are tailored for different requirements, a fact which is mentioned rather coyly in the manual. Together with their various flags this family of file-searching, pattern-matching tools prove very useful, and some time spent learning what they are capable of will be well repaid later. Which version you need for any given job obviously depends on the task in hand, ultimately the decision is up to you.

6.7. Sort

Sort isn't as well appreciated as it should be, which is a shame. If you've got any sorting problems to solve, there's a good chance that you

---

†We learn during the editing of this manuscript that the term was coined by the mathematician S.C.Kleene and does have a precise definition. We apologise for our ignorance.

can get it done by **sort** without having to 'descend' to the level of actually having to write a special sorting program. The manual is fairly good at describing this tool, so we won't spend much time on it. A couple of brief examples ought to show a little of its flavour. Do you remember the **who** command, which tells you who is logged in? The output from **who** is sorted into alphabetic order on the name of the teletype where the user logged in. To sort it into alphabetic order keyed on the user name (in fact the whole line – the user name is the first part), pipe it into **sort**:

    who | sort

the way **sort** decides the ordering of letters and numbers depends on the way your hardware implements its character set. Any half-decent computer nowadays uses the ASCII character set; the only users who will get funny results are the poor devils who have to use mainframes like IBM with the EBCDIC character set.

Sort will sort into numerical or alphabetic order, forwards or reversed, it can be told exactly how records are split into fields, which field to key on; there are a lot of options. **Sort** is such a useful tool that we highly recommend you to learn it well, even if it's only to get the pleasure of watching someone banging their head on a wall when you tell them that their highly complex, special purpose three-week's-in-development data massaging suite is completely replaced by **awk, fgrep** and **sort** with a handful of flags.

6.8. Awk

Awk is a very underused utility at our installation, and we suspect the same will be true at yours. Many people are put off by its apparent complexity and never learn the delights of awk's flexibility.

The **awk** command is an interpreter for a pattern matching and text manipulation programming language. **Awk** uses a more general approach than the commands **grep, egrep** and **fgrep** (and can replace them if programmed correctly, although the result will be slow); the possible actions on finding a matching line are considerably more powerful than merely printing it.

As with the grep commands, **awk** will scan one or more input files looking for lines which match a pattern. Several patterns may be specified, along with actions to be performed for each successful match. The set of patterns plus actions constitutes an **awk** program; this may

107

either be given in the command line, or, more usually, the program is stored in a file and then read by **awk.**

An **awk** program is made up of one or more statements, each having the form

    pattern { action }

Each line of input is tested for a match against each of the patterns in turn, successful matches causes the associated action(s) to be performed. Either the pattern or the action may be omitted: matching lines are simply copied to the output if there is no action; and if there is no pattern then the action is performed for every line in the input. The trivial **awk** program

    { print }

copies its input to the standard output.

An **awk** pattern can be built up from a variety of expressions: regular expressions, such as used by **ed** and **grep;** arithmetic relationships, very similar to the syntax of C; string-valued expressions; and boolean combinations of all of these.

Several variables are built-in to **awk** to make the matching of parts of lines easier. The input is split into records for matching; by default the record separator is a newline, so each record is one line of the input file. The number of the current record is available as variable 'NR'. Similarly, each input record is split into fields by the field separator (default is white space). Individual fields are referred to as $1, $2, ..., etc; the whole input record is $0. The number of fields in the current record is available as 'NF'. The variables 'RS' and 'FS' refer to the input record and field separators, so they may be changed at any time.

For example, the following simple **awk** program will print all lines with more than 10 characters before the first colon in the line; when all the input has been read it prints the total number of such lines.

```
BEGIN           { FS = ':'; a = 0 }
length($1)>10   { print length($1) $0
                a = a + 1 }
END             { print "Total lines found = " a }
```

The program is executed by first creating a file (e.g. 'progfile') containing the text of the program and then typing

    awk −f progfile [textfile ...]

Awk will scan the text in 'textfile', or if a filename is missing it will read the standard input. Alternatively, the **awk** program may be typed directly as part of the command line.

awk program [textfile ...]

This method is useful for short program or when then **awk** program is generated from a shell script file

The special symbols 'BEGIN' and 'END' are matched before any input is read, and after the end of input has occurred respectively. So, the first statement in the program above sets the field separator to a colon, and gives a value of zero to variable 'a'. Variables come into being when first mentioned; they may contain numeric or string values depending on the context. By default, variables are initialised to a null string, which is the same as the numerical value zero: this makes the initialisation of 'a' superfluous, but we have included it for clarity.

The pattern from the second statement matches all lines having a first field of more than 10 characters. 'Length' is a built-in function returning the length of a string of characters, in this case $1. There are many more functions available, 'print' for example; all of them may be used with an argument, as in the case of

length($1) or print $2

When no argument is given then $0 is assumed; 'length' on its own returns the number of characters in the current record.

The action specified in the second statement first prints the actual length of the first field, and then prints the whole line. Finally it increments variable 'a' by one to count the line.

Awk would take a chapter to itself if we were to explain it in the detail it deserves. The power of this tool is considerable and there aren't many text manipulation problems where it can't help; **awk** is one of the tools that you hardly notice when you use it, but miss terribly when you have to use a system without it.

6.9. Make

There comes a point in most software projects when the scale of the whole thing gets too much to hold in your head. Then it is very easy to lose track of the interdependency between files; when one source file is changed others may need recompiling.

Make allows you to keep track of these dependencies and maintain up-to-date versions of programs and data files. The sequences of operations that result in the creation of certain files may be expressed easily using **make** syntax. If this information is stored in a file named 'makefile' then the command

    make

will search to determine what work is necessary and execute the appropriate commands.

A simple example will serve to illustrate how a 'makefile' is constructed. The program 'gron' depends on five files; 'main.c', 'gron.c', 'subs.s', 'defs.h' and 'gron.h'. Both main.c and gron.c use declarations from the header file defs.h, but only gron.c uses declarations from gron.h; file subs.s depends on no other information, it contains assembly language subroutines used by both of the C files. So, file main.c contains the lines

    #include "defs.h"
    #include "gron.h"

and gron.c contains the line

    #include "gron.h"

By convention the object versions of the three source files will be found in main.o, gron.o and subs.o; these are linked together with functions from the 'lplot' library to produce the executable program 'gron'. The following **make** text describes this relationship and sequence of operations

    gron: main.o gron.o subs.o
        cc main.o gron.o subs.o − lplot − o gron
    main.o: defs.h gron.h
    gron.o: gron.h

The first line says that 'gron' depends on three files: main.o; gron.o and subs.o: the second line in the makefile describes how to construct gron assuming that these files are available. The third and fourth lines show the header file dependencies of gron.o and main.o; there is, however, no corresponding line to describe how to make these object files, **make** is able to take an educated guess as to what is needed.

Make uses three sources of information when operating: the description from a makefile; the times of last modification of files described therein; and a set of built-in rules when the makefile leaves gaps in the explanation. A search of the file system will reveal that two of the '.o' files have C source files (.c), and the third contains assembler statements (.s). Make uses its built-in knowledge to generate an object file from a source file; for C it issues a 'cc − c' command, and for assembler it uses 'as − o'.

A simple macro substitution facility is available from **make;** macros are defined either by makefile description lines containing an equals sign. The following defines a macro 'OBJECTS' to be a string containing the names of the three object files which comprise the program 'gron'.

OBJECTS = main.o gron.o subs.o

Alternatively, a macro may be defined via the command arguments

make "LIBS = −lplot −lS"

The use of quotation marks is necessary to prevent the interpretation of the embedded blanks as argument separators. The previous makefile may be rewritten to use macro facilities

```
OBJECTS = main.o gron.o subs.o
LIBS = −lplot
gron: $(OBJECTS)
        cc $(OBJECTS) $(LIBS) −o gron
main.o: defs.h gron.h
gron.o: gron.h
```

Comparing this version with the previous shows that a macro is substituted into either a dependency line or a command by parenthesising its name and preceding it with a dollar sign.

To summarise: a makefile contains descriptions of file dependencies and sequences of operations needed to reconstruct a particular file, or files. Dependency lines start with the name of the target file, terminated with a colon (other forms are possibly, but this is the simplest). Names following the colon are those files opon which the target is dependent; a dependency that is too long to fit on one line may be continued further using a backslash at the end of the line. Command lines to be executed must immediately follow, starting with a tab character. Comments may be introduced into the makefile by preceding the comment with a sharp (#) character.

The documentation available for **make** isn't altogether easy to read, and like so many of the powerful tools it takes quite a lot of effort to learn how to use it properly. If you can find any, you'll probably discover that reading 'makefile' files is one of the best ways to discover the strengths (and weaknesses) of **make**.

6.10. Conclusion

In this chapter we've introduced and discussed some of the heavily used UNIX tools. Much of the popularity of UNIX stems directly from the tools that it's supplied with, and they all deserve study. The power of some of the tools is almost awe-inspiring. Nobody who designs software systems that use a formal 'language' of their own can afford not to know **yacc** and **lex**. The effect of such tools is often suprising. By removing the tedium from programming, these high level tools make it *likely* that difficult projects will be completed when previously they were merely *possible*. These techniques look set to have an important future. Learn them if you can!

Chapter 7

Text Preparation

Whether we like it or not, a fundamental part of all programming tasks is that of documenting our work. So important is this that one should consider most programs useless without some descriptive material, possibly in the form of a manual, which will explain to our colleagues how this marvel of modern science can benefit them. We also need to ensure that we can re-use this software tool in a few months time without repeating the learning curve.

By producing the text on-line, each iteration of the document will improve the finished product. Alterations are easily achieved, so there is an incentive to keep it up to date and hence accurate. In this chapter we will examine the way in which careful use of UNIX tools will lead to a more polished document with the minimum of effort.

7.1. Simple Text

By now you will have mastered the first and most important stage in preparing text: use of the editor. UNIX is very kind in that all (ordinary) files have the same status: they may be used to contain program source, executable programs (binary), or text as part of a document. This means that the editor commands used to enhance our text file may be the same as those needed to create and amend a program; after all both files are just streams of characters.

In the simple case we can create a file with the editor and type in the text as required. This is fine up to a point, but if you examine most reasonable documentation, it will soon become clear that everything is easier to read if it is presented in a uniform way: straight left and right margins; pagination (skipping the folds in continuous stationery); standard titles on the head of each new page etc.

Using the editor to justify margins or paginate text would be extremely tedious at the very least; almost impossible should an extra word be added at the head of an already prepared page. You have probably gathered by now that there is a tool to assist us in this task, known as a 'text formatter'. A text formatter is a program to layout a document in a uniform way, thus making it clearer and easier to read.

7.2. Using the Formatter

There is more than one such program available under UNIX. Which one to select might be a problem but we suggest you start by using the program called nroff on your system, unless of course local wisdom dictates otherwise in which case many of the examples presented here may not work. As the name suggests, **nroff** is a new version of the program 'roff' whose name is a convenient form of 'runoff', a more common name for the text formatter on non-UNIX systems. While on the subject of names, we should mention that **nroff** has a sister, **troff**, whose output is designed specifically for a phototypesetter; the commands are almost the same but with a few extensions. We will not make any further reference to **troff** since it is beyond the scope of this book and very few UNIX sites have access to a typesetter anyway.

Nroff has been developed over a number of years to run under various versions of UNIX which has resulted in there being some compatibility problems. This chapter is aimed at the novice so the examples will be restricted to those that we believe will work on all versions; if an example doesn't quite work as described, try asking your local expert for some help. It may be that you have a version of **nroff** we haven't come across. In any case you should obtain a copy of the "Nroff/Troff User's Manual" [9] applicable to your system. Try not to be overwhelmed by this enormous document, but do keep it handy for reference and later use. Incidentally, the tutorial examples found in it should be studied when you have completed this chapter.

7.2.1. Introduction to Formatting

Nroff reads the contents of the file(s) supplied as arguments, processes the text it finds, and writes the result on the standard output.

nroff [options] [file ..]

If no files are given as arguments, **nroff** will read the standard input and can thus be used as a filter.

Each line in the source file is either text to be processed or a 'request line' which comprises a command to **nroff**. Request lines must start with either the primary, or secondary, control character, usually these are the period '.' and prime ''' respectively, but either may be altered. This should be followed by a one or two character command name. Commands are the way in which the operation of the formatter is controlled. Most of them will alter the layout of some part of the rest of the output. As a trade-off between brevity and mnemonic value, nroff uses two character command names, each name is an abbreviation of the full command.

Nroff is designed to be as simple in use as possible so that a file containing no commands at all will still be formatted in some reasonable fashion. Of course this won't suit everyone, but try it with your text file as a first shot.

7.2.2. Formatting Terminology

There are certain keywords used when describing text formatting that are rarely utilised elsewhere; we will attempt to explain the important ones here.

In the first place it helps to understand something of the way in which the formatting process operates. There are two particularly important parameters: the left and right margins. The former is usually expressed as the *indent* value – how far from the real left of the paper should the text be indented. The latter is controlled by altering the length of lines that the formatter is requested to produce.

The formatter operates in words, collections of printable ASCII characters, separated by one or more spaces. It reads words from the input and places them on the output line, one at a time. As many words as possible will be placed on each output line within the constraints of the left and right margins. The resultant text is known as 'filled text'. The effect of this operation will be to produce a straight left margin and a fairly even right margin, each line only differing in length by a few characters dependent on the size of the last word encountered when it was decided that the current line was full.

The irregularities in line length may be evened out somewhat by attempting to hyphenate the word that just wouldn't fit on any particular line. Some people don't like to read hyphenated text, so this operation may be suppressed. The result of allowing hyphenation will be lines whose lengths differ by one, two or a few characters at most.

This final irregularity may be eliminated by placing the last word, or partial word up to the hyphen, on each line such that it ends exactly on the right margin; the extra spaces created in so doing are then evenly distributed throughout the remaining gaps between words on the line. This type of finish is known as 'adjusted' text. Clearly, there is little point in adjusting text if filling is turned off, although the converse is not necessarily true. Normally, **nroff** will both fill and adjust text.

The formatter is expected to split the text into pages, ready to be printed. **Nroff** produces a single output stream for its efforts, so some provision has to be made for skipping over the perforations between each 'form' on the real paper. Typically an appropriate number of blank lines, or the ASCII formfeed character will be generated at the end of each page. This operation is known as 'pagination'.

You will probably have noticed that books tend to have some form of title at the top of each page. These are known as 'running headers', or 'running footers' at the bottom of the page; collectively 'running titles'. All this can be done automatically, on a personalised basis, by the formatter, rather than the user re-typing the headers for every new page.

7.3. Commands

Having experimented with **nroff** using straight text, you have probably come across some things you would like to alter in the final layout. It is time to learn some commands.

7.3.1. Generating Breaks

A *break* is any text or command that causes the formatter to break from its usual routine of filling output lines and to output any incomplete lines immediately. A sort-of 'flush' command really. A break may be caused explicitly by the command

.br

or alternatively by either a blank line in the input text or use of any of the commands that imply a break. A break that is caused implicitly may in general be suppressed by introducing the command by the 'no-break' control character instead of the period; it is not uncommon for this to be altered from the ''' to the ',', which is less likely to cause any difficulty.

Since **nroff** is designed to operate in a sensible manner, even on input that contains no commands, blank lines and any indents in the input will always be preserved. This implies that all lines starting with a space (including blank lines) will cause a break.

7.3.2. Some Examples

We will start by examining some relatively simple commands and see precisely what happens when they are used. The space command

.sp 2

causes **nroff** to leave, in this case, 2 blank lines in the output; incidentally so would 2 blank lines in the input file but typing blank lines becomes somewhat tedious when you need a lot of them.

Suppose you wish to underline a word of your file to emphasise it, then the sequence:

A line which will have one word
.ul
underlined
in it.

will appear in the output as:

A line which will have one word <u>underlined</u> in it.

This does of course assume that we were in *fill* mode at the time, otherwise the lines would not have been joined up as shown. With filling turned off, the result would be:

A line which will have one word
<u>underlined</u>
in it.

Notice the difference between the ".sp" command that was supplied with a parameter on the same line as the command itself, and the ".ul" command that affected the next line of text encountered.

Most commands operate in a similar way to those in the examples either causing some temporary effect (such as ".ul") or a permanent alteration such as the 'no fill' command ".nf" that turns off text filling.

7.3.3. Page Size Alterations

There are three values that govern the area of text produced by a formatter: the left and right margins and the length of the page.

The left margin is set by altering the *indent* value. This may be done on a permanent basis by use of the indent command ".in"

.in 10   \" indent to character position 10
.in +10   \" indent 10 MORE characters
.in −5   \" obvious? − indent 5 LESS characters

which will affect all subsequent lines of output as indicated. The first command causes an absolute indent, whereas the other two will alter the indent level relative to the current setting. Many of the commands share this syntax.

The example above serves to illustrate comments within request lines. Comments are introduced by the special character sequence "\"" (backslash double-quote) which indicates that the rest of the line should be ignored.

In some cases it is only one line that you wish to alter, for example the first line of a new paragraph, and so the temporary indent command ".ti" would be used.

```
.ti 10      \" indent next line 10 characters total
.ti +4      \" indent next line 4 MORE characters
.ti −6      \" indent next line 6 LESS characters
```

This will only operate on the next line of text to be output; after this the previous value of indentation will be restored.

All commands may be used in conjunction with each other. For example, to start a section of text with a left hand margin an additional 8 spaces in width, the following commands could be used

```
.in +8      \" all text indented 8 more characters
.ti  +3     \" next line by an extra 3 more
```

which when applied to the source text

```
This is the end of the outer level.
.in +8
.ti +3
And this is the start of the new paragraph.
There is now a lot more text to follow
all of which will be at the new level
eight characters further in on the page.
.in −8
Back again.
```

would produce:

```
This is the end of the outer level.
        And this is the start of the new
    paragraph. There is now a lot more text to
    follow all of which will be at the new level
    eight characters further in on the page.
Back again.
```

Notice that the ".in" command causes a break which is why the "Back again" is not on the previous line. What would happen if the ".in −8" command were to be replaced with " 'in −8"?

The right margin is far simpler and is governed by the length of the line: **nroff** will fill and pad each line to produce an even right margin according to the current line length. This is set by use of the ".ll" command.

```
.ll 72     \" set the line length to 72 characters
```

which does what the comment suggests. Notice how easy it is to read and understand the request lines if they are well commented.

The page length is set with the ".pl" request:

```
.pl 66     \" 66 lines per page
```

There is one more important request for use in page control, the page offset command, ".po". This will offset the entire page in either direction and will preserve all the indent values. It is useful when every other page needs to be positioned differently on the paper as for typesetting a document to be printed double sided, where the size of the left margin needs to be greater for the right-hand page than the left one to allow for binding. It is hardly desirable that the typist should need to be aware of which page the text will finally appear on. Imagine the problems when one additional page is added at the start of a long document. The ".po" command allows the page offset to be altered at the top of every printed page, automatically.

```
.po 10     \" shift page 10 characters right
.po        \" return to the original setting
.po −10    \" 10 characters left shift
```

Notice that the ".po" command may be used without a parameter as in the second example. Quite a number of **nroff** commands operate in this way. Either the command has a default setting which will be utilised in the event that there is not a parameter or, as in the case above, the previous value of the setting to which the command refers is remembered for possible later use. Usually, only one such value is stored.

As with most aspects of computing, the only real way to learn is to experiment. Most of the commands operate in a way similar to that shown in the examples. You should therefore study the Nroff User's Manual to see what commands are available and then try to write a report.

7.4. Macros

Having become familiar with the basic operation of the formatter, it is time to begin exploring some of the more exotic features. It is about now that many people shy away and leave it to the 'experts'. We make no claims that **nroff** is an easy animal to tame, but once in captivity its power is immense and occasionally demonstrated by its desire (and ability) to escape.

There are two aspects of macros: writing them and using them. Both will be covered; even if you don't intend to write any, using existing ones will undoubtedly make your formatting task easier.

7.4.1. What is a Macro?

A macro is a collection of **nroff** commands or other macros that is given a unique name. Once defined, a macro may be 'invoked' in precisely the same way as a command is issued. When **nroff** encounters a line begining with one of its two command control characters, it takes the next two characters on the line and looks them up in its internal name table. When a macro is defined, its name is entered into this table. The only difference between a macro name and a command name is that when a macro name is encountered, a copy of the contents of the macro will be inserted into the source, precisely as though each individual command that comprises the macro definition actually appeared in the source.

This feature is immensely powerful and essentially allows the formatter to be personalised to suit the needs of anyone. You can create a set of formatting macros to suit your applications, which can then be included in subsequent documents as required.

7.4.2. Macro Packages

The basic **nroff** commands available are intended to be primitive thereby imposing no restrictions on your final product. In order to make a good job of a fair sized document, you will find that macros are essential; unless you enjoy typing in the same series of commands over and over again.

For this reason there are a number of macro packages, (collections of well tested, useful macros), available under UNIX. Unfortunately there is no one standard package available, so you should consult your UNIX Programmers' Manual to see what is recommended locally.

7.4.3. Including Other Source Files

A macro must be defined before is is used. It is usually convenient therefore to define a collection of macros in a separate file which can then be included with all documents by use of the ".so" command.

The source command, ".so", allows the input source file to be switched temporarily, exactly like "#include" in C.

    .so macro__file

will cause the entire contents of "macro__file" to appear as part of the input at the point the ".so" command is encountered. The only functional difference between this command and "#include" is that the name of the file containing the macros must **not** be surrounded by double quotes, as distinct from the case for C. A command similar to that above should be placed at the start of your document so that all your macros are available when needed and only have to be defined once in the 'macro__file'.

As an alternative, 'standard' macro packages available on your system can be included by calling **nroff** with the " −mmacros" option.

    nroff −mmacros file ..

will cause the file "/usr/lib/tmac.macros" to be pre-pended to the input files.

7.4.4. Simple Macro Examples

We are now ready to construct some macros. Consider starting a new paragraph: the same sequence of commands will always be needed, so a macro seems reasonable.

    .de pg   \" define paragraph macro called "pg"
    .br   \" force out last paragraph text
    .sp 2   \" leave 2 blank lines
    .ne 3   \" need 3 lines to start paragraph
    .ti +2   \" indent first line by 2 characters
    ..   \" end of macro definition

The body of a macro comprises all the lines (not necessarily commands as shown) between the ' .de" request and the line ".." which terminates this macro definition. Hopefully, the comments explain the intended operation of the macro with the possible exception of the ".ne" command. This tells **nroff** that at least 3 lines are required on the current page; if these are not available, a new page will be thrown automatically.

The reason for this is to prevent a new paragraph from being started with only one or two lines at the bottom of a page.

This macro could be used in the following way:

Here is the text of the first paragraph.
.pg
And here is the second paragraph.

and so on for every paragraph in the text.

This was a very simple, but powerful, example of the way in which macro expansion enables us to solve a problem once and for all. The paragraph macro can be tested then used anywhere; one line of typing in the document instead of four.

7.4.5. Macros with arguments

Now that the paragraph macro is working, we will consider a macro to produce section titles. Let us assume that all titles are to be underlined and that following a new section we always want to start a paragraph. One possible macro definition could be:

```
.de se      \" define section macro "se"
.br         \" finish previous text
.sp 2       \" 2 blank lines between sections
.ne 4       \" must have at least 4 lines left
.ul         \" underline next input line
\\$1        \" place first argument here (see on)
.pg         \" start new paragraph
..          \" terminate the definition
```

This macro could be used as follows:

```
.se "My First Section"
This is the first paragraph in this new
section. It better be short to leave room
for other examples.
.se "Section number 2"
And the second section.
```

Notice that the text string supplied as a *parameter* in the macro call was enclosed in double quotes. This is so that the spaces form part of the one string to be passed to the macro; without the quotes the three words "My", "first" and "section" would each have been separate parameters since spaces are used as the parameter separator.

Now to explain the definition of our "se" macro. All very simple and obvious with the exception of that mysterious line

122

```
\\$1
```

which was apparently to be underlined. The presence of the special string ''\\$1'' is used to indicate to **nroff** that the first argument supplied in the call to the macro is to be placed at this point in the input stream. So, why all the backslashes?

7.4.6. Escape characters, the dreaded backslash

Not just within macro definitions but throughout the text processing operation, **nroff** can be requested to treat certain characters in a special way: one such character, the backslash, is used to introduce the special meaning to these other characters. It is known as the 'escape character'.

The choice of backslash as the escape character is unfortunate since it is also used by both the editor and teletype driver (that part of UNIX that controls your terminal) as an escape character. This means that it is not as easy to insert backslashes into your file as it is most other characters. Fortunately though, the backslash is seldom needed outside of macro definitions so regular typing of it can be avoided.

For a full list of the special characters and their meanings, the reader is referred to the ''Nroff User's Manual'' [11]. The one of interest here is the dollar. Its only meaningful use is within macro definitions as the argument indicator. It must be followed by a digit to indicate which argument to the current macro should be inserted into the text in its place. There are a total of nine arguments available within any one macro.

As explained above, all special characters must be introduced by the escape character to obtain their special meaning. This explains the formation of the string ''\$1'' (we are only interested in the first argument here), but why two backslashes?

The second backslash is inserted to delay the interpretation of the first. Remember the macro has first to be defined, then later on called. During the definition phase, **nroff** will process all escape sequences, **including the '\$1'**. However, at this stage there is no first argument since we are not inside a macro, but simply defining one; the string ''\$1'' will therefore copy as the null string into the body of the macro and not do what we intended when the macro is called. By using two backslashes in the definition, ''\\'' will copy as ''\'' so the string ''\$1'' is left in **nroff's** idea of the definition. When the macro is called, it will be supplied with a parameter (we hope) so the desired substitution will be achieved.

It is extremely important to appreciate the difference between the definition of a macro when **nroff** reads the request lines and stores them away for future use, and calling a macro which results in this definition being inserted into the input stream and re-read after any parameter substitution has taken place.

7.5. Page Titles

Unlike many text formatters, **nroff** does not provide any standard way of obtaining head and foot titles for pages, automatically. It is probably becoming clear by now that some macros will almost always be required, even if only for this purpose.

Macros may be invoked in one of two ways, either as previously illustrated by use of the macro name in a request line, or alternatively **nroff** will arrange to call a specific macro when a particular vertical position (line) on the output page is encountered. Macros invoked in this way are said to be 'sprung' by line traps.

7.5.1. 'Planting' Title Macros

It is conventional to define two macros, one triggered at the top of every page, the other just above the end of the page. The two examples that follow are sufficient to provide titles but we should mention that the trap mechanism has far greater powers beyond the scope of this book. The tutorial examples at the back of the Nroff User's Manual should be studied for further detail. The request lines

```
.wh 0 Th
.wh −3 Tf
```

state that macro "Th" (Title header) is to be run at line 0 on every page and that at a position 3 lines from the bottom of every page (negative distances are taken relative to the bottom of a page) macro "Tf" (Title footer) should be invoked.

The general form of the ".wh" (when) command is

```
.wh N xx
```

and should be expanded to read when at line N, run macro "xx".

Notice that there is no mechanism for passing parameters to macros invoked in this way.

7.5.2. Example Title Macros

If writing a package it is convenient to allow the user some freedom in the way titles are supplied, but by all means provide a standard. Here is a suggested pair of examples:

```
.de Th              \" header title
'tl 'Left Header'Centre Header'Right Header'
'sp 2
'ns                 \" turn on 'no-space' mode
..
```

The ".tl" request provides for three part titles as indicated; either part may be omitted, in which case no title will be printed for that part. The title command

```
'tl '''1st January, 1970'
```

will generate this date on the extreme right of the page with no other titles.

Note the use of the no-break control character for requests within the title macro that would normally cause a break. This is vital, otherwise any partially collected lines from the previous page will be forced out immediately, followed by 2 blank lines: not what was required. Care must always be taken to ensure that macros like this don't have side effects. It is wise to always use the no-break control character in macros unless you really mean you want a break. Even then, a specific ".br" is easier to understand later.

The request "ns" says turn on 'no-space' mode. This means any ".sp" or ".bp" requests that appear (at the start of a paragraph for example) will be ignored, since we already have a reasonable gap at the head of the page. No-space mode is automatically turned off when any text is output.

For the footer you might try:

```
.de Tf              \" foot title macro
'sp 1
'tl "Page %"
'bp                 \" begin page, without a break
..
```

The foot title printed will comprise the string "Page" followed by the page number, centered within the line; the character '%' used in the macro definition will be automatically translated into the current page number when the macro is invoked.

Again, note the use of the no-break control character. The request line "bp" (begin page) causes a new page to be thrown, but as we explained for the header macro shouldn't cause a break.

7.6. Additional Features

This section is certainly not aimed at the timid novice, rather it is intended to show the potential expert what else there is in store. Proceeding beyond here suggests you are becoming devoted to the exercise of taming **nroff**

7.6.1. Number Registers

Number registers are essentially variables that may contain any number. They may be used anywhere an ordinary number is expected. The requests

```
.nr a 1
.nr aa 2
```

declare two such registers; "a" is initialised to 1 and "aa" to 2. The values of the 'register variables' may be used in a request line as follows:

```
.sp \na
.ne \n(aa
```

meaning space 1 character, need 2. It is necessary to specifically request that the contents of a number register be used by introducing the register name by the special indicator "\n". If the register name comprises two characters, it is also necessary to introduce the two character name by the symbol '(' to prevent ambiguity between number register names and text. For example,

```
it is now \n(aaam,
it was \naam.
```

will print as:

```
it is now 2am,
it was 1am.
```

In order to allow numbered sections to be generated automatically, number registers may be automatically incremented (or decremented) by arbitrary amounts. The special character used to indicate 'auto-increment' mode is the plus sign '+'.

```
.nr x 2 M
register x has the value \n+x
```

will initialise "x" to 2 and auto-increment "x" by M every time "x" is introduced by the number register indicator immediately followed by '+'; if M is negative, the effect will be to decrement "x" my M. In general, M will be equal to 1 but should not be omitted from the declaration. It is important to appreciate that the number register will be auto-incremented **before** it is used. In the above example, if M is equal to 1 then the output will be

> register x has the value 3

Within macro definitions it is usually necessary to delay the interpretation of "\n" by use of "\\n".

There are several number registers maintained by **nroff** that are available to the user. Some are read-only; the rest may be modified although great care is generally needed since some have very unexpected side effects. You should study the Nroff Reference Manual to see precisely which registers are available.

7.6.2. String Variables

There are some special requests for defining and interpolating string variables which are essentially one line macros without the trailing newline.

The requests

```
.nr x 2
.ds S This is a string
.ds S2 String \nx
```

will define number register "x" and two strings "S" and "S2". They may be interpolated into the text as follows:

> String S was *S
> String S2 was *(S2

and would print as

> String S was This is a string
> String S2 was String 2

Note the use of '(' for two character names in a similar way to that used for number registers and that number registers and strings may be arbitrarily intermixed, even in definition lines. Once again, within macro definitions it is usually necessary to delay the interpretation of "*" by use of "*".

7.6.3. Diversions

Macros are reserved and uniquely named areas of store within **nroff** and may therefore be used as buffers. Text and requests may be copied from one buffer (macro) to another by a mechanism known as a diversion: the output stream instead of going to the standard output as normal, is internally *diverted* to another macro. In this way arbitrary lines of text may be stored and manipulated before being output, for example, in the generation of footnotes or figures. Two forms of the request to initiate a diversion exist:

.di xx \'' divert to macro "xx"; old "xx" is lost
.da xx \'' divert, but append to "xx"

in either case absence of an argument causes the current diversion (if any) to be terminated. In some versions of nroff it is possible to nest diversions but in practice this is seldom needed, and is certainly beyond the scope of this book.

Now that the diversion has been started, all the text that is read in from the current source file will be directed to the appropriate buffer; "xx" in this case. The diversion will be stopped when either ".da" or ".di" is encountered without an argument.

The difference between the two versions of the diversion request is that ".di xx" will cause the old contents of "xx", if any, to be overwritten, whereas ".da xx" will divert and append to the buffer "xx".

Once text has been diverted to a buffer it remains there indefinitely. The amount of text (number of lines – request lines don't count) directed is stored in the number register "dn" for later use, but beware, this is overwritten for each new diversion.

To output text saved in a diversion, the macro in which the text was stored is invoked, just like calling any other macro:

.xx \'' output (call) macro "xx"

Remember that when a macro is called, **nroff** interpolates the contents of the definition into the input stream. Therefore, in the case of a macro used to store diverted text, there is no difference on output.

It is often convenient to remove a macro once it has been output by use of the ".rm" command to save internal table space; assuming of course that it isn't required again.

.rm xx \'' delete macro xx

7.6.3.1. Diverting Formatted Text

It is important to appreciate that text is diverted in 'copy mode': that is all escape character processing will take place at the time of the diversion.

In the case that request lines are passed around in this way, it is vital to know how often a buffer (macro) will be processed to ensure that the correct number of backslashes are included so that actual interpolation of strings and number registers takes place when intended. Remember that the value of a variable can alter between the time a macro is created by a diversion, and the time it is finally output: which value gets used is clearly important. As a hint, particularly when dealing with filled text, always ensure that nroff is not going to process the text again when the buffer is finally output. A suitable sequence might be:

```
.eo        \" turns off escape processing
.nf        \" no filling
.xx        \" output the macro (buffer)
.ec        \" reset escapes
.rm xx     \" delete the macro
```

but you may prefer to leave escape processing on if your number registers or strings have yet to be dealt with.

7.6.3.2. Transparent lines

When creating request lines within a diversion, it may be desirable to delay their interpretation until the text is re-read. This may be achieved by use of the transparent line indicator "\!" at the start of the line.

```
.di xx
\!START
\!.br
\!.ul
\!A string \\*(xy
\!.br
\!an argument \\$1
.di
```

We call this using

```
.ds xy followed by
.xx "to prove it works"
```

which will cause the text

```
START
A string followed by
an argument to prove it works
```

to be output.

7.6.4. Conditional Input

Within a macro it is sometimes necessary to control which lines are processed, and in what order. To facilitate this, **nroff** provides the conditional command, ".if". The simple form of the conditional input command is:

.if *condition* line of text or commands

which causes the 'condition' to be evaluated and if the result is 'true', where true is defined to be non-zero, then the rest of the line of input is taken; if not the rest of the line will be ignored. The most common conditions involve arithmetic on number registers, string processing, or a test on one of the special number registers. In general, expressions of arbitrary complexity may be used. Here is an example of a simple header macro that prints a title on all but the first page:

```
.de Th              \" header macro
.if \\n%-1 'tl "Page %"
.if \\n%-1 'sp 2
'ns
..
```

In this case, 1 is subtracted from the current page number to form the condition. Notice that the ".if" command was introduced by the period: this is acceptable since ".if" does not cause a break because it was specifically designed for use in macros. As a further example, we will consider a slight modification to our ".se" macro so that it behaves in a sensible way when called without a parameter.

```
.de se
.br
.sp 2
.ne 4
.if \\w'\\$1' .ul        \" test for argument and
.if \\w'\\$1' \\$1        \" underline if present
.pg
..
```

The other comments have been specifically removed to emphasise the conditional lines. The condition being tested for here first involves the 'width' function, introduced by the special character "\w". If a parameter was supplied in the macro call, then the width function will return a positive result (the width of the string), otherwise it will return with zero which is a 'false' condition so the rest of the line will be ignored.

In the previous version of this macro, calling it without a parameter would have caused the first line of the next paragraph to be underlined. Do you see why?

The result of the conditional test may be inverted by prefixing it with the "!" character. The line

.if !\\w'\\$1' No parameter supplied

placed somewhere in the previous macro would output this message if no title was supplied.

There is a lot more that could be said about the ".if" command, but we suggest you try some examples of your own and make a further study of the Nroff User's Manual.

7.7. Hints on Writing Macros

This section is aimed as much at the novice who wants to experiment as the **nroff** junkie who aims to produce a macro package for everyone. A warning though if you fall into the latter category: all the users will complain and ask "why doesn't it do this?" The answer may be you didn't think of it, but it is more likely that you couldn't work out how many backslashes were needed to achieve it. Most complaints can be dealt with by presenting your assailant with a listing of the entire package and asking for their help.

The first golden rule when writing macros (or any programs for that matter) is use comments. There are very few commented sets of macros, consequently very few understandable ones. Don't be afraid to explain what you hoped you were asking **nroff** to do, even if it doesn't quite turn out that way.

Secondly, use meaningful variable and register names, although with only two character mnemonics, some will inevitably become strained; in any case, don't forget to comment your obscure name. Be careful to distinguish between internal names, those used only by your package, and external names by which macros are called and global variables named.

Avoid the use of built-in constants. If you need a constant, make it a number register with a suitable name then collect all these variables together in one 'profile' file and allow the user to alter it. No-one will like your exact formatting style, but most people will be glad of your macro package. The profile file should be included, along with the rest of the package at the start of each document.

Here is the paragraph macro designed for profiling:

```
\"  the profile file
.nr PI  2      \"  indent on first line of paragraph
.nr PS  2      \"  space between paragraphs
.nr PN  3      \"  need for a new paragraph

\"  paragraph macro
.de pg
.br
.sp  \\n(PS      \"  leave PS blank lines
.ne  \\n(PN      \"  need PN lines on this page
.ti +\\n(PI      \"  temporary indent PI spaces
..
```

Note the use of capital letters to avoid confusion with **nroff** commands and other macro names, and that all paragraph parameter registers start with "P" for ease of recognition.

Within the paragraph macro it is desirable to delay the interpretation of each of the number registers until the macro is called. If one of the backslashes were removed, the macro would still work but only with the values of the registers at the time the macro was defined. This means that it would not be possible to alter the format of the document without redefining the macro. By delaying the interpretation of the number registers, the variable name information is retained within the definition. We can now alter any of the number registers within the document for an immediate effect on all subsequent paragraphs.

As a hint on testing, a little used but invaluable command is the terminal message command.

```
.tm anything, including strings
```

will output it's arguments after processing all string and register variables to the standard error output. This is the only way to see exactly which macros are called where. There is no run-time debugger for **nroff**.

Within macro definitions remember that it is usually necessary to delay the interpretation of "\" by use of "\\".

7.8. Conclusions

This chapter was not intended to turn you into an **nroff** expert but hopefully to provide you with sufficient information to understand the manual and write simple macros. You may even complete some documentation one day, who knows?

Chapter 8

The Process Environment

The what?

8.1. Waffle

We've taken you gently by the hand in the first seven chapters and walked you carefully through some of the aspects of using UNIX, like a worried mother hen clucking around her chicks we've done our best to coddle you. We've tried to present enough to give you the background to understand the more difficult material in these next chapters. Here's where you grow up; from now on the gloves are off.

Some users will never read these chapters - you **can** use UNIX without understanding what you're doing – but we hope that you aren't that sort of person.

In this chapter we explain the action of some of the UNIX **system calls.** These are the interface between programs and the operating system, they are what actually do the work of the system utilities. Without them, programs are powerless to do anything except shuffle data around inside themselves. All external action, be it input, output, executing another program – all this has to be done using **system calls.** System calls communicate between programs and the bit of UNIX which really **is** an operating system: it's called the 'kernel' of UNIX. The kernel is the part of UNIX which looks after the processor for you, allocating memory and time to programs, handling the filestore and the communications.

Take the command to remove a file from a directory, **rm.** When you invoke this command a program is run; it looks at its arguments and deletes the directory entries you have specified. It checks each file (using a system call) to see if a) you own the file, and b) you have write permission on the file: it complains if either of these conditions aren't met. What it actually uses to remove the directory entries is the **unlink** system call. The system call performs none of these checks: if you have write permission in the relevant directory then **unlink** will remove that entry **irrespective of any permissions on the file itself.** That's why rm was written – to prevent you making silly mistakes. We really do want to emphasise the difference between utility programs which do their jobs by **using** system calls and the system calls themselves. If you don't understand this difference then think about it now; try hard to work out what we're talking about.

What actually happens when you give a command like **ls, cc** or your own **a.out?** What do they do? This is the chapter that tries to explain.

8.2. Running a program

The first stage in understanding how to use the kernel's services is to get some inkling of what happens when you give a command to your shell. The shell, you may remember, is the program started by 'login'. It reads the commands you type at the terminal and then carries them out, a few it has to do itself (when forced to), but the majority of commands are totally independent of the shell. The shell starts them running, giving them their arguments, then it waits for them to finish before giving you your next prompt.

We've said already that the shell is a perfectly ordinary program with no special privileges so it would seem that **any** program should be entitled to do this sort of thing. Right! This is exactly the case – all of the kernel facilities are available to any program that knows how to ask – no programs are treated differently from any others. What determines the rights of a running program is either the identity of the user running it, or in some cases the **owner** of the file where the program is kept; but we're getting ahead of ourselves.

We'll trace the execution of a simple command like **echo.** You see this sequence on your screen:

```
$ echo hi there
hi there
$
```

What happened?

The shell reads the line 'echo hi there' and sorts out the command **echo** from the two arguments. It then does a remarkable thing: it splits into two identical copies, a procedure known as a **fork.** Each copy has exactly the same files open and is the same program: the only difference is that each copy can find out whether it is the original or the new copy.

134

We pause here to introduce a new term, and to allow the thought of a **fork** to sink in. UNIX, in common with the usual terminology, calls each running program a 'process'. Processes are much more than just programs; programs are dead things with no powers – processes on the other hand have a life of their own and **obey** a program. If you like, the program is the DNA and the process is the living cell, controlled by the DNA. The state of a process is dynamic, it changes with time and perhaps in response to external stimuli, whilst a program is fixed and unchanging. Under UNIX, a process can elect to change its program as it runs by throwing away the old one then loading and starting a new program.

Back to the two copies of the shell. The original process is called the 'parent' and the new one is called the 'child'. The parent in this example immediately loses interest in the proceedings by saying to the kernel that it wants to **wait** until something happens to the child. It's the child that causes the action for the moment. It's still obeying the shell program but that doesn't last for long. The child says that it wants to **execute** a new program and gives a list of the arguments for the new program. The kernel intervenes, disposing of the memory allocated to the old program and loading a new program into this process; then starting it with the arguments provided. All that changes in this process is its program – nothing else, in particular all of the previously open files are still available to it. The new program is of course **echo,** which prints its arguments on the still open standard output file, your terminal.

This shows how the redirection of output is so easy to do under UNIX. If you had said

    echo hi there > fred

meaning that you wanted the output of this command to go to a file called 'fred', the shell would simply redirect its own output to 'fred' before executing **echo. Echo** would never know the difference.

Eventually, 'echo' executes the **exit** system call and dies. **Exit** is the UNIX form of suicide; any process which executes this call has all its files closed and is put into never-never land in a state known as a 'zombie' until its parent enquires about it.

The death of the child wakes up our waiting shell; it's told which of its children died and what status the child supplied to the **exit** call. **Execute** with its arguments and **exit** with its status are very similar to the function call and return arrangements found in C. Once the parent has received the exit status of the child, the ghost can be laid – what little is left of the zombie is tidied up and all last traces of the dead child disappear for ever.

Now that the child has finally gone, the parent gives you your next

135

prompt and waits for another command. Knowing this, it's not too difficult to see how the so-called 'background' tasks are carried out. Instead of waiting for its child to die the shell immediately gives you its next prompt. Any background tasks which terminate before you issue your next non-background command remain in their zombie state until the shell eventually issues a **wait** request.

8.3. Not done by mirrors

To find out how these tricks are done you'll have to be prepared to read some examples of C: although the same requests are available to the FORTRAN77 compiler it's usual to illustrate them from the viewpoint of a C program. The way that system calls actually work depends in large measure on the particular hardware you are using, but in each case the effect is eventually the same. A program issuing a system call causes control of the processor to be transferred to the operating system kernel – this almost always requires the use of a specialised instruction. On PDP11 computers this is a TRAP instruction, the Interdata machines call it a 'supervisor call (svc)' and other hardware knows it by yet other names. It's the job of the implementors of your system to hide all this in library routines; these are what we shall describe.

8.3.1. An example of fork

The **fork** system call is central to UNIX. It's the only way that a new process can come into being.

In the following example the program executes the **fork** system call, which returns a different value in the parent from the one in the child; this is the way they find out which one they are. The child is returned a value of zero, the parent gets the 'process identity' (pid) of the child. The pid is a number in the range 1 to 30000 which uniquely identifies the child; UNIX guarantees never to have two processes in the system with the same pid. If the system runs long enough to have more than 30000 processes pass through it then the numbers start back from 1, but UNIX checks that process n isn't still alive before re-allocating that pid.

The example also shows the program checking that the system call could be carried out: many system calls can fail for one reason or another; they usually return a value of -1 to indicate that a failure happened. We'll be looking deeper into that possibility later.

```
/* an example of fork and wait */
main(){
        int pid,status,died;
        switch(pid = fork()){
                case -1: printf("Can't fork\n");
                        exit(-1);
                case 0: /* child */
                        printf("I'm the child\n");
                        exit(3);
                default: /* the parent process */
                        died = wait(&status);
        }
        printf("child was %d\n",pid);
        printf("%d died\n",died);
        printf("exit value %d\n",status>>8);
        printf("exit status %d\n",status & 0377);
}
```

In this example the value returned from **fork** is assigned to the variable called pid. This value is used to select the next of 3 possible action, described below.

case -1:

If the process couldn't fork (perhaps there is no room in the system for it) it prints an error message and exits; there won't be a child if this is the case.

case 0:

The child sees a value of zero returned so it prints a message, then calls **exit** with an argument of 3 – this value is passed back to its parent later.

default:

The parent decides to **wait** for the child. When a child dies the parent is woken up (if it's waiting) and the pid of the child is returned from the call of **wait**, so parents with several children are able to find out which one has died. The argument to **wait** was a pointer to the variable called status; **wait** sets this variable to a value which shows two things. The high-order eight bits are the argument the child passed to **exit**, the low eight bits are set by the operating system to show why the child terminated. If the child died of natural causes (by its own decision), these low order eight bits will be zero; if the operating system had to intervene and stop the child because something illegal occurred, it sets these bits to indicate what the error was.

The parent prints all these values: the pid returned from **fork**, the pid of the child (which is the same number), the argument the child gave to **exit** and last of all, the status returned by the operating system.

If a process has several children, it has to perform a **wait** for each one to learn what happened to them. Children without a living parent are automatically inherited by the grandmother of all processes, process 1, which is given the task of **waiting** for all of these orphans: an important job because children which aren't waited for will eventually clog up the whole system with zombies. You'll become unpopular if you write programs which **fork** a lot without performing **waits** to pick up these terminated processes. Eventually you will be stopped from executing any further **forks** until you have done something about dead children; each user is only allowed a certain number of processes and zombies still count until they have been cleaned up.

8.3.2. Errors in system calls

The case above illustrates that it's possible for a system call to fail, but it's not only **fork** that can go wrong. To indicate failure all system calls arrange to return an 'impossible' value, this is nearly always -1. To help you identify the reason for the failure, the C library routines set an external variable called 'errno' with a value which indicates what happened. The values and their names are given in appendix E. There is also a library routine called 'perror' which will print an appropriate message on the standard error output. Be careful about calling it though, since the message it prints always refers to the **most recent** error; successful system calls do not reset errno. Here's an example of both of these being used in a short program which guarantees to get an error from the system call **stime** as long as you are an ordinary user.

```
extern errno;
main(){
        int res;
        res = stime(0);
        printf("returned %d\n",res);
        printf("errno is %d\n",errno);
        perror("tried to set time");
}
```

Try it on your system: if it doesn't fail you'll be most unpopular because you've just set the date and time to something extremely silly. The perror routine is very handy, we use it a lot in our own programs.

8.4. Personal belongings

As we've said, there's a lot more to a process than just its program. Most of a process' attributes are inherited from its parent: things like open files; who owns it; its current directory; and more besides. Here we look at some of them to see what they mean.

8.4.1. Inherited files

Unless special action is take to do otherwise (very rare), a process which **forks** passes on all its open files to the child: both processes have equal access to them. If either of them decides to close a shared file then only the process that executes the close actually loses touch with the file. The other (or others if there are several) still have that file open. Files inherited in this way only have one read/write pointer† which is shared between all the processes – if one process moves the pointer by, say, reading from the file, then the pointer has moved for all of them. This is rarely a problem but we mention it for completeness; you'll find more about read/write pointers in the section on i/o. Usually the only files still open by the time a process decides to **fork** are its standard input, output and error files; these you **want** to share.

8.4.2. User and Group ID

Processes carry with them, like a passport, their 'user identity' (uid) and 'group identity' (gid), numbers which allow the operating system to see which user and group the process belongs to; they decide what access this process has to the filestore. The filestore protection arrangements have already been mentioned; the tie-up between them and a process is that the uid of a process says who its owner is, the gid says which group it belongs to, both are checked against the permissions of a file when an attempt is made to open it.

The uid and gid of your shell are set when you log in; the values used are taken from the password file by **login**. The kernel doesn't know about user or group names, only numbers; they are passed on to all your shell's children, and their children and so on – the uid and gid set at login decide the ownership of every process you ever execute. The result of this, as you might expect, is that it's easy to tell who owns every process in the system. To UNIX, it's the uid that decides who a user is: the name you log in by has no relevance to the operating system and is almost a fictitious

---

†This is not what the standard i/o package calls a file pointer.

thing. Utilities like **ls** keep up the pretence when they tell you who owns a file, but even they have to find the uid and gid of a file first, then look up the username associated with the uid by searching the password file.

The system calls **getuid** and **getgid** allow a process to find out what its uid and gid are, you can find out yours with this example program.

```
main(){
        int uid,gid;
        uid = getuid();
        gid = getgid();
        printf("uid= %d, gid= %d\n",uid,gid);
}
```

In fact every process has **two** uids and gids. The two known as the 'effective' ones are the ones actually used to check filestore accesses, the 'real' pair are the ones identifying the owner and group of the process. To find the effective pair, replace the system calls in the previous example with **geteuid** and **getegid** instead. Most of the time the effective and real ids are the same, so your access permissions are what you would expect from examining your own user and group codes. Why bother to have these different ids? Read on.

The really neat part about having two versions of each id is that they **don't** have to be the same. Some executable files have the 'setuid' (suid) or/and the 'setgid' (sgid) modes set on them – these modes are easily set by the owner of the file in the same way as the access permissions. When a process executes a file with either of these modes set, its effective ids are changed, according to the setuid or setgid mode, to those of the file. As a result, the process appears to take on the identity of someone else; almost as if it became **privileged** in the same way as that other person.

The setuid/setgid modes are useful for implementing complicated protection schemes beyond those normally provided by UNIX. For example, a database which is only to be accessible to people who know the right password is not implementable using the ordinary filestore protections. It can be done, though, by providing special programs whose job is to check the password and then perform the file access themselves. Make all the secure files accessible by only one user and arrange that your access programs have the correct setuid mode and ownership set: you've done it! It's then your 'privileged' programs that do the access checking; you can make them as complicated as you like.

The UNIX **passwd** utility is a prime example of this sort of user-implemented access control. It's owned by a user with write permission on the password file and has the setuid mode: it's **passwd** that checks for itself whether or not what you are trying to do is reasonable and does the job for you if it agrees. This is a very simple idea, and one which is easy to use. Anyone can make use of it.

Processes unhappy about their current effective ids can attempt to modify them with the **setuid** and **setgid** system calls. Ordinary processes can only set their effective ids to correspond to the real ones, throwing away privileges†; but there is one user called the 'super-user' with extra powers. A process with an effective uid of zero (the super-user) may set both its real and effective user or group ids to any value it likes, using the **setuid/setgid** system calls. This is how **login** arranges for your shell to take on your own uid and gid. Just before executing your shell, **login** sets its own user and group ids to yours; that's how you become yourself when you log in.

Sometimes it's useful for a privileged process to see what access the real user has to a file. The **access** system call allows it to check, the access permissions are checked with respect to the real, not the effective ids. This function call

        access("xyz",mode);

returns zero if the file 'xyz' is accessible depending on the values of the 'mode': 4 for reading; 2 for writing; 1 for execute. A return of −1 indicates an error. Files may not be executable even if they have execute permission − it takes more to make an executable binary program than just that! Incidentally this raises an interesting point. A process whose effective and real ids differ may not be able to access files that the real user can − permission is **only** calculated by looking at the effective ids, no note being taken of the real ones.

8.5. Loose ends

8.5.1. Current directory

Every process has something called its 'current directory'. This is the starting point for pathnames which don't begin with a /; it's set originally by **login** so that your shell starts up in what's called your 'home' or 'login' directory‡. Processes can change their current directory with the **chdir** system call:

        chdir("/usr/fred");

---

†They couldn't be allowed take on any ids they like - this would make a mockery of the whole filestore security!
‡You can find out what yours is by looking at the $HOME variable in your shell.

will change the current directory of the process executing it to /usr/fred, provided that the permissions on that directory allow it. A return value of −1 from the function indicates it wasn't entitled to do any such thing, probably because the directory didn't exist or didn't have execute permission set on it (execute permission on a directory means you may mention its name as part of a pathname − directories aren't actually executable).

Because the current directory is inherited by the children of a process, rather than being some sort of 'global' system variable, your shell has to perform **chdir** for itself when you issue the **cd** command. Work out why − the answer is straightforward.

8.5.2. User mask

This is another inherited feature, and quite useful if you are security conscious. Most system utilities are relaxed about security when they create files for you; in general they allow the whole world to read your files but give only you write permission. This is what is wanted in most systems − few users have anything to hide and it's very handy to be able to 'lift' ideas from other people. Most UNIX systems actively encourage this.

If you are worried about the sensitive nature of your programs or data, and want to discourage these utilities from giving everyone permission to pry, the **umask** feature is the way to go about it. Setting this mask allows you turn off certain permissions in files created by your children. A call such as this

umask(7);

forces the low order 3 bits (7 = 111 binary) of the mode of all files created from now on to be zero: bits that are a one in the user mask will always be a zero in the mode of any file created. So, with a mask of 7, all files created will have no permissions at all for users in the category of 'other'.

Since the mask is an inherited feature, your shell has to execute **umask** for itself.

Don't confuse the **command** with the **system call**. The command is recognised by the shell, but the process is actually actually carried out using the system call; though their names are the same, there's a world of difference between them.

8.6. Execute

Off with his head!

You've now found out how to make your programs manipulate their environment and you should have had several things explained. If your head is swimming, this is a sensible time to pause. If not, on we go. It's time to learn about the execution of programs.

As we've said, a process is entitled to change its program. This is done using one of the several variants of the **exec** system call, often after a process has decided to **fork**. Here's a short program which doesn't bother to fork, but calls the system utility **echo**.

```
main(){
        execl("/bin/echo","echo","hello there",0);
        printf("The exec failed\n");
}
```

The call of printf should never occur since if the **execl** works, the program containing it will have been abandoned. Instead, the **echo** utility should have been loaded and started with the arguments 'echo' and 'hello there't. The first argument is always the same as the name of the program, this is done by the agreement of all programs under UNIX, it isn't actually **insisted** upon but you would be silly to ignore the fact. **Echo** prints its other arguments on its standard output (still the terminal because it wasn't closed) and in this case prints just the one. In this form of the system call, you give a list of character pointers terminated by a zero. The first is the name of the file to execute, the rest are the arguments to be given to it.

Remember that executing a new program may change your effective uid or gid if the program being executed has the appropriate modes set.

If you don't know how many arguments you want to provide (the shell doesn't), you can use the flexible **execv** form of the call, where the first argument is again the name of the program, but the second is a pointer to an array of character pointers. The last member of the array is zero, all the others are the arguments.

```
/* this is an initialised array
   of character pointers */
char *arglist[] = {
        "echo",
        "hello there",
        0};
main(){
        execv("/bin/echo",arglist);
        printf("Cock up\n");
}
```

---

†The pathname of the command should be /bin/echo unless your system is unusual.

Being able to call other programs from one of your own is one of the great strengths of UNIX. If, for example, it wanted to create a directory, manipulate some files within it, then delete them and remove the directory it wouldn't be allowed to: only the super user may create and unlink directories because of the checking needed to maintain the filestore structure. Instead, your program can fork and execute the privileged program (/bin/mkdir) which does the job for it – no need to be privileged, no need to worry about performing the checks for yourself. The status returned will tell you whether or not the creation was successful. It's even easier if the library routine **system** is adequate for your purposes; look at its description in the manual or appendix D. If you want to get really clever, you can arrange for the output of these programs to be readable from the program which invokes them; a bit of messing around to direct their standard output into a **pipe** (which your program reads from) will do it.

Both of the system calls we've shown are really stripped-down versions of the real thing – **execle** and **execve** but they are too fancy to go into here. In essence, they pass yet another list of arguments called the **environment** to the new program. Look it up in section two of the manual.

8.7. Signals

All processes are liable at some time or another to receive 'signals'. Signals can be generated internally from the process itself, or externally. An example of an external signal is SIGINT – when you press the INTERRUPT key, every process run from your terminal is sent that signal. Internal signals can be due to a number of unusual conditions such as attempting to execute illegal instructions or access nonexistent memory.

What happens when a process receives a signal depends on what the process has said previously about that signal. If the process has said it wants to 'ignore' that signal, then the worst that can happen is that there may be a premature return from certain system calls†. The process may have said nothing about that particular signal; if this is the case it is terminated forthwith and the process **waiting** for it is told about the signal. Certain signals cause a 'core dump', where the entire image of the process is copied into a file called 'core' in the process' current directory; the core file can be inspected later to see what caused the problem.

---

†Read or write on slow devices like teletypes but NOT disc files; also the **pause** and **wait** calls.

The other option open to the process is to 'catch' signals. Caught signals act like a hardware interrupt, transferring to a previously specified location in the program. The library 'signal' routine is used to specify a function to be called on receipt of a signal, the signal number being passed to that function as an argument.

The signal mechanism explains how (amongst other things) the INTERRUPT key works. Ordinary processes neither catch or ignore this signal, so they terminate on receiving it. Your shell catches the signal (then does nothing with it) and as a result it doesn't terminate, which is just as well. You don't want to be logged out every time you press INTERRUPT. Processes run in the background mode have interrupt ignored – the shell does this just before executing them, it works because ignored interrupts are still ignored after an **exec**. Caught interrupts are reset if you do an **exec** because it wouldn't make sense not to.

Try this program to see signals in action. It catches the INTERRUPT signal and exits on the fifth one; the routine catching the signal has to re-catch it each time because the default action (termination) is restored whenever one of these signals is caught. Ignored signals do not suffer from this.

```
#include <signal.h>
int nsigs;
main(){
        int onintr();
        signal(SIGINT,&onintr); /* catch INTERRUPT */
        for(;;)
                sleep(100); /* do nowt for 100 secs */
}
onintr(sig){
        signal(SIGINT,&onintr);
        printf("signal %d received\n",sig);
        if(++nsigs >= 5)
                exit();
}
```

The header file <signal.h> used in that example contains some useful definitions including the names of signals, these are covered in appendix E. Two arguments of the correct type for the signal function are also defined – calling signal with a second argument of SIG__DFL resets the default action of terminating the process, giving SIG__IGN as the argument causes the signal to be ignored.

Returning from the function which caught a signal will resume in the main program at the point where it left off. Beware, though, of performing floating point arithmetic in the signal-catching function; it may cause some undesired side effects if the main program also uses floating point quantitiest.

8.8. I/O

The most heavily used system calls are the ones used for input/output (i/o). UNIX i/o is exceptionally simple to use and places very few constraints on programmers; reading and writing are the most common operations but we'll look at how to open files first – you can't read from a closed file!

8.8.1. Open, Close and Creat

UNIX has three methods of opening files and one trick that looks like an open but isn't. We'll look at two called **open** and **creat**.

Open is used to open a file for reading, writing or both; as long as the file already exists. The system call returns an integer known as a 'file descriptor' which is used to refer to the file in subsequent operations. There are two arguments to **open**, the file name and the mode. The file name is a string – the name of the file, the mode is an integer which is 0 for reading, 1 for writing and 2 for both. To open 'fred' for read/write acess:

> fildes = open("fred",2);

A return of −1 indicates an error. Most UNIX systems limit the number of files a process may have open concurrently to around 20, but don't bank on more than 16. By convention, file descriptors 0,1 and 2 refer the standard input, output and error files in that order.

If the file doesn't exist already, the **creat** system call will attempt to both create it and open it for writing; it too returns a file descriptor unless an error prevents it from working. Attempting to **creat** an already existing file will truncate it to zero length, then open it. When files are created this way, it's necessary to specify the 'mode' of the file – this is the mode which determines who can access it, and how. To create 'fred' with read and write permissions to everybody, the call will look like this:

> fildes = creat("fred",0666);

---

†This depends on your hardware and the library routines. On PDP11 machines the standard signal library routine omits to save and restore the floating point registers during the signal.

146

The mode may of course be modified without your knowledge depending on the state of the process' **umask**. The call will fail if the file already exists but you don't have write permission on it.

Closing files is simple – call **close** with the file descriptor to be closed as its argument.

```
close(1);   /* close standard output */
```

Close is handy for processes that have too many files open and are in danger of running out of file descriptors.

8.8.2. Reading and writing

UNIX treats files as sequential arrays of bytes. You can read or write an arbitrary number of bytes from/to any point in the file. Trying to read past the end of a file isn't possible, but writing beyond the end of a file merely extends it to make room – the operating system will allocate space until it runs out of disc. Any number of processes may have a file open and perform read or write operations to suit themselves†. All files on UNIX systems are accessed in exactly the same way; processes neither know nor care what 'sort' of file they are using. Some ludicrous operations, say reading from a line printer, are not permitted, but in general all file i/o is consistent no matter what the actual file is: teletypes, disc files and magnetic tapes (as well as pipes) need no special treatment from the program's point of view.

Both **read** and **write** system calls are used in the same way. You supply a file descriptor, the address of the data area in memory, and a byte count. The system then transfers up to that many bytes (if it can), and reports how many bytes it could. When you're writing to a file the system will transfer the whole count requested unless an error occurs (perhaps the end of a tape was reached, or the disc drive failed). The byte count is often less than requested when you're reading from a file: teletypes usually return only one line of information at a time, the operating system will also stop a **read** when it reads to the end of a file. In no case will more data be transferred than you asked for. A value of zero bytes read from a file indicates that you are already at the end of the file – this can be simulated on teletypes by pressing the EOT key described in chapter 1.

Every open file has a 'read/write pointer' which is moved by n bytes every time n bytes are transferred; this means that in practice the file

---

†Simultaneous writing on a file by several processes can be a nuisance. Standard UNIX permits it, but some look-alikes have implemented methods of 'locking' files to prevent this. See your documentation for details.

appears to be sequential. The pointer can easily be moved, or its position found, using the **lseek** system call – thus random access is equally easy to perform.

Lseek requires three arguments: a file descriptor, a 'long' variable known as the 'offset' and a 'whence' argument. Calling this routine results in the read/write pointer being set to the value of offset if whence is 0, to its current position plus offset if whence is 1, and to the size of the file plus offset if whence is 2. These combinations are all that is needed to perform completely general random access i/o. **Lseek** returns the previous value of the r/w pointer, or -1 if you try to seek backwards past the beginning of the file. Put this example in xyz.c, for later use.

```
main(){
          int fildes;
          long old,new;
          fildes = open("xyz.c",0); /* open for reading */
          if(fildes = = -1){
                    perror("xyz.c");
                    exit();
          }
          new = 5;
          old = lseek(fildes,new,0); /* seek to fifth byte */
          printf("old pointer %D\n",old);
}
```

We'll use this example later.

We said earlier that **read** and **write** are easy to use. This program copies its standard input to its standard output, counting characters. It uses a character array (buf) to store the data on the way through.

```
main(){
          char buf[512];
          int nread,ccount;
          ccount = 0;
          while((nread = read(0,buf,512)) != 0){
                    ccount + = nread;
                    if(write(1,buf,nread) != nread){
                              perror("writing");
                              exit(-1);
                    }
          }
          printf("%d characters read\n",ccount);
}
```

148

Contrast this with the version using the standard i/o package in chapter 4. As with that one, use it on itself, then combine it with the example of **lseek** to try to get it to read itself starting at the fifth byte.

The choice of the magic number 512 in the previous example wasn't an accident; many UNIX implementations are at their most efficient when they're transferring data in chunks of this size. Don't worry if other lengths are more convenient for your particular application – 512 isn't essential, just a good idea when it's handy. We wouldn't recommend transferring a lot of data on a byte-by-byte basis though, single character i/o really is rather inefficient. The 'getc' and 'putc' of the standard i/o package get around this by buffering the transfers internally.

The other two ways of getting file descriptors are using **pipe** (which returns two, the read one and the write one) and **dup** which copies an existing file descriptor. **Dup** doesn't get you a new read/write pointer! You need several **opens** or **creats** to get several r/w pointers into one file.

8.8.3. ioctl

The **ioctl** system call is an open-ended sort of thing. It's used to set parameters in various output device handlers and will vary considerably from one piece of hardware to another. It gets used, in particular, to turn off echoing at a user's terminal while they type in their password. Your system documentation will be more forthcoming on the details of its implementation on your hardware. Programs can find out (if they want to), whether or not their standard i/o channels are connected to teletype-like devices by using **ioctl**.

8.9. Summary

We've looked at some system calls in detail and hope that you've learnt something about them. No serious UNIX programmer can afford to ignore them, an understanding of their purpose and use is essential to make the best of what UNIX has to offer.

For reference, a list of system calls, signals and error numbers is given in appendix E.

Chapter 9

Libraries

The language C, unlike Pascal or FORTRAN, has no built-in input/output facilities; unfortunately most programs interact in some way with their external environment. The UNIX 'open', 'read' and 'write' system calls may be used for all program I/O, but they tend to be both primitive and processor dependent. For example, any assumption of the order in which bytes are stored will lead to errors if the program is moved from a PDP−11 to a M68000.

In this chapter we'll take a look at the library functions provided by UNIX, including the standard I/O package (SIO). The SIO functions are intended to provide you with a convenient and uniform interface to the operating system. What's more, they are **portable**; a program using just SIO routines should execute correctly no matter what machine it is running on. Before we delve too deeply into the Pandora's box it might be a good idea to take a look at how you get at these library routines.

9.1. The Preprocessor

Many library functions require you to include a header file into your source program; any C program which uses routines from the SIO must contain the line

    #include   <stdio.h>

near the beginning. Header files contain macro and variable definitions used by the library funtions; they are 'included' into your source file by the compiler 'preprocessor'. The C compiler contains a pre-first pass capable of macro substitution, conditional compilation and inclusion of named files. Any source line commencing with a '#' in column 1 is picked up and interpreted by the preprocessor.

9.1.1. Token Replacement and Macro Substitution

A line of the form

#define   identifier   string

causes the preprocessor to replace all subsequent instances of 'identifier' with the given 'string'. A macro may be similarly defined

#define   identifier(arg1, .., argn)   string

Subsequent references to the 'identifier' are replaced by the 'string'. Each argument mentioned in the definition parameter list is replaced with the corresponding argument from the call; the number of actual and formal (definition) parameters must match.

Text occuring inside a quoted string or a character constant isn't replaced by the preprocessor. After replacement the line is scanned again to see if any more defined identifiers can be found. A long definition may be continued onto further lines by writing '\' at the end of the line to be continued

```
#define LONG – DEF This is a very long definition and \
so has to be continued onto several further lines. It \
will probably cause problems when substituted but \
nevertheless serves to illustrate the principle.
```

When the identifier is replaced the long string is placed on one line. Token replacement is most useful for defining constants

```
#define BUFSIZE 400
#define EOF (−1)
#define NULL 0
...
char buffer[BUFSIZE], *bp, ch;
...
        bp = buffer;
        while ((ch = getchar()) != EOF) {
            if (bp <= &buffer[BUFSIZE])
                *bp++ = ch;
            else {
                printf("buffer overflowed\n");
                ...
```

and macro definitions for commonly used logical tests

```
#define isaplha(c)   (c> ='a' && c< ='z')
...
char *acp;
...
        if (isalpha( *acp )) {
          ...
```

When using macros with pointers as the actual arguments care must be taken to avoid using auto increment/decrement. The following would give strange results

```
        if (isalpha( *acp+ + )) { ...
```

A line of the form

```
#undef identifier
```

causes the previous definition of 'identifier' to be forgotten.

9.1.2. Conditional Compilation

Source file lines may be conditionally ignored or compiled using lines of the form

```
#ifdef identifier
```

The 'identifier' is checked to see if it's currently defined, that is, it has been the subject of a #**define** line;

```
#ifndef identifier
```

checks to see if the identifier is currently undefined; and

```
#if constant-expression
```

checks to see if the 'constant-expression' evaluates to non-zero (true). Each of these variations is followed by one or more lines, possibly containing

```
#else
```

and terminated by

```
#endif
```

If the checked condition is true then any lines between #**else** (if one exists) and #**endif** are ignored. Conversely, if the condition is false then any lines between the test and an #else, or a #endif, are ignored. An identifier may be defined in the **cc** command line using the flag − **D**identifier; thus

```
cc  − Dfred file.c
```

would cause the condition

```
#ifdef fred
```

to become true.

A Word of Warning

These constructions should be used sparingly, otherwise a highly unreadable program will be produced.

9.1.3. File Inclusion

A line of the form

```
#include "filename"
```

causes the preprocessor to replace that line with the entire contents of the file 'filename'. The search for the include file commences in the current directory and, if not found there, continues in a sequence of standard places; for most UNIX systems this will be just the directory '/usr/include'. If the current directory is not to be searched then

```
#include <filename>
```

will search only the standard places. The compiler's idea of where this standard place exists may be modified by means of the .b − Idir-name flag; thus

```
cc  − I/usr/andy/include file.
```

would cause a line of the form

```
#include <defs.h>
```

to be replaced with the file '/usr/andy/include/defs.h'. These files are called 'header' files and by convention have the extension '.h' as in 'stdio.h'. The files in the directory '/usr/include' contain system dependent information, for example the structure of an i-node. You may create your own header files containing macro and/or token definitions, but perhaps the most useful application is when splitting your C program into several source files.

At some point in the construction of a program it may get so large that the listing becomes unwieldy. It's a good idea to keep only related functions together in one file; for example the symbol table manipulating routines for an assembler. The collection of functions that comprise a C program may occur in any order; the source may be spread over several files so long as no function is split, each source file is given the extension '.c'. Suppose a program is made up by the three files 'main.c', 'pass1.c' and 'pass2.c', then the command

        cc main.c pass1.c pass2.c

will individually compile the three files and place the resulting relocatable object code in 'main.o', 'pass1.o' and 'pass2.o'. These object files are loaded along with any necessary library functions into an executable file called 'a.out'. If only one source file, pass1.c, needs to be recompiled, then the command

        cc pass1.c main.o pass2.o

will compile pass1.c and load the resulting object file along with main.o and pass2.o. The convention '.c' is used by the C compiler to distinguish source files from object files which have the extension '.o'.

If you wish to compile one of the source files on its own without producing an executable file, the ' − c' flag should be given to **cc;**

        cc − c pass2.c

will compile pass2.c and if there are no errors produce the object file pass2.o .

Any global variables referenced by functions within the separate source files must be declared in each one. To save on typing, and to make modifications easy, all the declarations may be collected together into one file, let's call it 'global.h', and included into each of the source files

        #include "global.h"

9.2. The Loader

Although the **cc** command appears to produce the executable file 'a.out', this task is actually performed by the loader, **ld. Ld** combines several object files onto one, resolves all external references and searches libraries for functions not declared, but referenced, in the object files. The output is left in the file a.out unless **ld** is explicitly told otherwise; it's made executable only if no errors occurred. **Ld** accepts numerous flag arguments specifying options for loading. They are too many to be detailed here; in any case **cc** supplies the correct set of arguments so there's no need to worry unless you want to do something out of the ordinary.

154

One of these flags is ' − lx', where 'x' is a string specifying a library file to be searched; the file /lib/lib **x.a is first looked for and then** /**usr/lib/lib x.a.** The ' − lc' flag is given by **cc** which causes **ld** to search the library file '/lib/libc.a'; this contains all commonly used functions (system calls, standard I/O, etc).

We have already looked at system calls in the previous chapter; although all the examples shown use C, the method of access to functions from FORTRAN 77 is no different. For reference we now provide a list of the other contents of /**lib/libc.a.** We won't attempt to give a full description of each function; you'll have to look in section 3 of your manual for more details. However, some functions, particularly **printf** and **scanf,** deserve a detailed explanation. The Manual lists library functions in alphabetical order; we'll deal with them under the four headings − standard I/O; Maths; Miscellany; and specialised libraries.

9.3. Standard I/O

Each source or sink of data is referred to by the SIO package as a 'stream'. All processes started by the shell automatically inherit three open streams − the standard input (**stdin**), standard output (**stdout**), and the standard error (**stderr**). SIO functions manipulate pointers to streams using the predeclared type 'FILE'. These identifiers, plus others, are declared for you in the header file 'stdio.h', which must be included in every program using functions from this package. We'll take a look at SIO by examining some of the functions; all of them are described in detail in appendix D.

Before any I/O can be performed on a file it must be opened using **fopen. Fopen** takes a filename plus a mode, haggles with the operating system for a file descriptor and then returns a pointer to a stream to be used for further operations on the file. The stream is actually a structure containing information such as the UNIX file descriptor, the location of an array to be used for buffering of data, the current position within that array, whether the file is being read or written, and so on. The mode of opening is a string containing a single character; "r" to open for reading; "w" to create for writing; and "a" to append onto the end of an existing file. So to open file 'fred' for reading

```
FILE *fp;
fp = fopen("fred", "r");
```

Note that FILE is a type just like 'int' or 'char'. If for any reason the open

155

fails, like opening a file for reading that doesn't exist, then the 'NULL' pointer is returned.

```
if ((fp = fopen("fred", "r")) == NULL) {
printf("cannot find fred\n");
exit(); }
```

Once you have opened a file, the next thing you will want to do is read or write; **getc** and **putc** are the simplest methods of I/O. **Getc** returns the next character from the file described by the supplied FILE pointer. It returns the value 'EOF' when it runs out of data to read

```
int ch;
FILE *fp;
while ((ch = getc(fp)) != EOF) {
        ...
        do something with the characters
        ...
}
```

Note, **getc** returns an integer value even though it's producing characters; this is necessary for compatibility with the other SIO functions.

Putc is the reverse of **getc**; it puts a character onto the file described. If an error occurs, for example when the file is full (about to exceed the file size limit), **putc** returns the value EOF

```
char ch;
FILE *fp;
if (putc(ch, fp) == EOF)
        printf("Failed to put a character\n");
```

The corresponding functions to handle words are **getw** and **putw**.

Terminal I/O can be performed using the SIO package by means of the two functions **getchar** and **putchar** which read and write a single character to or from the terminal respectively. These functions use the FILE pointers **stdin** and **stdout** which are normally connected to the terminal, but they may be redirected to files or pipes using the dup(II) system call. **Getchar** and **putchar** are defined in the file 'stdio.h' in terms of **getc, putc, stdin stdin** and **stdout**

```
#define getchar() getc(stdin)
#define putchar(c) putc(c, stdin)
```

character by character using **putc**. Fortunately, the function **fputs** exists to do this for you; it sends the characters from a zero-terminated string to the file described by the supplied file pointer.

```
FILE *fp;
fputs("hello sailor", fp);
```

Puts outputs directly to **stdout** and appends a newline, so

```
puts("hello sailor");
```

will print the string

```
hello sailor\n
```

onto the terminal.

Apart from just reading and writing characters, words (integers) and strings, the SIO package contains routines to format output, and input. The function **printf**, and the corresponding one for input **scanf**, are very powerful; they allow the translation to and from character representations of numerical quantities. They are in fact so powerful that not many people come to grips with all the facilities. The only way to get to know **printf** and **scanf** is to practice using them; type in and run our examples and then try some of your own.

Printf converts, formats and prints its arguments onto the standard output under the control of a format string. The functions **fprintf** and **sprintf** places their output onto the specified stream, and into a string (character array), respectively. It's up to you to ensure that there's enough free space in the string for **sprintf** to operate.

```
char *control, *s;
FILE *fp;
printf(control, arg, ...);
fprintf(fp, control, arg, ...);
sprintf(s, control, arg, ...);
```

The 'control' string contains two types of objects, ordinary characters which are simply copied, and conversion specifications, each of which causes the next successive argument, 'arg', to be examined and converted. A conversion specification is introduced by the character '%' and, in the simplest case, consists of a single further character.

d = decimal	o = octal
x = hexadecimal	u = unsigned integer
e, f & g = float	c = character
s = string ·	% = print a '%'

For example, to print a single integer value in the three forms: decimal; octal; and hexadecimal

```
int a;
a = 10;
printf("%d — %o — %x\n", a, a, a);
```

which will result in

```
10 — 12 — a
```

Don't forget, the control string is printed verbatim, except for conversion specifiers. The three forms of the float conversion character print the value in different formats, for example

```
float x;
x = 560.0
printf("%f — %e — %g\n", x, x, x);
```

when executed will print

```
560.000000 — 5.600000e+02 — 560
```

The string and character conversions work as expected, the following program extract

```
char *acp, *bcp, ch;
acp = "Example of a string printed using %s\n";
bcp = "The ascii code for character '%c' is %d\n";
ch = 'a';
printf("%s", acp);
printf(bcp, ch, ch);
```

will print

```
Example of a string printed using %s
The ascii code for character 'a' is 97
```

You may specify a field width and precision by placing characters between the '%' and the conversion character. A digit string specifies a minimum field width, padding occurs if there are fewer characters in the converted field; a preceding minus (−) sign indicates that left adjustment in the field should take place. A digit string preceded by a dot (.) indicates a precision to be used when printing float values, or character strings. For example

```
int a; float x;
a = 12; x = 560.0;
printf("%2d — %−4d — %6d\n", a, a, a);
printf("%.0f — %.2f — %2.2f\n", x, x, x);
```

will print

```
12  -  12   -  12
560 - 560.00 - 560.00
```

Notice that although the last float format specified a field width less than the number of characters to be printed, they did in fact appear. In general, if the field width is too small then it's ignored. Specifying a precision smaller than the number of decimal places required for a float will cause the value to be rounded

```
float x;
x = 42.647;
printf("x = %.2f\n", x);
```

and will result in

```
x = 42.65
```

The full set of possible conversion specifications is presented in appendix D for your edification; most of them are 'fairly' obvious from the explanation. One exception is the precision as related to strings. The following shows a variety of effects that may imposed onto the string 'hello sailor', we have put colons around each printed field to show its extent

```
%s        : hello sailor:
%5s       : hello sailor:
%-7s      : hello sailor:
%20s      :        hello sailor:
%-20s     : hello sailor    :
%10.5s    :      hello:
%-10.5s   : hello     :
%.10s     : hello sail:
```

Warning

Printf, fprintf and **sprintf** use their control format argument to decide how many more arguments follow and what their types are. They'll get confused, and your program is likely to fail (core dumped because of bus error or segmentation violation) if there are not enough arguments or they're of the wrong type.

The **scanf** function is the converse of **printf,** it provides the same conversion facilities, but in the opposite direction. Characters are read from some source, analysed according to the format of a control string, and the resulting values then stored using the remaining arguments. The control format is a string containing conversion specifications just as for **printf;** the result arguments MUST be pointers to variables of the appropriate type. **Scanf** reads the standard input, **fscanf** reads from a specified stream, and **sscanf** reads from a zero terminated string.

```
char *control, *s;
FILE *fp;
scanf(control, arg, ...);
fscanf(fp, control, arg, ...);
sscanf(s, control, arg, ...);
```

The control string may contain objects of several types, the simplest case consisting of ordinary characters (not %), each of which must match the next character in the input. White space characters (blanks, tabs, newlines) in the control format may optionally match white space in the input; put simply, any white space is ignored.

Conversion specifications are again introduced by the character '%'. The '%' and the conversion character may be separated by a number specifying a maximum field width, and/or a '*'. The conversion characters are almost the same as for **printf**

d = decimal	o = octal
x = hexadecimal	h = short integer
c = character	s = string
f, e = float	% = a '%' must be matched

Conversion specifications grab characters from the input source until their requirements are satisfied; the next specification carries on from the character after the last one used by the previous conversion. Characters used up by any particular conversion make up an input field, each conversion specification directs the interpretation of the next input field and any result is placed into the location pointed to by the corresponding argument. If the character '*' appears in a conversion specification then this field is simply skipped and no value assigned.

Input fields are strings of non-white space characters, extending to either the next white space character or until the field width, if specified, is exhausted. Enough of the theory, let's have a go; type in the following program

```
main() {
        int a; char ch;
        float x, v;
        scanf("%2d %*d %f %1s %f", &a, &x, &ch, &v);
        printf("a = %d\n", a);
        printf("x = %f\n", x);
        printf("ch = %c\n", ch);
        printf("v = %e\n", v);
}
```

160

compile it and execute with

    4267   42.67   T   53.806e − 12

as input; we hope your printed output looks something like

    a = 42
    x = 42.669998
    ch = T
    v = 5.3806e − 11

The first specification, ''%2d'', directs **scanf** to interpret the first two characters as a decimal integer and to place the resulting value into variable 'a'. Then '67' is skipped by the '%∗d' specification, any white space following these two characters is ignored, so the next character to be looked at from the input is '4'. The third specification in our format causes the characters '42.67' to be interpreted as a floating point number and the result placed into variable 'x'. Of course, floating point numbers are only an approximation to the truth; this is why '42.66998' was printed.

The next specification may look slightly strange, why not just use '%c' we hear you asking ? The 'c' conversion character is special in that the normal, skip over white space action is suppressed, causing the next character from the input to be used, this would place a blank into the character 'ch'. What we want is the letter 'T', so the specification '%1s' (meaning a single character string) is used instead. In general, if you require non-blank characters then use '%ns', where n is the number of characters wanted. Finally, the last conversion specification, '%f (which is a synonym for 'e'), interprets the characters '53.806e − 12' as a float value and places this value into variable 'v'. Try this next example

```
main() {
        int a; float x;
        char ch[3], wd[20];
        char ∗s = "X-values are 1, 2.7 and 14.6zzn";
        sscanf(s, "%s %3s %d, %∗f and %f", wd, ch, &a, &x);
        printf("word = %s\n", wd);
        printf("ch = %c %c %c\n", ch[0], ch[1], ch[2]);
        printf("a = %d\n", a);
        printf("x = %f\n", x);
}
```

when compiled and executed it should print

    word = X-values
    ch = a r e
    a = 1
    x = 14.600000

Can you work out why ?

A variation on the string conversion specification is '%[...]'; this indicates a string not delimited by white space characters. The left bracket is followed by a list of one or more characters, which make up the string; the string is terminated by any character not from the set within the brackets. If the first character in the set is ' ∧ ' (circumflex) then the string is delimited by one of the characters from the remaining set. This latter construction may be used to specify your own string delimiters. For example, the program

```
main() {
        float x;
        char word[20];
        char *string = "The value of x = 563.703\n";
        sscanf(string, "%[ ∧ =] = %.3f\n", word, &x);
        printf("word = '%s'\n", word);
        printf("x = %f\n", x);
}
```

when executed will print

```
word = "The value of x "
x = 563.703
```

When using the '%[∧ ...]' notation the terminating character isn't copied from the input and must be explicitly matched. In the above example, the '=' sign is used to terminate the string 'word'; this character is not copied from the input and so remains to be used. Try the above example again, this time removing the second '=' from the control format string. What is printed for the value of x ? Why ?

Just to emphasise the last point, here is program extract which may be used to split up comma separated fields into separate strings. It may look complicated, but believe us, it's necessary. A program containing

```
char string1[20], string2[20], string3[20], string4[20];
scanf("%[ ∧ ,], %[ ∧ ,], %[ ∧ ,], %[ ∧ ,]", string1,
                        string2, string3, string4);
```

when executed with the input

    it can be seen, therefore, that if, under certain conditions, ...

will result in

```
string1 = "it can be seen"
string2 = "therefore"
string3 = "that if"
string4 = "under certain conditions"
```

Warning

The result arguments to **scanf** MUST be pointers to variables of the appropriate type; also, it's up to you to ensure that there's enough space available to accommodate the largest possible input string. One of the most common mistakes is writing

```
float x;
scanf("%f", x);
```

instead of

```
scanf("%f", &x);
```

This is bound to lead to the dreaded 'Core dumped' message.

When you have tired of reading and writing your streams of data, you may wish to close them. To reuse an input stream it's sufficient to close it using **fclose,** the stream then becomes available for I/O on a different file. It's unnecessary to close input streams if the program has finished as the exit procedure does this for you.

```
FILE *fp;
fclose(fp);
```

However, output streams are a very different kettle of fish; due to the buffering mechanism employed by the SIO package some data may be waiting to be written out to the file. If you merely use **fclose** then this information is lost forever. **Fflush** must be used first to flush out any buffered data before **fclose** is called, either explicitly or, as the effect of an **exit.**

```
FILE *fp;
fflush(fp);
fclose(fp);
```

Some versions of SIO buffer terminal output on a line by line basis. This is o.k. until you want to print out a partial line, say as a prompt. The line will not appear as the SIO routines are waiting for a line-feed before writing out the characters. To get round this use a fflush after the print, or putc.

```
printf (" - >");
fflush (stdout);
```

9.4. Math Functions

Functions from the library '/lib/libm.a' are loaded automatically by the FORTRAN compiler; C programs need the ' – lm' flag to **cc**. Any program using math functions should include the file **math.h**, that is, they should have the line

#include <math.h>

near the beginning; this is necessary for correct typing of the functions.

Appendix D gives details of the routines available from this library. They include Bessel, trigonometric and hyperbolic functions. Besides returning an error value, functions from this package also set **errno** to indicate the nature of the fault.

EDOM   the argument to a function was out of the domain of the function. For example, arguments of magnitude greater than one to **asin** or **acos**

ERANGE the value of a function can't be represented within the available machine precision. For example, the singular points of **tan**.

9.5. Miscellany (Section 3 of the manual)

Functions coming under this heading make up the bulk of the library 'lib/libc.a, which is searched by the link editor, **ld**, automatically when called from the C or the F77 compilers. We have listed in appendix D all those functions supplied with UNIX for a PDP – 11; your installation should have most of them. For further details consult section 3 of your local manual.

9.6. Special Libraries

Various specialised libraries exist, often peculiar to an installation. You will have to consult your local documentation for details, both **cc** and **f77** must be told if you use any functions from these libraries. We will give a short description of the two special libraries distributed with standard (Bell) V7 UNIX; they may or may not be available at your site. For particular details see appendix D.

9.6.1. Multiple Precision Arithmetic

Functions from this library can perform arithmetic on integers of arbitrary length. Values must be stored using the predefined type 'mint';

pointers to 'mint' may be initialised using the function **itom,** which sets an initial value. Routines are available for the usual operations $(+, -, *, /)$, plus square root and raising to a power.

9.6.2. Graphics Interface Routines

This library contains functions to generate graphical output in a relatively device independent fashion. Various loader flags may be supplied to **cc** depending on the destination of the graph; '−lplot' produces output to **stdout,** which can then be filtered using one of the **plot (l)** commands for a particular device. Alternatively, output may be generated directly for a restricted range of graphical terminals, for example, the flag '−l300' produces plotting commands for a GSI 300 terminal, and '−l4014' will drive a Tektronix 4014.

Before any plotting functions are used **openpl** must be called to initialise the output stream. Functions are available to draw lines (.b line), circles (**circle),** and arcs (**arc);** to move the plot position (**move);** to plot a point (**point);** and many more. When the graph is finished **closepl** must be called to flush any pending output and close the output file.

9.7. The Archiver

You may create your own libraries of functions using the **ar** command, which combines several files into a single 'archive' file. **Ar** is most commonly used for maintaining libraries of object files to be used by the loader, **ld;** it has the capability to create, add, extract, list, move and/or delete files from/to an archive file. There is no reason, though, why it should not be used to create a library of files containing any arbitrary information.

The contents of a library to be used by **ld** must be in relocatable object format, such a file is produced using the '−c' option to **cc** and **f77.**

    cc −c libfile.c

or

    f77 −c libfile.f

Both these commands will produce 'libfile.o'. The 'r' flag is used with **ar** to add such object files to a library file; if the library file doesn't exist then it's created, and if the entries specified already exist in the archive they are replaced. The command

```
ar r mylib file1.o file2.o file3.o
```

will create 'mylib', if it didn't exist already, and place into it the entries 'file1.o', 'file2.o' and 'file3.o'. The 't' flag is used to list the contents of an archive file

```
ar t mylib
```

should produce something like

```
file1.o
file2.o
file3.o
```

You may now use functions from your library just by giving its name to the C or FORTRAN compiler, the loader can tell that this file contains archived entries and will search for referenced functions in the normal fashion. For example

```
cc prog.c mylib
```

will compile 'prog.c' and then search the library 'mylib' for any needed functions.

Chapter 10

Maintenance

10.1. Introduction

As far as we're concerned, 'maintenance' does **not** mean poking about inside the processor with a soldering iron; it doesn't mean software maintenance either, in the usual sense of the term. What we talk about in this chapter covers a whole range of both software and techniques that don't fit into any of the other chapters.

We talk about the sort of things that don't necessarily interest casual users of UNIX, covering topics like the starting and stopping of a UNIX system, filestore checks and backup, the printer spooler and other matters. This doesn't mean to say that you ought to ignore what's in here if you just want to use UNIX to run software packages bought off the shelf from a commercial supplier, though if that's the case you're probably safe if you **do** ignore it. As well as maintenance of a UNIX system, a lot of the detail of the workings of the operating system are described and will go a long way towards illustrating what is really happening as you use UNIX. You don't need to know it, but it helps if you do; for anyone who will be responsible for the day to day running of a UNIX installation it's indispensable.

10.2. Starting and stopping UNIX

Instead of simply giving a list of instructions telling you how to stop or start UNIX, we prefer to discuss the way in which the software operates. This has the advantage of masking the fact that a list of "do this then do this" instructions is impossible to provide because of differences between various UNIX implementations; it also gives us the chance to describe a number of important aspects of UNIX, especially the **init** program. Let's now go through the whole procedure – from a cold start right through to shutdown – and see what's happening.

10.2.1. Starting UNIX

Getting UNIX started on a dead processor is sometimes reminiscent of black magic rites: various secret incantations to be muttered; shaking a bag of bones over the power supplies; appeasement of the gods and the sacrifice of a virgin – you know the sort of thing. The exact steps to take will vary considerably depending on your hardware and the software implementation so we can't be specific at this point; your own system might not need the bones and the sacrifice, but this is still a solemn process and ought to be approached in the proper frame of mind.

If you do have to start UNIX running then you'll have to inspect your local documents to find what steps should be taken; but in each case once you've followed them you end up with a copy of the UNIX kernel being loaded into memory and being given control of the processor. The first time you do this it helps to have someone around who's done it before and will be able to hold your hand.

We'll describe the steps taken to start Standard Version 7 UNIX on a PDP-11 processor purely as an example of one way it's done, knowing that the details will differ substantially on other systems. At the same time we'll try to explain what the software is up to; these details should be almost invariable no matter what system you're using.

Starting PDP-11 UNIX is pretty straightforward, following exactly the same steps you'd take to start any operating system on one of those machines. After you've pressed the right buttons on the console or the processor the UNIX bootstrap program runs and gives you an '@' as a prompt. There are a number of 'stand alone' programs which can be run at this point, disc formatters, diagnostics and similar stuff, but you usually want to start UNIX going.

Starting UNIX is a two-stage job involving an intermediate program called 'boot', whose job is to find the real UNIX and start it. On our machine the dialogue is this:

```
@boot
   boot
   : rf(0,0)unix
```

the 'boot' program prompts you with 'boot' and the colon, you tell it the name of the disc, which drive and which segment of that drive it should search for the program called 'unix'.

Once loaded and started, UNIX initialises itself and eventually starts a single shell running on the console terminal; this shell belongs to the super user and should be used to run the filestore checks described later.

You should always check the filestore when UNIX is started because there's no guarantee it was stopped properly. Involuntary halts (power failure or software problems) have a nasty habit of leaving the filestore in a state of confusion, which will rapidly get worse if the system is allowed to run for any length of time before the problems are sorted out.

In brief the startup procedure is this: press the right buttons, say the right things and check the filestore. If the filestore is really screwed up UNIX may not even be able to start. We've yet to see this happen on our own system but perhaps we've been lucky. UNIX needs the early part of the directory hierarchy and several files to be intact for it to be able to give you the first shell prompt; if your system won't start, or only gets half way to starting, then is the time to suspect major disaster; if you haven't got any way of recovering from it you've got big trouble!

When you're sure the filestore is intact, set the date (see the 'date' command, section one of the manual) and type EOT to the first shell; this will cause the system to come up in its normal multi-user state. Try not to get the date wrong. As well as being misleading, an incorrect date can make a mess of the file backup system and is a thorough nuisance.

10.2.2. Init

The startup and subsequent operation of a UNIX system is dependent on a rather special program called **init. Init** is a strange thing, being an ordinary user process in some ways, and part of the operating system in others – a half-and-half process with one leg in heaven and the other in hell. When UNIX is started the operating system itself becomes the first process and gets the special process identity (pid) of zero, even though it isn't really a process in the normal sense of the word. This pseudo-process forks and produces the first real process, with a pid of 1; by a highly devious piece of trickery the first action of this process is forced to be an **exec** system call which executes the program '/etc/init'.

It's the job of this first process to provide the shell that you see as the first obvious sign of the operating system doing something; the shell is a child of **init**. When the shell exits, **init** assumes that the whole system is ready for multi-user operation and starts the necessary steps. The first step is to fork and execute a super user shell which obeys the commands held in the file '/etc/rc'; the commands will probably clean out your temporary directories, mount extra filesystem volumes and start a couple of housekeeping processes going†.

---

†See notes on 'cron' and 'update' in section 8 of the user manual for details of two common housekeeping processes, or read further.

The final step taken by **init** is to read the '/etc/ttys' file, where it finds out about all the terminals where a user may log in. For each of these it forks once. Each child opens one of the terminals three times, getting its standard input, output and error file descriptors allocated to that terminal, then the program '/etc/getty' is executed. **Getty** is the first program to talk to a user and attempts to do things such as automatic speed detection and working out whether or not the terminal is upper-case only; it sets the terminal characteristics according to what it thinks is correct. The first 'login' message you see is provided by **getty** which reads your response to that prompt and then executes the real login with your response as an argument; a lack of lower-case characters in the response will make **getty** think you have no lower case. You know what happens from the 'login' stage.

The parent **init**, process 1, does nothing but wait for children to die. **Init** is a special process which inherits any orphan processes (those with no parent still existing); when it learns of these through the **wait** system call it ignores them. The ones it's interested in are the processes it forked for user's terminals: whenever one of those dies, another must be forked to provide another 'login' message.

The path outlined above means that when you log in, your shell is in fact one of these children of **init**. Because of this, simply by exiting, your shell ensures that another 'login' will be provided at your terminal.

Without **init** a UNIX system would never even get started, let alone run properly. It's obvious that this process is rather special to the operating system and must never stop. Some UNIX systems have other special processes too; the VAX virtual memory UNIX system we know of uses process 2 for internal business. Your local documentation will probably be able to tell you more.

10.2.3. Stopping UNIX

Given that the system works in the way outlined, you shouldn't find it hard to understand how to stop the system: persuade **init** not to fork any more, then kill off all the other processes in the system. This is conveniently done for you by **init** itself when it receives the hangup signal, SIGHUP. To send this signal to **init** you have to log in as the super-user and use **kill** to send the signal:

kill −1 1

init will receive the signal, kill off everything else in the system and return to single user mode with a shell running on the console terminal. Use this shell to execute **sync** a couple of times, then stop the processor. The

sync is important, ensuring that the filestore on the disc system is up to date when the machine is halted; forgetting to **sync** is a good way of getting a corrupt filesystem.

10.3. The ttys file and getty

The file '/etc/ttys' plays an important part in a multi-user UNIX system, defining what sort of terminals are attached and what should be done with them. When the system starts up in multi-user mode **init** reads this file to discover how many **login** processes are needed, then using the procedure outlined above it forks and provides them.

In a standard UNIX system the format of this file is simple – one line per terminal. The first character on a line determines whether or not a given terminal is to be used: a '1' means the terminal is to be used, a '0' means it isn't. The second character is passed to **getty** as an argument by **init** and indicates what special characteristics this terminal has. The rest of the line is the name of the terminal special file in the /dev directory. For example, a line in /etc/ttys looking like this:

    10tty1

means that /dev/tty1 is to be given a **login** process.

Init only reads the ttys file when the system starts up – the file isn't inspected regularly to see if any changes have been made, so editing it to reflect a new arrangement and then waiting for the change to be noticed won't work. To make **init** take another look at the file you have to send it the SIGTERM signal, e.g.

    kill 1

The second character of each line in the ttys file is passed on to /etc/getty. What **getty** does with it depends on your system; look at your documentation to find out. The normal use of this character is to indicate special terminal features such as parity, speeds and so on.

Getty prints the 'login' message on it's terminal and waits to see what the response is. If a 'break' is detected on the terminal line, a new speed setting is tried. A range of speeds is cycled through in this way, so users dialling in from outside keep pressing 'break' until they get the 'login' message printed correctly: the speeds must then be right for their terminal. Whatever is typed in response to the 'login' is inspected. If it only contains upper-case characters **getty** assumes your terminal is upper-case only and sets the terminal mode to map upper-case into the lower-case equivalent. If the reply was terminated by 'return' and not 'newline' (the usual case), **getty** also notes this fact in the terminal mode setting and from now on 'return' will be interpreted as 'newline'.

The last step taken is to execute **login** and pass your reply to it as the argument: from now on **login** is controlling the terminal. Bad luck if the terminal modes were set incorrectly!

10.3.1. The process group

If it's not already a member of a 'process group', a process is automatically given a process group as soon as it opens its first teletype for i/o. The process group is inherited by all the children of a process and they aren't allowed to change it, so all the processes you run from a terminal are bound to be members of the process group associated with that terminal — they're all descended from the child of **init** which first opened the terminal. The terminal is called the 'controlling terminal' for that process group. The controlling terminal is what determines the handling of the INTERRUPT key; press that key on a terminal and a SIGINT signal is sent to every process whose controlling terminal it is, even if that process doesn't belong to you.

10.3.2. Excuses

We've described Standard UNIX here because we think it's important to know how the startup and login sequences work. We must warn you though that this is one area which is often tinkered with by system implementors; yours will probably be slightly (maybe considerably) different in detail, so be prepared. Read the **init, getty** and **ttys** sections of your manual thoroughly to find out what your versions do.

10.4. Checking the filestore

We said earlier that you should check your filestore for consistency every time you start the system running. Why?

Presumably your files are precious to you and you won't be all that happy if they get lost. The filestore demands a certain amount of care and respect if this isn't to happen. The UNIX filestore is a highly structured collection of data which only works properly if that ordering is correctly maintained; in normal circumstances the operating system looks after it and **does** keep things properly ordered, but there are times when things can go wrong. Faults are normally the result of one of two possibilities: either a physical disaster such as a disc head crash, or hardware malfunction – the most common being power failure. We would prefer to leave unmentioned the possibility that some fool scribbles all over a disc by accident; the filestore protections must be set to prevent direct write access to filestore discs.

Hardware failure matters because there's a high likelihood that important data such as the contents of modified directories will not have been written to disc since the modification was made. The likelihood is compounded by UNIX's habit of keeping this important information in memory for speed of access: it won't be written out to disc unless it's forced out either by external means, or when the memory is required for something else. The **sync** system call **does** force this updating to occur and most fully started UNIX systems run a process (/etc/update) whose only job is to execute a **sync** every thirty seconds or so, keeping the discs relatively up to date. The **sync** command will force an update in the same way and should always be the last command executed prior to halting your processor.

The UNIX filestore doesn't contain the safety features found in some other operating systems; features such as duplicated directories and file checksums are **not** part of the usual UNIX implementation (although there's no reason why they shouldn't be – future UNIX systems might have them). The only checks that can be made on a filestore of the usual organisation is that its **structure** is consistent; there's no way of checking that individual files are uncorrupted. There's nothing to stop individual users from implementing their own checksums, safety copies or whatever, it's just that this isn't done automatically.

The philosophy underlying the UNIX approach is that a) you can't protect against total loss of data (as in the case of a serious head crash), and that b) providing the redundancy/checksum features would seriously slow the whole system and not be worth the cost in view of the reliability of UNIX systems in general. We tend to agree with this, but that's just our opinion.

10.4.1. Icheck and Dcheck

The two utilities most widely used to check a filestore are **icheck** and **dcheck;** you should read their manual entries carefully if you ever need to use them. We use them to check each disc of our system in turn, applying first **icheck** and remedying any problems it finds, then **dcheck** to perform the final checks. To be able to appreciate what they do and how they do it you must have an understanding of the way that filestore discs are organised: go and look it up before you try to use these commands.

173

Icheck is used to check that the allocation of blocks on a disc is still sensible. For example, blocks shown to be available for re-allocation (in the **freelist**) must not also be part of a file; neither should one block be in more than one file. Checks are also made to ensure that neither the freelist nor files contain blocks which lie outside the range of legal block numbers (on a 10000 block disc you can't have block number 10001). Blocks which don't appear in either the freelist or any files are treated as 'missing blocks', these also cause complaints. **Icheck** should never be used on discs which are part of currently running filestore or all sorts of spurious error reporting is likely. Discs should always be checked and errors corrected before they are made part of the running system.

On our system we have three RK07 discs. Their entries in the /dev directory are: rf0, rf1 and rf2 for the 'block' versions of these discs; rrf0, rrf1 and rrf2 for the 'character' or 'raw' versions. **Icheck** is faster if it checks the 'raw' disc because it can read large chunks at time; the speedup is quite noticeable. We would use the command

    icheck /dev/rrf1

to check the middle of the three discs.

Icheck will always report certain statistics about the state of each disc; this output should be inspected to see if any problems have arisen. Missing, duplicate or bad blocks in the freelist are easily dealt with by re-running **icheck** with the ' − s' flag; this causes it to rebuild the freelist and the problem should go away. Duplicate or bad blocks which are associated with an i-node are much more trouble and the i-node (i.e. the file) is probably beyond hope.

If, say, i-node 153 is reported as containing bad or duplicate blocks, the first step you should take is to find out what names it goes by; the **ncheck** command will tell you the names of all the links to that particular i-node. In this case, then,

    ncheck −i 153 /dev/rrf1

would be used to find out what the i-node is called. If the file is important you might try to take a copy of it by mounting the disc and copying the file, (see **mount(1)** and this chapter later), but if it contains bad blocks the copy will fail. The i-node should now be cleared using **clri** and a note made of the names reported by **ncheck** so that these directory entries can be dealt with later. The **clri** command will be

    clri /dev/rrf1 153

after which the i-node is shown as being free − the file has gone for ever. Clearing i-nodes in this way almost always results in a 'missing' diagnostic on the next run of **icheck** so the ' − s' option will definitely need to be used soon.

To summarise: check the disc, note the names of each problem i-node (there are as many names as there are links to the i-node), clear each problem i-node with **clri** and then re-run **icheck** with the ' − s' flag to rebuild the freelist, e.g.

icheck − s /dev/rrf1

then run **icheck** yet again to see if you got it right. You may have to iterate this process a number of times. Do the whole thing for each disc in your system.

Dcheck is the next step in the checking procedure. It ensures that the number of links claimed by each i-node is matched by an equivalent number of directory entries; only discrepancies will be reported. If an i-node is reported with more links than entries the situation isn't critical and can be left if you don't mind. The reverse − an i-node with less links than entries is a different proposition and needs urgent attention. Once again you must find out what names it goes by (**ncheck** again), take a copy of it if you really need to (by mounting the disc etc.), unmount the disc, clear the i-node(s), mount the disc again and delete the directory entries. Finally you can copy the file back from wherever you put it and re-forge the old links with the **ln** command.

The important steps are the clearing of the i-node and the deletion of any directory entries which refer to it.

If the **dcheck** phase resulted in the use of **clri** you'll have to repeat the **icheck** because you will have introduced more missing blocks.

As a rule of thumb, you can tolerate a few dozen missing blocks and a handful of i-nodes with more-links-than-entries until you get fed up with seeing the diagnostics. All other anomalies need treatment.

A last word on **icheck**. It uses the filesystem 'superblock' to tell it what values are reasonable for disc block and i-node numbers; it'll get horribly upset if the superblock is deranged. You might be able to patch the superblock with **adb** but in the circumstances we think we would probably give up and rebuild an empty filesystem on the disc using **mkfs,** then restore a backup copy onto it. Also, if you ever have to fix up the running system disc with **icheck,** you must halt the processor immediately afterwards **without executing sync**. If you don't, the old, bad, kernel copies of the disc information get written back onto it and your good work is undone!

Various attempts have been made with varying degrees of success to produce an automatic filestore corrector. The Berkeley **fsck** is apparently a good one – it's worth trying to get a copy – but none are perfect because it's impossible to cater for every possible malfunction. This is one area where human intervention will be important for a long while to come; to quote from the manual "experience and informed courage count for much".

10.4.2. Building an empty filesystem

From time to time you'll find yourself needing to build an empty filesystem on a disc, usually just before you restore a backup filestore copy onto it. The **mkfs** command is used to put the right structure there; although it's capable of much more sophisticated use we only ever use it to build a completely empty filesystem. On our UNIX system the command

/etc/mkfs /dev/rrf1 50000

builds an empty filesystem on the disc /dev/rrf1, using the first 50000 blocks. We then use the **restor** command to restore magnetic tape backups onto it.

10.5. Backup

You're happily using your one-disc system, congratulating yourself on saving money by getting just the one disc and no tape drive. The system runs perfectly (though a little slowly) and has been ticking along for months and months without a hitch. Then, one day, perhaps influenced by a hangover, the super user accidentally writes directly onto the system disc; scribbling over the bootstrap, the superblock and the first few hundred i-nodes. You haven't got a backup disc – the system uses a fixed winchester – what can you do? Answer: Cry.

UNIX systems come complete with two utilities to help you take backup copies of your filestore, they're called **dump** and **restor**. They are both explained in obscure detail in section one of the manual. In brief, they both expect you to have a magnetic tape drive available and it's this which they manipulate, although they can be made to treat any other block-structured device (maybe an exchangeable disc) as if it were a tape.

If you ever contemplate buying a UNIX system **insist** on being given full details of the backup arrangements before you part with money.

We can give details of how we handle our own backups; we don't pretend to having studied the matter in depth, all we can say is that we've never lost anything important yet. In three years we've only had three major failures which needed recourse to the tape backups; that's on an experimental machine into the bargain, two of the failures being caused by modifications to the kernel which didn't quite work. Failure is so rare that perhaps we don't give backup the attention it deserves.

10.5.1. Dump

Each of our discs is dumped separately, so we keep a family of tapes for each of the three. It's advisable to dump a filestore while it isn't actually doing anything, to avoid the problem of dumping a file which is in the process of being re-written and only getting half of it. Our dumps are taken at the dead of night; for us that happens to be convenient and a time when the system is unlikely to be busy.

Read the following description in conjunction with a copy of the **dump** page of the manual.

The first time round, a full dump is taken of each disc:

```
dump 0u /dev/rf0
```

dumps our system drive and the tape is marked as such. The next dump of this drive is a 'level 9' dump onto a different tape and only contains files modified since the last full dump:

```
dump 9u /dev/rf0
```

these incremental dumps are placed on tapes which are used in the sequence 1 2 3 1 2 3... each day. When the incremental dump reaches about a third the size of a full dump another full dump is taken onto the second full dump tape; these are also used in the order above. This procedure has been quite adequate for our needs and means that we only have to lose one day's work even if the entire filestore is lost on disc.

10.5.2. Restor

Restoring a dump is simple. In the case of a disc so corrupt we can't or won't patch it up, we first of all initialise the disc using **mkfs,** e.g.

```
/etc/mkfs /dev/rrf1 50000
```

then restore the most recent full dump onto it (having mounted the right tape in the tape drive)

```
restor r /dev/rf1
```

When that has finished, we restore the most recent incremental dump using exactly the same command but of course the right tape. That completes the restoration. Although it's apparently possible to extract individual files from the dump tapes we never bother and can't say how it's done.

10.5.3. Summary of backup

Secure backup of your filestore is the single most important job for the administrator of your system. We've told you what we do; this may not be good enough for someone who has real security needs. **Dump** and **restor** are highly flexible in this respect, provided that you have a tape or equivalent device. If security matters to you, make sure you have full details about filestore backup before you contemplate buying a particular hardware configuration. We neatly sidestep the issue by allowing those of our users who are paranoid about the security of certain files to take their own backup copies too, using their own tapes and the **tar(1)** command. In the paranoid class comes ourselves with respect to the text of this book.

In practice our system is so reliable that we haven't had any serious trouble yet.

10.6. Special files

"Special files", you cry, "I thought all files were the same". Indeed one of the criteria used by the designers of UNIX was that there would be no 'special' file formats: a file should be a file and contain whatever you want to put in it. The design of UNIX does exactly that: there **are** no restrictions on what you put in a file, or how you choose to arrange the data; what UNIX calls a 'special file' is something that most operating systems don't give you at all – access to actual hardware devices.

There are three main types of file supported by UNIX (we're ignoring 'multiplex files' because they're experimental and not present in all UNIX systems). There are the ordinary files you've met already; there are pipes which are used to connect the output of one process to the input of another; the only difference between these and ordinary files is that pipes have a limited length (often 4096 bytes) and are strictly sequential in their operation. You aren't allowed to **seek** in a pipe. Special files are handled in exactly the same way as any other file (**open, read, write** etc.) but what happens in each case depends on the piece of hardware that you're talking to. If, say, your system has a line printer connected, it's name is likely to be '/dev/lp'. This is the pathname of the special file which refers to the printer hardware. If the permissions permit it, you can open this file just as if it were any other; opening this file and writing to it will result in the data you write being printed on the printer. Of course, it makes no sense to try to read from the printer or to **seek** to some position within the file; this special file is strictly sequential in performance and silly operations aren't allowed.

All of the hardware devices available to your system will have a special file entry somewhere in your filestore hierarchy, nearly always in the directory '/dev'. All the terminals, discs, tape and printers should be found there with permissions set according to the safety of allowing users access to them. Some devices will be available to everyone but on a 'single user' basis; once they've been opened for use further attempts to open them will fail until they are closed. The printer and magnetic tape drives are usually handled in this way because of the inconvenience caused to all if several users try to write on them at once†.

A detailed description of each special file will be found in section 4 of your user manual and should be read carefully before you try to use any of them. They're usually simple to use, doing exactly what you expect them to **but** they depend on the capabilities of the hardware involved and this often leads to whimsical restrictions on their use or aberrations in operation. Perseverance and experimentation are the only way to get round any peculiarities not explicitly covered in the documentation. It's impossible for us even to try to explain a particular example here; yours will be different enough to make the effort a waste of time.

10.6.1. General features of special files

A special file requires an entry in the filestore to give it a name; this implies that an i-node is needed, together with a link to it (usually in the '/dev' directory). They're created with the **mknod** system call, which is restricted to the super user; see your manual for details. The easiest way of using **mknod** is by using the program '/etc/mknod' which does a lot of safety checks for you. Each special file has three main qualities which have to be specified: whether it's a 'character' or 'block' file; its 'major' device number and its 'minor' device number.

The major device number is used to select a given type of device; the

---

†This single access policy can lead to *deadlocks* Reference [1], p94-99. UNIX takes no steps whatsoever to avoid this possibility, it becomes the responsibility of the user's software. The **lpr** line printer spooler helps reduce the likelihood of it, in practice we have yet to see deadlock occur for this reason.

ones driven by the same piece of software (the 'device driver') within the operating system. The minor device number selects an individual member from this group of similar devices. If you don't have access to the kernel source code there's no way you can find out or change what a given major device number refers to; it's built into a table inside the kernel. Your documentation may be helpful here, but don't bank on it: the whole lot may be hidden, although if you know the pathname of a given special file you can find the major and minor device numbers by using **ls(1)** with the '−l' flag.

The device driver is selected by the major device number, that software then uses the minor device number to work out which device to drive. As an example, our system has three disc drives which all share the major device number of 2. The minor device numbers of the three drives are 0, 1 and 2 for the first, second and third drives respectively.

You only need to know about the device numbers when you create the filestore entry for these devices. They're needed by the system but not the user; users refer to these files by their filestore name, as with any file.

Historically, special files were either block structured devices (disc, tape) or not (teletype, printer). The I/O mechanisms driving them were, and still are, different enough to make it worth while distinguishing between them; as a result they're known as either 'block special files' or 'character special files'. The distinction is made odd by the fact that most if not all block structured devices are also accessible as character special files. What's the difference?

Block special files are accessed just like ordinary files. Fully buffered random access I/O is supported on all these devices unless it's physically impossible: you can't perform random access writes to normal magnetic tape, though random access reads are legal.

Character special files are essentially unbuffered and all non-block-structured devices must be one of these. Most of the block structured devices can also be accessed as character devices **but there are some important differences in the way they're handled.** All I/O in this case is forced to start on a block boundary within the device and transfers are made directly between the device and user memory; **seeks** to the middle of a block only actually get to the start of the block, which has surprised several programmers who weren't prepared for it. Very long read/write transfers are fast because the whole transfer is a single operation even if it's several device blocks in length. Long transfers on block special files are done one block at a time and are slow by comparison.

Your system filestore discs will also be accessible as special files. They shouldn't be readable or writeable by ordinary users unless you don't care about filestore security since access to the physical discs means, obviously, access to the files stored on them (if you know how to do it).

A problem with making discs unreadable by rank-and-file users is that the **ps** command needs to be able to read the disc area used for memory swapping if it's to find out about swapped-out processes. Making **ps** a setuid command owned by someone who has got read permission on the disc is a solution.

Write permission on these discs is VERY DANGEROUS and will only be allowed if you're mad.

For more information about special files you might like to read "UNIX implementation" by Ken Thompson, in volume 2b of the user manual. Some of you might understand it, too.

10.6.2. Mount

UNIX filesystem volumes can be absorbed into your 'live' filestore using the **mount** system call and removed with **umount**. It's normally done using the programs '/etc/mount' and '/etc/umount' which perform checks and some bookkeeping.

The action of **mount** is simple. The filesystem volume concerned can be mounted at any point in the directory structure of your filestore – it's normally spoken of as 'mounting the disc on a directory' – once done, all references to the directory are transformed into references to the root directory of the mounted volume.

Any pathnames which contain the name of a mounted-on directory are now directed through the mounted disc; the old directory name now referring to the root directory of the mounted device. On our system, the command

/etc/mount /dev/rf1 /usr/tmp

causes the pathname '/usr/tmp' to mean the root directory of the disc whose special file name is '/dev/rf1'; any files on that disc can now be accessed through the pathname '/usr/tmp'.

Unmounting discs is equally easy, but the system refuses to unmount any device until all the files on it have been closed. The **mount** and **unmount** commands maintain in the file '/etc/mtab' a table of the names of devices which are currently mounted. Any complaints they make about the contents of this table ('device not in mount table') can be ignored. The table can get out of step with the real state of affairs, especially after a crash: it's only there for the sake of interest and doesn't matter.

Be careful about mounting discs on a directory which isn't empty; the entries in that directory become invisible for the duration of the mount because the directory name has been hijacked and no longer refers to what it used to be. Read what the manual has to say about **mount** and **unmount,** and pay particular attention to the 'read-only' flag. Unless your tape drive permits random-access writes, magnetic tapes **must** be mounted read-only or they will be destroyed.

10.7. Housekeeping

We mentioned the **cron** and **update** utilities a little while ago. Their full names are '/etc/cron' and '/etc/update', both are normally started by **init** as a result of entries in the '/etc/rc' file which specifies actions to be taken when the system starts running.

Update is very simple; its only job is to execute the **sync** system call every 30 seconds. This ensures that the filestore on disc is kept relatively up to date and helps to prevent horrific failures if the processor stops suddenly.

Cron is a more complicated beastie. Every minute it examines a file called '/usr/lib/crontab' to see if any commands should be carried out at that time. It's convenient for scheduling automatic processes such as filestore backup, accounting, dial-out network message handling or anything else you feel like doing. The manual entry tells you how to specify particular processes for execution but most ordinary users use **at(1)** to do the dirty work for them.

On our system **cron** is used to turn on and off execute permission on the system games programs at certain times of the day, and to clean out any old files (more than two days old) which are still hanging around in the '/tmp' directory. **Cron** in UNIX systems is used to do the jobs that would have otherwise needed manual intervention, allowing routine hourly/daily/weekly scheduling of software. Being able to run commands at set times can make the administration of your system less of a chore and certainly helps to reduce the demands on operations staff.

10.7.1. Lpr

Lpr is the command used to print stuff on the system printer. Users aren't allowed to share this device for obvious reasons, so to reduce inconvenience the **lpr** command acts as a 'software printer'; it can either be given a list of file names to print, or failing that, it will read and then print its standard input. As with most other commands **lpr** has a number of options which can be selected by flags – they're described under **lpr(1)** in the manual. The files to be printed are queued by the insertion of appropriate entries in the directory '/usr/spool/lpd'; this is done automatically by **lpr**. The actual printing of the files is done by a program called '/etc/lpd', known as the 'printer daemon', which simply looks for a file to be printed by searching the directory '/usr/spool/lpd'; whenever it finds a file to print, it prints it. The daemon will exit if there aren't any files to print (this means there is no permanent overhead associated with it), so it has to be started running by **lpr** every time a file is to be printed. The daemon is the only process ever to open the printer special file and ordinary users won't normally have access to this device.

To ensure that there aren't two daemons running at once, the first daemon to start will create the file '/usr/spool/lpd/lock'. Any further daemons which start will exit immediately if they find this file exists, so the current daemon has to remove the file just before it exits: this method of synchronising the software isn't ideal and does in fact contain a subtle bug which needs a 'semaphore't to solve the problem properly. Much more noticeable is that if the daemon ever stops without removing the lock file (software failure or a system crash while the daemon is running) then subsequent daemons will think one is already running, and exit. If your printer suddenly stops and won't re-start, this could be your problem. Use **ps(1)** to see if the daemon is still running – if it is, then your printer has broken and the daemon has hung up waiting for the printer to say it's ready. If the daemon has vanished and the lock file still exists, remove the lock file; the next use of **lpr** should restart the printing.

10.8. New users

A surprising omission from Standard UNIX is the software to install and remove users. Most UNIX installations have done something about this, but there's no agreed piece of software to do it, so we'll describe what you ought to do by hand. If your system comes complete with the software to do it automatically you might still be interested to find out what goes on.

Installing a new user is a three stage process. First you modify the password file, then the group file, then you make a directory for the user. Removing a user is the reverse process.

Let's say you want to install a user and have decided to call her 'eva'.

†Reference [1], p16-23.

The first task is to check that there aren't any other users of that name already installed; you have to look for that name in the file '/etc/passwd'. **Grep** is handy for this:

    grep eva /etc/passwd

will print all lines containing 'eva'.

The password file contains lines of this format:

    xyz:xxxxxx:7:5::/usr/xyz:

a number of fields separated by colons. This line describes a user whose login name is 'xyz', whose encrypted password is 'xxxxxx', whose uid and gid are 7 and 5 respectively and whose login directory is '/usr/xyz'. The password file is described in section 5 of the manual if you want a closer look at what each field means.

Using other entries in the password file as a guideline, make an entry for your new user. Select whatever uid and gid you think appropriate – the uid should be unique but the gid will depend on the way you've chosen to allocate groups on your system. You can use **ed** to edit the file provided you're the super user. Leave the password field blank – our user's entry will be something like

    eva::22:5::/usr/eva:

when you've finished.

Having edited the password file you now have to amend the file '/etc/group' to show that there is a new member in whichever group you selected for 'eva'. This is done by appending ',eva' (don't forget the comma) to the list of members already in that group. The group file shows which group(s) a given user is entitled to enter; if eva is to be allowed to use the **newgrp** command to change her current gid to something else, then the group file will need an entry for her name in each of the groups she's entitled to. Oddly, although there is provision for passwords to be included in the group file there seems to be no easy way of setting them; certainly there's nothing which will work for group passwords analogous to the **passwd** command. If you're in doubt which group a user should belong to you'll find it helps to know that nearly all users should belong to the group called 'other' – put them there to start with.

Your last step is to make a directory for the user with the **mkdir** command. Remember to change it's ownership to that of the new user or she won't be able to create her own files!

Removing users is, as we said, the reverse of the procedure above, with the added burden of having to delete the user's files. Log in as the super user and change your directory to the login directory of the user you're deleting. The command

    rm −rf *

will delete all the files and directories below the current one. Now change directory to somewhere else and remove (with **rmdir**) the user's login directory. This change of directory stuff isn't essential but a good safety precaution. Executing that 'remove everything' command in the wrong place will be acutely embarrassing.

There's a snag with the apparently simple business of editing the password file which is caused by the **passwd** utility. **Passwd** edits the password file too and we've grounds for suspicion that the two procedures can interact unfavourably if both occur at the same time, although we haven't investigated this fully. If there is a problem here, then it won't be seen to happen very often; the only chance of getting a corrupted password file is if both re-write the file simultaneously.

General Commands

Most UNIX systems provide the user with many commands. We will give a short form listing of the more general of those available with standard UNIX. You should find a more detailed treatment of each command, along with many more, in section 1 of your local manual, which is often referred to as the 'UNIX Programmer's Manual'. Section 6 of the manual may contain commands peculiar to your installation.

The syntax of each entry in our list generally conforms to that used by the UNIX manual. Items within square brackets, '[' ']', are optional parts of the command, and a list of single characters means that one or more may be selected from the list. A row of dots, '...', indicates that any number of the immediately preceding item may be given. Words printed in bold are key words, and must be reproduced exactly as shown.

adb – symbolic debugger
  adb [−w] [objfil] [corfil]
     −w = open 'objfil' and 'corfil' for both reading and writing; defaults, objfil = 'a.out', corfil = 'core'

ar – archive & library maintainer
  ar [**dmpqrtx**] [**abciluv**] [posname] archive file ...
    d = delete
    m = move to end or relative to 'posname'
    p = print
    q = quick (don't check)
    r = replace
    t = list contents
    x = extract

    a = after 'posname'
    b = before 'posname'
    c = suppress create message
    i = before 'posname'

    l = use local temporary file (not in '/tmp')
    u = update
    v = verbose (give message for each operation)

as – assembler
  as [−] [−**o** objfil] file ...
    − = make undefined symbols global
    −**o** = use next argument as output file default: 'a.out'

at – execute commands at later time
  at time[**apnm**] [day][**week**] [file]
    time = up to 4 digits specifying hours (and mins)
    a = AM
    p = PM
    n = noon
    m = midnight
    day = month name followed by a day number or day of the week
    week = activation of command is delayed for 7 days
    file = take input from 'file' rather than stdin

awk – pattern scanning & processing language
  awk [−**Fc**] [−**f** progfile] [prog] [file] ...
    −**Fc** = use 'c' as a file separator
    −**f** = use next argument, 'progfile', as prog

bas – basic interpreter
  bas [file]
    file = take input from 'file' before terminal

basename – strip filename affixes
  basename string [suffix]
    string = string to be stripped of pathname prefix
    suffix = if present also delete this suffix

bc – arbitrary-precision arithmetic language
  bc [−**l**] [−**c**] [file ...]
    −**l** = load the function library
    −**c** = compile only (don't execute)
    file = take input from any files specified before reading the terminal

cal – print calendar
  cal [month] year
    month = month number (1–12)
    year = year number between 1–9999

calendar – reminder service
  calendar [−]

      − = send all users their calendar entries

cat − concatenate & print files
  cat [−**u**] file ...
    −**u** = cause output to be unbuffered

cb − C program beautifier (pretty printer)
  cb

cc − C compiler
  cc [−**c**] [−**p**] [−**f**] [−**O**] [−**S**] [−**P**] [−**o** output] [−**D**name = -
  def] [−**U**name] [−**I**dir] file.c ... [−**I**] ofile ...
    −**c** = compile only (produce a '.o' file)
    −**p** = profile
    −**f** = use floating point interpreter
    −**O** = optimise
    −**S** = compile to assembler only ('.s' file)
    −**P** = preprocess only (send output to 'file.i')
    −**o** = send output to 'output'; default is 'a.out'
    −**D**name = def = define preprocessor variable
    −**D**name = set 'name' to value 1
    −**U**name = undefine preprocessor variable 'name'
    −**I**dir = use 'dir' when looking for include files
    −**I** = loader options(eg −lm for /lib/libm.a)

cd − change directory
  cd directory

chgrp − change group-id of files
  chgrp group file ...
    group = either decimal gid or a group name

chmod − change protection permissions on files
  chmod mode file ...
    mode = either symbolic representation: [**ugoa**][+ − =][**rwxst**] or
        the logical OR of the octal permission numbers (see
        Chapter 5)

chown − change ownership of files
  chown owner file ..
    owner = either decimal uid or a login name

cmp − compare 2 files
  cmp [−**l**] [−**s**] file1 file2
    −**l** = print byte number and differing bytes
    −**s** = print nothing; return exit status; 0 = same; 1 = different;
        2 = bad arguments

col – filter reverse line feeds
   col [**–bfx**]
      –b = do not output backspaces
      –f = output half line feeds
      –x = leave tabs alone (don't convert to space)

comm – print lines common to two files
   comm [**–123**] file1 file2
      –1 = suppress lines only in 'file1'
      –2 = suppress lines only in 'file2'
      –3 = suppress lines in both files

cp – copy files
   cp oldfile newfile
   cp file ... directory

crypt – encode/decode text
   crypt [password]
      password = key for transformation

date – print or set the date
   date [yymmddhhmm[.ss]]
      date is set to arg (if present) — super–user only
      yy = year   (2 digits)
      mm = month   ,,
      dd = day   ,,
      hh = hour   ,,
      mm = minute   ,,
      ss = seconds   ,,

dc – desk calculator
   dc [file]
      file = take input from 'file' before reading terminal

dd – convert & copy a file
   dd [option=value] ...
options:
      if = input file
      of = output file
      ibs = input block size (default 512)
      obs = output block size (,,)
      bs = block size (both input & output)
      cbs = conversion block size
      files = copy only n files from input
      skip = skip n input records
      seek = skip n output records

        count = copy only n input records
        conv = **ascii, ebcdic, ibm, lcase, ucase, swab, sync, noerror**

deroff – remove text formatting commands
    deroff [– **w**] file ...
        – **w** = output word list

diff – differential file comparator
    diff [– **befh**] file1 file2
        – **b** = ignore trailing blanks
        – **e** = output script of **ed commands**
        – **f** = produce a reverse script to – **e**
        – **h** = fast, superficial comparison, used with large files

diff3 – 3-way differential file comparison
    diff3 [– **ex3**] file1 file2 file3
        – **e** = output **ed** script to add changes between 'file2' and 'file3' to
            'file1'
        – **x** = output script for changes in all 3 files
        – **3** = output script for changes in 'file3' only

du – summarise disk usage
    du [– **a**] [– **s**] [file ...]
        – **a** = give an entry for each file found
        – **s** = give grand total only

echo – echo arguments
    echo [– **n**] [arg ...]
        – **n** = don't output a newline

ed – editor
    ed [–] [– **x**] [file]
        – = don't print a character count
        – **x** = file is encrypted

eqn – typeset mathematics
    eqn [– **d**xy] [– **f**n] [– **p**n] [– **s**n] [file] ...
        – **d**xy = use 'x' & 'y' as delimiters
        – **f**n = use 'n' as font
        – **p**n = use 'n' for subscript size changes (default 3)
        – **s**n = use 'n' as point size

expr – evaluate arguments as an expression
    expr arg ...

f77 – FORTRAN 77 compiler
    f77 [– **c**] [– **p**] [– **O**] [– **f**] [– **o** output] [– **onetrip**] [– **u**] [– **C**]

$[-w]$ $[-w66]$ $[-F]$ $[-m]$ $[-Ex]$ $[-Rx]$ file.f ...
$[-l]$ ofile ...
- **c** = compile only (produce a '.o' file)
- **p** = profile
- **O** = optimise
- **S** = compile to assembler only (produce a '.s' file)
- **o** = send output to 'output'; default is 'a.out'
- **onetrip** = compile loops that execute at least once
- **u** = variables are undefined by default
- **C** = compile code to check subscripts
- **w** = suppress warning messages
- **w66** = no FORTRAN 66 warning messages
- **F** = run EFL and Ratfor processors; output to 'file.f'
- **m** = run M4 preprocessor
- **Ex** = use 'x' as an EFL option
- **Rx** = use 'x' as a Ratfor option
- **l** = loader options

factor – factor a number
  factor [number]

file – determine file type
  file file ...

find – find files
  find pathname expression
    pathname = starting directory for search
    'expression' is made up of the following primitives;
    n is integer; $+n$ means $>n$; $-n$ means $<n$

	true if
−**name** filename	'filename' matches current file
−**perm** onum	permission flags = 'onum'(octal)
−**type** c	file type is b, c, d, f
−**links** n	file has 'n' links
−**user** uname	file belongs to 'uname'
−**group** gname	file belongs to group 'gname'
−**size** n	file is 'n' blocks long
−**inum** n	file has i-node number 'n'
−**atime** n	file has been accessed in 'n' days
−**mtime** n	file has been modified in 'n' days
−**exec** command	if exit status of 'command' is 0
−**ok** command	like −exec but asks
−**print**	prints current pathname (always true)
−**newer** nfile	'nfile' was modified before 'file'

The above may be combined with the following operators

  ! not
  −a and
  −o or
  () parentheses for grouping (must be escaped with \)

graph – draw a graph
  graph option ...
options:

  −**a** = automatic abscissae
  −**b** = disconnect after each label
  −**c** c = use 'c' as label for each point
  −**g** n = 'n' is grid type; 0 = no grid; 1 = frame + ticks; 2 = full
  −**l** lab = label graph with 'lab'
  −**m** n = 'n' is mode; 0 = disconnected; 1 = connected; default = 1
  −**s** = save screen, don't erase before plotting
  −**h** f = 'f' is fraction of space for height
  −**w** f = 'f' is fraction of space for width
  −**r** f = 'f' is fraction of space to move right
  −**u** f = 'f' is fraction of space to move up distances −r and −u are
              moved before plotting
  −**t** = transpose horizontal & vertical axes
  −**x**[l] = next 3 arguments are lower, upper & spacing limits for x;
              l for logarithmic x axis
  −**y**[l] = next 3 arguments are lower, upper & spacing limits for y;
              l for logarithmic y axis

grep – search a file for a pattern
  grep [option] ... expr [file]
  egrep [option] ... [expr] [file]
  fgrep [option] ... [strings] [file]
options:

  −**b** = print block numbers
  −**c** = print a count of matches
  −**e** expr = use 'expr' for matching
  −**f** file = use 'file' for matching (**egrep, fgrep**)
  −**h** = don't print filename headers
  −**l** = list files with matching lines
  −**n** = print line numbers of matching lines
  −**s** = don't print anything, just return an exit status
  −**v** = print all but those that match
  −**x** = output only those line matching totally (**fgrep**)
  −**y** = fold upper & lower case (**grep**)

join – relation database operator
  join [option] ... file1 file2
options:
       'n' is 1 or 2
       – an = output unpaired lines in file 'n' also
       – e s = use string 's' for white space replacement
       – jn m = join on 'm'th field of file 'n'
       – o n.m = output 'm'th field of file 'n'
       – tc = use 'c' as separator

kill – terminate a process
  kill [– signo] processid
    processid = id of the process to which the specified signal is to be
             sent
signo:
      1 = hangup(SIGHUP)
      2 = interrupt(SIGINT)
      3 = quit(SIGQUIT)
      4 = illegal instruction(SIGILL)
      5 = trace trap(SIGTRAP)
      6 = IOT(SIGIOT) – PDP11 specfic
      7 = EMT(SIGEMT) – ,,
      8 = floating exception(SIGFPE)
      9 = kill(SIGKILL)
      10 = bus error(SIGBUS)
      11 = segmentation violation(SIGSEGV)
      12 = bad system call(SIGSYS)
      13 = write on a pipe with no one to read(SIGPIPE)
      14 = alarm clock(SIGALRM)
      15 = software terminate(SIGTERM) – default
      16 = unassigned

ld – loader
  ld [**– sulxXrdnioeOD**] file ...
    – s = strip symbol table & relocation bits from output
    – u name = make 'name' undefined
    – lx = load library '/lib/libx.a'; 'x' is a string
    – x = do not save local symbols
    – X = save local symbols except those whose name start with 'L'
    – r = generate relocation bits
    – d = define common storage
    – n = make output shareable
    – i = separate instruction am data spaces

     − o output = use 'output' as output file not 'a.out'
     − e symbol = use 'symbol' as the name of the entry point (default 0)
               point (default is location 0)
     − O = overlay file
     − D num = 'num' is the data segment size

learn − computer aided instruction
     learn [−directory] [subject[lesson[speed]]]

lex − lexical analysis generator
     lex [−**fntv**] [file]
     − f = fast compilation; limited to small programs
     − n = no summary; default
     − t = send result to standard output not 'lex.yy.c'
     − v = print summary of generated analyser

lint − C program verifier
     lint [−**abchnpuvx**] file ...
     − a = report assignment of long values to int variables
     − b = report 'break' statements that cannot be reached
     − c = report unportable casts
     − h = use heuristic tests
     − n = don't check for compatibility with standard library
     − p = check portability to IBM & GCOS C
     − u = don't report defined but unused variables
     − v = don't report unused function arguments
     − x = report 'extern' variables not used

ln − link to a file
     ln oldname [newname]

login − sign on to UNIX
     login [username]

look − find lines in a sorted list
     look [−**df**] string [file]
     − d = dictionary order (alphanumerically)
     − f = fold upper case to lower case
     file = file containing lines; default '/usr/dict/words'

lookbib − search bibliographical data base for references
     lookbib [file] ...
     See **refer**

lorder − find ordering relation for object library
     lorder file ...

ls – list contents of directory
    ls [−**acdfgilrstu**] [name ...]
        −**a** = list all entries
        −**c** = sort on last i-node change
        −**d** = list only directory names (not entries)
        −**f** = interpret all entries as directories and list in the order found
        −**g** = give group id instead of owner
        −**i** = print i-node number
        −**l** = long listing format
        −**r** = sort in reverse order
        −**s** = give size in blocks
        −**t** = sort by time modified
        −**u** = sort on last access time

m4 – macro processor
    m4 [file]

mail – send or receive mail
    mail person ....
    mail [−**f** file] [−p] [−**r**]
        −**f** = use 'file' instead of 'mbox'
        −**r** = first-in, first-out order of messages
        −**p** = don't ask questions

make – maintain programs
    make [−**f** mfile] [−**iknrst**] file ...
        −**f** = use 'mfile' instead of 'makefile' or 'Makefile'
        −**i** = ignore returned statii
        −**k** = on bad status, continue unrelated branches
        −**n** = trace & print, don't execute any commands
        −**r** = no suffix list'
        −**s** = don't print command lines before execution
        −**t** = touch (update time) files

man – print sections of the manual
    man [−**ekntw**] [chapter] title ...
        −**e** = run eqn
        −**k** = output for Tektronix 4014
        −**n** = output to standard output using nroff
        −**t** = phototypeset
        −**w** = print pathnames only

mesg – permit or deny messages
    mesg [**ny**]
        n = forbid messages via write
        y = allow messages
        if no argument just report current permissions

mkdir – make a directory
  mkdir dirname ...

mv – move or rename files
  mv oldname newname
  mv file ... directory

neqn – typeset mathematics for nroff
  neqn [option] ... [file] ...
    See **eqn**

newgrp – log in to a new group
  newgrp group

nice – run a command at low priority
  nice [– number] command [arg ...]
    number = priority from 1 to 20; lowest 20, default 10

nm – print name list
  nm [– **gnopru**] [file]
    – **g** = print only global symbols
    – **n** = sort by value, not name
    – **o** = print filename on each line
    – **p** = don't sort
    – **r** = sort in reverse order
    – **u** = print only undefined symbols

nohup – run a command immune to hangups(SIGHUP)
  nohup command [arg ...]

nroff – text formatter
  nroff [option] ... file ... options:
    – **e** = produce equally spaced words in adjusted lines
    – **h** = replace spaces with tabs to conserve file space
    – **i** = read standard input after files
    – **m**name = prepend macro file '/usr/lib/tmac/tmac.name'
    – **n**n = number first generated page 'n'
    – **o**list = print only pages whose numbers appear in the comma
                separated list
    – **q** = invoke simultaneous input/output mode
    – **r**an = set number register 'a' to the value 'n'
    – **s**n = stop after 'n' pages; default 1
    – **T**name = prepare output for terminal type 'name' 37, tn300, 300s,
                etc.

od – dump a file
  od [– **bcdox**] [file] [+] [offset[.][b]]

> −**b** = print bytes in octal
> −**c** = print bytes in ascii
> −**d** = print words in decimal
> −**o** = print words in octal
> −**x** = print words in hexadecimal
> offset = start location, default octal; . for decimal; b for blocks

passwd – change login password
  passwd [name]

plot – graphics filters
  plot [−**T**term [raster]]
    term = 4014, 450, 300, 300S, ver

pr – print files
  pr [option] ... file ... options:
    −**n** = 'n'−columned output
    +n = begin with page 'n'
    −**h** string = use 'string' as header for each page
    −**l**n = use 'n' as page length; default 66
    −**m** = print each file in a separate column
    −**s**c = separate columns with character 'c'
    −**t** = don't print header or trailer
    −**w**n = use 'n' as page width; default 72

prof – display profile data
  prof [−a] [−l] [−v] [−low [−high]] [file]
    −**a** = report all symbols
    −**l** = order ouput by symbol value
    −**v** = report only graphic profile
    low, high = percentages for plotting; default 0, 100

ps – process status
  ps [**aklx**] [namelist]
    a = give all processes with terminals
    k = use '/usr/sys/core' instead of '/dev/mem'
    l = give long status listing
    x = give all processes
    namelist = file containing system namelist; default is '/unix'

ptx – permuted index
  ptx [option] ... [input [output]] options:
    −**b** break = use characters from file 'break' to separate words
    −**f** = fold upper case to lower case for sorting
    −**g** n = use 'n' for column gap; default 3
    −**i** ignore = don't use keywords from file 'ignore'

        − o only = use only keywords from file 'only'
        − r = use 1st word on each line as a referenece
        − t = use phototypesetter
        − w n = use 'n' for line width; default 72

pwd – print working directory
  pwd

ranlib – convert archives to random libraries
  ranlib archive ...

ratfor – Ratfor compiler (preprocessor)
  ratfor [− C] [− h] [− **6**x] [file] ...
      − C = copy comments to output
      − h = convert quoted strings to hollerith form
      − 6x = use 'x' as continuation character
            (placed in column 6)

refer – find & format references in documents
  refer [option] ...
options:
      − ar = reverse the first 'r' author names
      − a = reverse all author names
      − b = omit all flags
      − cs = capitalise fields whose key-letters are in string 's'
      − e = accumulate references
      − kx = use labels specified with 'x'
      − lm,n = label with 'm' name letters and 'n' year digits
      − p f = use file 'f' as reference
      − skeys = sort by fields whose key-letters are in the string 'keys'

rev – reverse lines of a file
  rev [file] ...

rm – remove files
  rm [− **fir**] file ...
      − f = do not ask questions
      − i = interactively remove each file
      − r = recursively remove directory entries

rmdir – remove directories
  rmdir dir ...

roff – text formatter
  roff [+ **n**] [− **n**] [− **h**] [− **s**] file ...
    + **n** = start with page 'n'
    − **n** = stop after page 'n'

−**h** = replace space with tabs when possible
−**s** = pause before printing each page

sed − stream editor
   sed [−**e** script] [−**f** cmdfile] [−**n**] [file] ...
      −**e** = next argument is editor command
      −**f** = use next argument as command file
      −**n** = only print lines operated on by p command

sh − shell : command interpreter
   sh [option] ... [arg] ...
options:
      −**c** string = interpret 'string' as a command
      −**e** = if non-interactive, exit on bad returned status
      −**i** = shell is interactive
      −**k** = place all keywords in the environment for a command
      −**n** = read commands, but don't execute
      −**r** = restricted environment
      −**s** = read commands from standard input
      −**t** = exit after executing one command
      −**u** = treat unset variables as error when substituting
      −**v** = print input lines as they are read
      −**x** = print commands & args as they are executed

size − size of an object file
   size [ofile] ...

sleep − suspend execution for an interval
   sleep seconds
      seconds = an integer specifying sleep time; 1 − 65535

sort − sort or merge files
   sort [−**cmubdfinrtx**] [+m.n [−m.n]] ... [−**o** name]
             [−T dir] [name] ...
      −**c** = check order but don't sort
      −**m** = merge only, files should be sorted already
      −**u** = output only one copy of repeated lines
      −**b** = ignore leading blanks
      −**d** = dictionary order (alphanumeric) for sorting
      −**f** = fold upper case to lower case
      −**i** = ignore characters outside ascii range (040–0176)
      −**n** = sort on an initial numeric string
      −**r** = reverse order of sort
      −**tx** = tab character is 'x'
      +m.n = skip 'm' fields and 'n' characters

$-$m.n = end of key (used with $+$m.n)
$-$**o** name = output to file 'name'
$-$**T** dir = use directory 'dir' for temporary files

spell – find spelling errors
  spell [$-$**b**] [$-$**v**] [$-$**x**] [file] ...
    $-$**b** = use British spelling
    $-$**v** = output words derived from list
    $-$**x** = print stems

spline – interpolate smooth curve
  spline [$-$**a**] [$-$**k**] [$-$**n**] [$-$**p**] [$-$**x**]
    $-$**a** = automatic abscissae, next argument is spacing
    $-$**k** = next argument is used to compute boundary value
    $-$**n** = next argument is number of intervals between limits
    $-$**p** = make output periodic
    $-$**x** = next 1 or 2 arguments are lower am upper x limits

split – split a file into pieces
  split [$-$**n**] [file [name]]
    $-$**n** = output 'n' lines per file; default 1000
    name = use 'name' as the stem of output filenames; default is 'file'

strip – remove symbol table and relocation bits
  strip file ...

struct – structure FORTRAN programs
  struct [option] ... [file]
options:
    $-$**a** = turn else if sequences into switch
    $-$**b** = generate goto's, not breaks
    $-$**en** = 'n' is loop control parameter
    $-$**i** = don't make computed goto's into switches
    $-$**n** = generate goto's, not nexts
    $-$**s** = input in standard form

stty – set terminal modes & options
  stty [$-$]option ...
    options are preceeded by $-$ to indicate negation
    even   allow even parity
    odd   allow odd parity
    raw   raw mode input
    cbreak   pass characters on as received
    nl   accept only newline to terminate lines
    echo   echo all characters typed
    lcase   map upper case to lower case

tabs	terminal has hardware tabs
ek	reset erase & kill to default
erase c	set erase character to 'c'
kill c	set kill character to 'c'
hup	hangup phone line on last close
0	hang up immediately
crn	set delay for carriage return
nln	set delay for linefeed
tabn	set delay for tab
ffn	set delay for formfeed
tty33	terminal is Teletype model 33
tty37	terminal is Teletype model 37
vt05	terminal is DEC VT05
tn300	terminal is GE TermiNet 300
ti700	terminal is Texas Instruments 700
tek	terminal is Tektronix 4014

50 75 110 134 150 200 300 600 1200 1800 2400 4800 9600 exta
extb set baud rate

su – substitute user id temporarily
  su [name]
  name = login name from password file

sum – sum a file
  sum file ...

tabs – set terminal tabs
  tabs [−n] [terminal]
  −n = don't indent left margin
  terminal = terminal name

tail – print end of file
  tail [[+−]number[**lbc**]] [file]
  number = **l**ines, **b**locks or **c**haracters from begining(+) or end(−)
      of file

tar – tape archiver
  tar [key] [name] ...
  key = a string containing at most one function and
  optionally several modifiers
functions:
  c = create new tape (implies r)
  r = write files on end of tape
  t = list contents of tape
  u = update

x = extract files from tape modifiers:
0,....,7 = tape drive number
b = use next argument as blocking factor
f = use next argument as tape device
l = complain on unresolved links
w = wait for user response before each operation
v = verbose

tbl – format tables
  tbl [file] ...

tc – phototypesetter simulator
  tc [−**t**] [−**s**n] [−**pl**[**picP**]] [file]
    −**t** = don't wait between pages
    −**s**n = skip the first 'n' pages
    −**pl** = set page length to 'l'
        p = points
        i = inches
        c = centimeters
        P = picas (default)

tee – pipe fitting
  tee [−**a**] [−**i**] [file] ...
    −**a** = append to file, don't overwrite
    −**i** = ignore interrupts

test – condition command
  test expr
  'expr' is constructed of the following primitives

	true if
−**r** file	'file' is readable
−**w** file	'file' is writable
−**f** file	'file' is not a directory
−**d** file	'file' is a directory
−**s** file	'file' longer than 0 bytes
−**t** [fildes]	'fildes' is a terminal; default 1
−**z** s1	length of string 's1' = 0
−**n** s1	length of string 's1' not 0
s1 = s2	string 's1' = string 's2'
s1 != s2	string 's1' != string 's2'
n1 op n2	ints 'n1' & 'n2' are algebraically equal
op = −**eq**, −**ne**, −**gt**, −**ge**, −**lt**, −**le**	

The above may be combined with the following operators
! = unary negation

         −**a** = binary and
         −**o** = binary or
         () = parentheses for grouping

time – time a command
    time command [arg] ...

tk – paginator for Tektronix 4014
    tk [−**t**] [−**n**] [−**p**] [file]
         −**t** = don't wait between pages
         −**n** = 'n' column output
         −**p** = set page length to 'l'

touch – update modification date of a file
    touch [−**c**] file ...
         −**c** = don't create file if it doesn't exist

tp – tape archiver
    tp [key] [name] ...
         key = a string containing at most one function and optionally
                 several modifiers
functions:
         d = delete
         r = replace
         t = list
         u = update
         x = extract modifiers:
         0,....,7 = tape drive number
         c = create new tape
         f = use first file name instead of tape device
         i = ignore errors
         m = mag tape, default is DECtape
         v = verbose
         w = wait for user response

tr – translate characters
    tr [−**cds**] [string1 [string2]]
         −**c** = complement characters in 'string1'
         −**d** = delete all characters in 'string1'
         −**s** = remove repeated characters from 'string2'

troff – text formatter for phototypesetter
    troff [option] ... file ...
options:
         −**a** = send printable approximation to standard output
         −**b** = just report if phototypesetter is busy

−**f** = don't feed paper or stop phototypesetter at end
　　　−**g** = output for GCOS
　　　−**i** = read standard input after files
　　　−**m**name = prepend macro file '/usr/lib/tmac/tmac.name'
　　　−**nn** = number first generated page 'n'
　　　−**o**list = print only pages whose numbers appear in the comma
　　　　　　separated list
　　　−**p**n = print all characters in size 'n'
　　　−**q** = invoke simultaneous input/output mode
　　　−**r**an = set number register 'a' to the value 'n'
　　　−**s**n = stop after 'n' pages; default 1
　　　−**t** = send output to standard output
　　　−**w** = wait until the phototypesetter is available

tsort – topological sort
　tsort [file]

tty – get terminal name
　tty

uniq – find repeated lines in a file
　uniq [−**cdu**] [+n] [−n] [input [output]]
　　　−**c** = output repetition count with each line
　　　−**d** = output one copy of each repeated line
　　　−**u** = output lines not repeated
　　　+n = skip first 'n' fields in each line
　　　−n = skip first 'n' characters in each line

units – scale conversion program
　units

wait – wait completion of process
　wait

wc – word count
　wc [−**clw**] [file] ...
　　　−**c** = just count characters
　　　−**l** = just count lines
　　　−**w** = just count words

who – who is on the system
　who [who−file] [**am i**]
　　　no arguments = print who is on
　　　1 argument = examine 'who-file'
　　　2 arguments = print who you are

write – write to another user
  write user [ttyname]
    user = login name from the password file

yacc – yet another compiler-compiler
  yacc [−**dv**] [grammar]
    −**d** = generate file 'y.tab.h' with 'define' statements
    −**v** = make output file 'y.output'

The Editor

This appendix is intended for use as a reference by users of ed. If you want detailed descriptions and examples of the use of most of the features listed below, they are to be found in chapter 3.

Calling ed:
ed – filename
The optional ' – ' prevents ed from reporting how many characters are read or written; useful in command files which invoke ed.

If **filename** is present ed will read from the file and use that name as the default in a subsequent **w** command.

Commands.

a – append.
line-no a
Text following the **a** is appended after **line-no**. Dot is assumed if **line-no** is not given. The text being appended is terminated by a single '.'. Dot is set to the last line appended.

c – change.
first,last c
Lines numbered **first** through to **last** are changed to the text provided on the lines following the **c** command, as with the append command. A single line number will change just that line, no line numbers imply line dot. Dot is set to the last line changed.

d – delete.
first,last d
Delete lines **first** through to **last** inclusive. A single line number means just that line, if no line number is given then dot is deleted. Dot is set to to the line **last + 1** unless $ was deleted; in that case dot is set to the new $.

e – edit.
e filename
Start editing a new file. Any previous editing is thrown away

(unless it had been written with **w**); if you haven't performed a **w** since the last change you made a warning is issued. The filename is remembered for use later.

E

Just like **e** but ed won't complain if no **w** has been issued since the last amendment you made; this is not in common use.

f – file.

f filename.

Set the remembered filename to **filename.** This will be the default for subsequent **w** commands. By itself, **f** will print the remembered filename.

g – global.

g is used in two contexts. The first is to execute commands on any lines containing a context search expression:

first,lastg/expression/commands

lines **first** through to **last** are checked to find and remember those which contain a match of **expression.** The **commands** are then applied to those lines. The commands part may be several lines long if all but the last line are terminated with a backslash. If the **first,last** part is missing, the whole file is searched.

The **s** command also uses **g** as a qualifier, where it means that the substitution is to be applied to every occurrence of the **s** pattern match on a line. See the relevant section.

i – insert

line-no i

The same as **a** except that text is inserted before the line specified. Dot is set to the last line inserted.

j – join.

first,last j

Lines **first** through to **last** are joined together to make one long line. If only one line number is given, then that line is joined to the one after it OR nothing happens; this depends on your particular version of ed. If in doubt, try it out. The Standard one does nothing. If no line number is given, dot is joined to the next line in all known versions of ed.

k – mark.

line-no k lower-case-letter

This command attaches a **mark** to the line specified, or dot if no line number is given. The lower-case-letter may be used wherever a line number is valid provided it is preceded by an apostrophe (e.g. 'a means the line marked by the command **ka** .) The ability to mark

207

lines helps get around the problem caused by line numbers changing when stuff is inserted or deleted in front of them. It is not possible to mark two lines with the same letter.

l – list.

> **first,last l**
> List lines **first** through to **last**. If only one line number is given then only one line is listed; if there is no line number then dot is listed. Dot is set to the last line listed. List makes non-printing characters 'visible' and is used to find out if a line contains garbage characters. Tab characters print as >, backspace as < and other rubbish is printed in octal (form feed would be printed as \014). For other notes see the **p** command.

m – move.

> **first,last m after**
> Lines **first** through to **last** are spirited away and placed back following line number **after**. Only one line number before the **m** moves only that line, none means move dot. Dot is set to the last line moved.

p – print.

> **first,last p**
> Lines **first** through to **last** are printed, without any attempt to make non-printing characters visible. If only one line number is given, only one is printed; no line number means print dot. Dot is set to the last line printed. Both **p** and **l** may be put on the end of most commands (usually but not necessarily substitute commands) to see what happened.

q – quit.

> This command causes the editor to terminate without writing out the file. If the file has been modified since it was last written out, ed complains.

Q

> This is just like **q** but no complaint will be made.

r – read a file.

> **line-no r filename** The file is read, its contents being put after line **line-no** in the current file. If no line number is supplied $ is used ($ is the last line of the current text). Dot is set to the last line read. If the filename is missing, the remembered filename is used – if there isn't a remembered filename, then one must be supplied; the one supplied is remembered for use in further commands. A **line-no** of 0 is permissible, implying that text will be read at the front of the current text.

s – substitute.

> **first,last s /ab/cd/gp**

On lines **first** through to **last** substitute for the pattern **ab** the pattern **cd**. If only one line number is given the command only applies to that line; if none is given then the line affected is dot. A **g** following the command means all occurrences of **ab** , otherwise only the first occurrence on the line is substituted. An optional **p** or **l** may also be supplied, meaning that the result should be displayed appropriately. If **ab** is an empty pattern (no characters) then the last expression used in a **s** command or context search is used instead. An ampersand (&) in the **cd** causes the thing matched by the **ab** to be inserted at that point. The '/' delimiters may be replaced by any non-special non-blank character. Dot is set to the last line changed.

t – transcribe.

Transcribe works just like the **m** command, but copies lines rather than moving them. This is often useful to save re-typing lines which occur repeatedly or have much in common.

u – undo.

Restore the effect of the last **s** command, provided it was applied to the current line. Convenient for idiots.

v – ??.

See the notes on **g** except that the commands are applied to lines which didn't match the expression.

w – write.

first,last w filename

Write the specified lines out to the file. If no name is given, then the name remembered from the last **e** or **r** command (or the name given when ed was invoked) will be used. The filename is remembered for later if none was supplied before.

W

Just like the **w** command, but the text written is **appended** to the file.

x - encrypt.

The **x** command will prompt you for a key which is then used to encrypt or decrypt text subsequently read or written. The algorithm used is described in **crypt,** see section one of the user manual.

! – unpronounceable.

! any unix command

The ! allows a temporary escape from ed and executes the command given. Ed is suspended until the command terminates.

Context Searching

Forwards:

/expression/

The entire file is searched from .+1, wrapping around from the bottom to the top if necessary, until a match is found for the expression or the search gets to dot. The construction is exactly equivalent to a line number; it is the line number of the first line to contain a match for the expression.

Backwards:
?expression?
This is the same as the forward search, but goes backwards from .−1.

In either case, if the expression is zero characters long, then the last expression used in an **s** command or context search is used instead.

Line numbers:
These can be numeric (1 2 3 etc.) or context searches as above. There are two special line numbers, dot (.) and dollar ($). Dot is the number of the current line and changes as editing proceeds. Dollar is always the number of the last line in the file. Simple arithmetic is permitted if you want to use relative addressing within a file; for example $−5 means the line 5 lines before the end of the file.

Expressions

Expressions are used in context searches and substitute commands. They are built by combining ordinary and special characters. Ordinary characters at a particular position in an expression match an occurrence of themselves at the same position in the string being checked for the match. For example /a/ matches a single letter a. The special characters are used to match groups or classes of characters. A list of the special characters and their use is given below.

$ −   matches the end of the line.
∧   −   matches the start of the line.
.   −   matches any single character.
*   −   match any number of the character before the *, including none.
[−   followed by a list of characters and terminated by a] in any but the first place. Matches any one of the characters in the list. [1–5] is shorthand for [12345]. Special characters are not special in the list and need not be escaped by a backslash. If the first character in the list is carat (∧) then the whole meaning is reversed: [∧ 1–5] matches any character except 1 2 3 4 or 5.

Any part of an expression in a substitute command may be enclosed by the brackets \(and \). In the right hand side of the command, a \1 will then refer to the pattern matched by the first such enclosed expression, \2 to the second and so on.

s/\(a\)b\(c\)/\2q\1/

will thus change 'abc' to 'cqa', for example. This feature is understood rarely and almost never used.

Ed ignores ASCII NULL characters and anything after the last newline in a file. Lines being edited may be up to 512 characters long; files must be less than 128k characters in size. Each line in a file requires an extra word of memory for the editor, restricting the practical maximum file size – especially on 16 bit processors.

The error message ?TMP means that an error has occurred in the temporary file used to store the text being edited – usually a size problem.

Appendix C

Shell Syntax

The **shell** is both a command language and a programming language that provides the user interface to UNIX.

Commands

Simple commands consists of one or more words separated by blanks and terminated by either newline or semicolon. The first word is the name of a command to be executed; any remaining words are passed on as arguments to the command, which may choose to ignore or use them.

C.1 Input-Output Redirection

Output that normally appears on the terminal ('standard output') may be redirected to a file by writing

    command > filename

Similarly input that is normally taken from the terminal keyboard ('standard input') may instead be read from a file

    command < filename

Output may also be appended to an existing file

    command >> filename

If the file did not exist already then it is created. Other UNIX I/O channels may be used instead of the standard output or standard input. For redirection of output the specified file descriptor is duplicated and used as the standard output

    command >&2 filename

In the above example, the standard error channel is redirected to file 'filename'. Similarly, the standard input may be duplicated

    command <&3 filename

If one of the above forms is preceded by another digit then that file descriptor is created rather than the standard output or input. For example

command 2 > &1 filename

will result in both standard output and error output of the command going to file 'filename'.

One further use of the redirection characters is to close the standard output and/or input just before the command is executed. To close the standard input

command < & −

and to close the standard output

command > & −

C.2 Background Commands

To execute a command without waiting for it to complete, place an ampersand, '&', at the end of the command line

command &

When a command is started with '&' the shell reports its unique process number; a list of currently active processes may be obtained with the **ps** command.

C.3 Pipelines

Commands which read the standard output and then write to the standard input are called 'filters'. They may be connected together into a 'pipeline' by writing the pipe operator, '|' between them

command-1 | command-2

C.4 Filename Generation (Pattern Matching)

Lists of filename arguments may be generated by specifying a general pattern to be matched. The character '*' is a pattern that will match any string including null.

echo *.s

will print all the filenames in the current directory whose names end with '.s'. The character '?' will match any single character in a string, e.g.

echo prog.?

will print all filenames starting with 'prog.' and followed by a single character. A sequence of characters enclosed between '[' and ']' will match any single character from the set; a pair of characters separated by '-' will match any character lexically between the pair. For example

    [a-z]*

matches any filename (in the current directory) that starts with one of the letters 'a' through 'z'. One exception to these rules is that a '.' at the start of a filename must be explicitly given.

C.5 Quoting

Characters such as '', '<', '*', '?', '|' and '&' are called 'metacharacters' and have a special meaning to the shell. This meaning may be temporarily overidden by preceding the character with '\'. Thus

    echo *

will print a single '*', and

    echo \\

will print a single '\'. The sequence *newline* is ignored to allow long commands to continue over one line.

When more than one metacharacter needs quoting it is often more convenient to enclose the entire string between single quotes

    echo ab'*\|*'cd

will print

    ab*\|*cd

Enclosing the string between double quotes will prevent interpretation of all but the metacharacters ($ ' \ ").

C.6 Shell Procedures

Commands may be stored in a file and the shell called to interpret them

    sh cmdfile [args ....]

Arguments are referred to from within 'cmdfile' using the positional parameters $1, $2 .... The number of arguments in the call is available as '$#', this includes the name of the file being executed which may be referred to using '$0'.

The parameter '$*' can be used to substitute for all arguments except '$0'. For example

    sort -nr $*

C.7 Shell Parameters

$0, $1, $2, ...

Positional parameters corresponding to the command arguments; $0 is the name of the command itself.

$#   The number of positional parameters.

$*   will match all of the supplied parameters, except $0.

$?   The exit status of the last command executed. Most commands return a zero exit status if they ran successfully, otherwise a non-zero status is returned. This status is used by commands such as **if** and **while**

$$ The unique process number of the shell. This may be used to generate a temporary filename

        cat file1 file2 file3 > /tmp/t$$

        ...

        ...

        rm /tmp/t$$

$!   The process number of the last process run in the background (started with '&').

$-   The current shell flags.

C.8 Here Documents

Standard input to a command invoked from a shell procedure may be taken directly from within the body of the procedure.

```
ed file  <<#
...
...
w
#
```

Lines of text between '<<#' and '#' are used as the standard input for **ed**. The string '<<#' is arbitrary, the 'here document' being terminated by a line that consists of the string following '<<'. Parameters are substituted in the document before it is directed to the command's input. For example, if the file 'rmline' contains

```
ed - $2  <<#
g/$1/d
w
#
```

then the command

    rmline string file

will remove all lines from 'file' that contain occurrences of 'string'.

Normal quoting methods may be used to prevent substitution of the special character '$'

```
ed - $3 << +
1,\$s/$1/$2/g
w
+
```

Parameter substitution may be prevented entirely by quoting the terminal string, this is more efficient if parameter substitution is not required.

```
grep $1 <<\@
...
...
@
```

C.9 Shell Variables

String variable names must begin with a letter and may consist of letters, digits and underscores. Variables may be given values by writing

```
mark=/usr/andy/bin/
flags=-O
xyz=abc
```

which assigns values to the variables 'mark', 'flags' and 'xyz'. The value of a variable is substituted into a command line by preceding its name with a dollar;

```
echo $xyz
```

will print **abc**. When using variables to provide a base string the notation

```
${var-name}
```

should be used, for example

```
mv a.out ${mark}newcmd
```

will move the file 'a.out' to the directory '/usr/andy/bin' and rename it as 'newcmd'.

The following variable names have a special meaning to the shell

$HOME This is the default argument for the **cd** command; it it usually set in the user's '.profile' file. Thus the commands cd   and   cd $HOME

are equivalent

$IFS   This is the set of characters used in blank interpretation;
that is splitting a command line into individual words. The
default values are blank, tab and newline.

$MAIL   When the shell is used interactively (i.e from a terminal)
the file specified by this variable is examined before it
issues a prompt. If the file has been modified since it was
last looked at then the shell prints 'You have mail.' before
prompting.

$PATH   is a list of directories to be searched when the shell
attempts to find a command to execute. If $PATH is not set
the the current directory, '/bin' and '/usr/bin' are searched
by default. Otherwise $PATH may be set to a string of
directory names separated by semicolons

PATH = :/usr/andy/bin:/bin:/usr/bin

$PS1   The primary shell prompt; by default '$'.

$PS2   The secondary shell prompt, when further input is needed;
by default '>'.

C.10 Control of Flow

The actions of the **for** loop and the branch are determined by data
available to the shell (usually arguments supplied to a shell procedure); whereas the **while** or **until** loop and the **if-else-fi** branch
actions are controlled by exit status returned from commands. Many
UNIX utilities return an exit status specifically for this purpose. The
control-of-flow commands may be used either from within a shell
procedure or typed in at the terminal. In the later case the shell will
change prompt to '$PS2' whilst you are in the middle of the
command.

For

The **for** command is used to loop through procedure arguments,
executing commands once for each argument

```
for name [in word]
do command-list
done
```

If 'in word' is ommitted then 'in $*' is assumed, for example

```
for i
do grep $i *.c
done
```

Case

A multi-way branch or command selection is provided by the **case** command

```
case word in
    pattern1) command-list;;
    pattern2) command-list;; ...
esac
```

The command-list associated with the first pattern that matches 'word' is executed.

If-Else-Fi

```
        if command-list
        then command-list
        [ elif command-list ]
        [ else command-list ] fi
```

The **else** part is optional and may be omitted. A multiple test **if** command may be implemented using the **elif** form of **else if**. The **if** command is commonly used in conjunction with the **test** command

```
        if test -f file
        then process file
        else do something else
        fi
```

A simple, and quite common, use of the **if** construction is to conditionally execute one command depending on the returned value from another.

```
        if command-1
        then command-2
        fi
```

The above is so common that a simpler form exists, it may be rewritten using the characters '&&' ('andf' symbol) to separate the two commands

```
        command-1 && command-2
```

Conversely, use of the characters '||' ('orf' symbol) will only execute command-2 if command-1 fails.

```
        command-1 || command-2
```

This latter form cannot easily be expressed using the **if** construction unless a further command is introduced to fill the **then** part.

```
if command-1
then true;        :  do nothing
else command-2
fi
```

Of course, both command-1 and command-2 may be command lists; the returned value is that produced by the last simple command in the list.

While

The condition for execution of the body of the **while** loop is the exit status of the last simple command in the list following **while**.

```
while command-list
do command-list
done
```

The loop termination condition may be reversed by replacing the **while** with **until**. For example

```
until test -f file
do sleep 30; done
further-commands
```

will loop until 'file' exists.

C.11 Command Substitution

The standard output from a command may be substituted in a similar fashion to parameters; the name of the command is enclosed within single reverse quotes (grave quotes).

```
path = 'pwd'
```

is equivalent to

```
path = /usr/andy/unixbook
```

if the current directory is '/usr/andy/unixbook' . Command substitution may be used in all contexts where parameter substitution is allowed.

C.12 Shell Grammar

empty:

word: A sequence of non-blank characters

name:	a sequence of letters, digits or underscores starting with a letter
digit:	**0 1 2 3 4 5 6 7 8 9**
item:	word input-output name = value
simple-command:	item simple-command item
command:	simple-command (command-list) { command-list} **for** name **do** command-list **done** **for** name **in** word ... **do** command-list **done** **while** command-list **do** command-list **done** **until** command-list **do** command-list **done** **case** word **in** case-part ... **esac**)if command-list **then** command-list else-part **fi**
pipeline:	command pipeline| command
andor:	pipeline andor**&&** pipeline andor|| pipeline
command-list:	andor command-list; command-list**&** command-list; andor command-list**&** andor
input-output:	> file < file > > word < < word
file:	word**&** digit **&** -

case-part:	pattern) command-list;;
pattern:	word
	pattern|word
else-part:	elif command-list**then** command-list
	else-part
	else command-list
	empty

Meta-characters and Reserved Words

a) syntactic

|	pipe symbol
&&	'andf' symbol
||	'orf' symbol
;	command separator
;;	case delimeter
&	background commands
()	command grouping
<	input redirection
<<	input from a here document
>	output redirection
>>	output append

b) patterns

*	match any character(s) including none
?	match any single character
[..]	match any of the enclosed characters

c) substitution

${..}	substitute shell variable
'..'	substitute command output

d) quoting

\	quote the next character
'..'	quote the enclose characters except for '
"..''	quote the enclosed characters except for $ ' \ ''

e) reserved words

if then else elif fi
case in esac
for while until do done
{ }

Appendix D

Standard Libraries

We will list the contents of libraries distributed with standard V7 UNIX; each function has an entry in the list showing the loader flag, if needed, and a page number where you can find a short description. Functions with no type declaration are 'int'.

MPX = multiplex files
SYS = system call
SIO = standard I/O

Function	Loader flag	Page No	
abort()		237	
abs(x)		237	
access(name, mode)		247	SYS
acct(file)		247	SYS
double **acos(x)**		236	
alarm(seconds)		247	SYS
arc(x, y, x0, y0, x1, y1)	− lplot	245	
asctime(tm)		238	
double **asin**(x)	− lm	236	
assert(expression)		237	
double **atan**(x)	− lm	236	
double **atan2**(x)	− lm	236	
double **atof**(nptr)		238	
atoi(nptr)		238	
long **atol**(nptr)		238	
attach(i, xd)		228	MPX
brk(addr)		248	SYS
cabs(z)	− lm	237	
calloc(nelem, elsize)		241	
double **ceil**(x)	− lm	237	
chan(xd)		228	MPX
chdir(dirname)		248	SYS

D.1 Obsolete System Calls

Certain of the system calls mentioned in the above table are either historic in origin, or peculiar to the PDP-11. They will certainly not be available in all implementations of UNIX and we include them in the table merely for completeness.

gtty, stty
These are the original forms of the system call for reading and setting terminal modes. They have been superceded by the **ioctl** system call, which should be used for any new software.

lock, phys
Lock allows a process to remain in primary memory, i.e. to prevent itself being swapped out. Obviously this will interfere with UNIX's memory allocation schemes and can lead to deadlock problems. A process can access physical memory directly using the 'phys' system call. Both these system calls are very dangerous and probably will not be a part of most UNIX systems.

tell
This is an obsolete function which was identical to

    lseek(fildes, 0L, 1)

it had the effect of returning the current file pointer position.

D.2 Multiplex Files

Multiplex files are an experimental part of UNIX with probably many bugs remaining. If they are available at your installation, and you think you need to use them, then read MPX(2) very carefully, and consult your local guru (if you have one).

D.3 Standard I/O

Every program file using functions from the standard I/O (SIO) library must have the line

    #include <stdio.h>

near the beginning.

D.3.1. Open a stream

FILE *fopen(filename, type)
FILE *freopen(filename, type, stream)
FILE *fdopen(fildes, type)
    char *filename, *type; FILE *stream;
Fopen opens the file given by the string 'filename' and returns a FILE pointer to be used for stream input or output. The string 'type' determines how the open is attempted

    'r'   open for reading
    'w'   create for writing
    'a'   append: if 'filename' exists then open for writing at end of file, otherwise create for writing.

Freopen causes any I/O on the open stream to be directed to or from the file given by filename. The original value of stream, which is closed, is returned. A common use of **freopen** is to attach I/O on **stdin**, **stdout** or **stderr** to named files. If the file cannot be accessed then both **fopen** and **freopen** return the pointer NULL. **Fdopen** allocates a stream to be used with a file descriptor obtained from a **open**, **dup**, **creat** or **pipe** system call.

D.3.2. Get stream status information

feof(stream)
ferror(stream)
clearerr(stream)
fileno(stream)
    FILE *stream;
Feof returns a non-zero (true) integer after an end of file has been read on the stream, zero otherwise. **Ferror** returns a non-zero (true) integer when an error has occurred on I/O involving the stream, zero otherwise. Unless cleared the error will remain until the stream is closed. **Clearerr** clears the error indication on stream, subsequent calls of **ferror** will return zero unless a further error occurrs. **Fileno** returns the UNIX file descriptor (not to be confused with a FILE pointer) associated with stream. It would be unwise to use this file descriptor for normal UNIX I/O, so doing is guaranteed to upset the SIO buffering.

D.3.3. I/O on a stream

fread(ptr, sizeof(*ptr), nitems, stream)

fwrite(ptr, sizeof(*ptr), nitems, stream)
        FILE *stream;
Fread and **fwrite** may be used for buffered binary I/O. The read or write is performed on a block of data beginning at ptr and involves nitems of type *ptr. The number of data items actually read or written is returned.

int getc(stream)
int getchar()
int fgetc(stream)
int getw(stream)
        FILE *stream;
The above functions return the next character (**getc, getchar, fgetc** or word (**getw**) as an integer from the stream. **Getchar()** is identical to **getc(stdin)**. **Fgetc** behaves exactly as **getc** but is an actual function, whereas **getc** is a macro; so

        FILE *fp;
        fgetc(fp + +);

will work correctly. All functions return the integer constant 'EOF' on end of file or read error.

char *gets(s)
char *fgets(s, n, stream)
        char *s; FILE *stream;
Gets reads a newline terminated string from **stdin** into the string pointed to by s and returns the value of its argument; newline is replaced by zero. **Fgets** reads at most n − 1 characters from the stream into s; the read is terminated by a newline character if this occurs before n − 1 characters have been read. The last character placed into s is followed by a zero to terminate the string. **Fgets** returns s. Both functions return the NULL pointer on end of file or error.

ungetc(c, stream)
        char c; FILE *stream;
Ungetc attempts to push character c back onto the stream, this character will then be returned by the next call of **getc**. At least one character must have been read from the stream. EOF is returned if **ungetc** fails to push a character back, any attempt to push EOF is rejected out of hand.

int putc(c, stream)
putchar(c)
fputc(c, stream)

putw(w, stream)
      char c; FILE *stream;

These functions place a character (**putc, putchar, fputc**) or word (**putw**) onto a stream; all return the value written. **Putchar(c)** is identical to **putc(c, stdout)** **Fputc** behaves exactly as **putc** but is implemented as an actual function rather than a macro, so a statement using auto increment/decrement will work as expected

      char *acp; FILE *fp;
      fputc(*acp+ +, fp);

Output to the stream **stdout** is unbuffered if it refers to a terminal. The integer EOF is returned by all functions on error; since this is a valid integer, **ferror** should be used to detect **putw** errors

puts(s)
fputs(s, stream)
      char *s; FILE *stream;

Puts copies the zero terminated string from s to **stdout** and appends a newline. **Fputs** copies the zero terminated string from s to the stream specified. Neither function copies the terminating zero.

D.3.4. Formatted I/O

printf(format [, arg ...])
fprintf(stream, format [, arg ...])
sprintf(s, format [, arg ...])
      char *s, *format; FILE *stream;

Each of the above functions converts, formats and prints its arguments (**arg** ...) under the control of the format given by the string 'format'. **Printf** places its output on **stdout**, **fprintf** places its output on a stream and **sprintf** places its output in the string pointed to by s, then appends the zero character (null).

The format string is examined character by character; it is printed out exactly as read until a '%' is found. This special character is used to introduce a format conversion which determines how the next argument (arg) is to be printed. The simplest specification is a single character following the '%':

    d   the integer arg is printed in decimal

    o   the integer arg is printed in octal

    x   the integer arg is printed in hexadecimal

    c   the arg is interpreted as a character

s	the arg is taken to be a character pointer (string). Characters are printed from the string until a null character is reached.
f	the float or double arg is printed out in the form [−]ddd.ddd
e	the float or double arg is printed out in the form [−]d.dd-de[+ −]dd
g	the float or double arg is printed in style %d, %f or %e, whichever is the shortest yet still giving full precision. Non-significant zeros are not printed
u	the integer arg is printed as an unsigned decimal number.

Any other character is printed exactly as it appears; thus '%%' may be used to print '%'

Between the '%' and the conversion character there may be optionally:

A minus sign, ' − ', which indicates left adjustment of the converted value in its field.

A digit string specifying a minimum field width; if there are fewer characters in the converted value then it will be padded to the left (or right if ' − ' has been given). The padding character is normally blank; if the field width begins with a zero then zero padding will be done.

A period, '.', which separates the field width from the next digit string.

A digit string specifying a precision for printing float or double numbers or the maximum number of characters to be printed from a string.

The character 'l' which indicates that a following **d**, **o**, **x** or **u** refers to a long integer arg. (An upper-case conversion character may be used instead. i.e. %ld is equivalent to %D.)

scanf(format [, ptr ...])
fscanf(stream, format [, ptr ...])
sscanf(s, stream [, ptr ...])
    char ∗s, format; FILE ∗stream;
The above variations of **scanf** provide the same conversion facilities as **printf** but in the opposite direction. Characters are read from some source and analysed according to the specification in the string 'format'.

The results are stored using the remaining arguments, which must be pointers to variables of the appropriate type. **Scanf** reads from **stdin**; **fscanf** reads from a stream; and **sscanf** reads from the zero terminated string pointed to by s.

The format string contains conversion specifications which are used to control the interpretation of input; it may contain:

Blanks, tabs or newlines ('white space') which may optionally match white space in the input. Otherwise they are ignored.

Ordinary characters (NOT **'%'**) which must match the next character in the input.

Conversion specifications, consisting of the character '%', followed by a conversion character. Between these two characters there may optionally be a number specifying the maximum field width and/or a '*' signifying that this field is to be ignored.

Also, optionally, the character 'l' which indicates that a following **d**, **o** or **x** refers to a long integer and the corresponding argument is a pointer to a long rather than an int. Similarly **c** or **f** may be preceeded by 'l' to indicate that a double rather than float is wanted. An upper-case conversion character may be used instead, i.e. %F is equivalent to %lf

The characters **d**, **o** and **x** may be preceded by 'h' to indicate a pointer to short rather than int. (There may be no difference on your machine.)

Input fields are strings of non-blank characters, extending to either the next blank character or until the field width, if specified, is reached. A conversion specification controls the conversion of the next input field, the result is placed into the location(s) pointed to by the corresponding argument. If assignment suppression, '*', is indicated then the field is simply skipped. Since the newline character is treated as blank (white space) **scanf** will read across line boundaries to find input.

The conversion characters are similar to those for **printf** and are interpreted thus:

d   a decimal integer is expected in the input; the corresponding argument should be an integer pointer.

o   an octal integer is expected; the corresponding argument should be an integer pointer.

x	a hexadecimal integer is expected; the corresponding argument should be an integer pointer.
c	a single character is expected; the corresponding argument should be a pointer to a single character variable. The normal skip over white space characters is suppressed, so use '%1s' to be sure of reading the next non-space character.
s	a character string is expected, which is terminated by either blank or newline. The corresponding argument should be a character pointer pointing to an array large enough to hold the string plus a terminating zero which is added.
f	a floating point number is expected; the corresponding argument should be a pointer to a float variable; the character 'e' is a synonym for 'f'. The format for floating point numbers is a combination of the 'e' and 'f' **printf** formats; it consists of an optional minus sign, a string of digits possibly containing a decimal point, followed by an optional exponent field consisting of an 'E' or 'e' followed by an integer (optionally signed).
[	a character string **not** delimited by white space characters is expected. The left bracket is followed by a set of characters which make up the string and a right bracket. If the first character in the set is ' ∧ ' (circumflex) then the string is delimited by one of the characters from the remaining set. Otherwise, the string is delimited by any character not in the set; that is, the string must comprise only those characters between the brackets. The corresponding argument must be a character pointer as for '%s'.

% a single '%' is expected, no conversion is done.

Scanf returns the number of successful matches, zero if there were none, and EOF on end of file.

D.3.5. Interprocess I/O (pipes)

FILE *popen(cmd, type)
pclose(stream)
    char *cmd, *type; FILE *stream;
Popen causes the shell command line contained in the string 'cmd' to be

executed with a pipe connecting the standard input and output of the command line to the calling process. The string 'type' contains either 'r' for reading on the pipe or 'w' for writing. A file pointer is returned which can be used to write to the standard input of the command or read from its standard output. **Pclose** should always be used to close a stream opened by **popen**, it waits for the command to terminate and then returns its exit status. A value of -1 is returned if the stream was not opened by a **popen** .

D.3.6. Stream manipulation

fseek(stream, offset, whence)
long ftell(stream)
rewind(stream)
      FILE *stream; long offset;
Fseek is the SIO equivalent of the system call **lseek**. The position of the next input/output operation is set to offset if whence is 0, current location plus offset if whence is 1, and size of file plus offset if whence is 2. Any previous effect of an **ungetc** is forgotten after an **fseek**. **Ftell** returns the value of the current offset into the file associated with stream. **Rewind(stream)** is equivalent to

      fseek(stream, (long)0, 0)

setbuf(stream, buf)
      FILE *stream; char *buf;
Stream buffers are normally allocated dynamically from calls to **malloc**, alternatively, **setbuf** may be used after the stream has been opened, but before any I/O is performed; it causes the array pointed to by buf to be used instead. If buf is the pointer NULL then I/O will be unbuffered.

D.3.7. Close a stream

fclose(stream)
fflush(stream)
      FILE *stream;
Fclose empties any buffers associated with the specified stream and then closes the file. **Fflush** writes out any buffered data for the stream which remains open. To close a stream that has been used for output **fflush** should be called, then **fclose**.

D.4 Math Functions

Functions from the library **/lib/libm.a** are loaded automatically by the

FORTRAN compiler; C programs need the '−lm' flag to **cc**. Any program using math functions should include the file 'math.h', that is, they should have the line

    #include <math.h>

near the beginning. This is necessary for correct typing of the functions.

D.4.1. Bessel functions

double j0(x) double x;
double j1(x) double x;
double jn(n, x) double n, x;
double y0(x) double x;
double y1(x) double x;
double yn(x) double n, x;
The above calculate Bessel functions of first and second kinds for real arguments and integer orders. Negative arguments cause y0, y1 and yn to return a huge negative value and set errno to EDOM.

D.4.2. Trigonometric functions

double sin(x) double x;
double cos(x) double x;
double tan(x) double x;
double asin(x) double x;
double acos(x) double x;
double atan(x) double x;
double atan2(x,y) double x,y;
Sin cos and **tan** take radian arguments and return the appropriate trigonometric function. The value returned by **tan** at its singular points is huge and errno is set to ERANGE. **Asin** returns the arc sine in the range −pi/2 to pi/2. **Acos** returns the arc cosine in the range 0 to pi/2. Both **asin** and **acos** return 0 for arguments of magnitude greater than 1 and errno is set to EDOM. **Atan** returns the arc tangent in the range −pi/2 to pi/2. **Atan2** returns the arc tangent of x/y in the range −pi to pi.

D.4.3. Hyperbolic functions

double sinh(x) double x;
double cosh(x) double x;
double tanh(x) double x;
The above return the corresponding hyperbolic functions for real arguments. A huge number of the appropriate sign is returned if the correct value would overflow.

D.4.4. Euclidean distance functions

double hypot(x, y) double x;
double cabs(z) struct { double x, y; } z;
Both functions return

    sqrt(x*x + y*y)

D.4.5. Miscellaneous

double ceil(x) double x;
Ceil returns the smallest integer not less than x.

double exp(x); double x;
The exponential function of x is returned.

double fabs(x) double x;
The absolute value of the integer x is returned.

double floor(x) double x;
The largest integer not greater than x is returned.

double log(x) double x;
double log10(x) double x;
Log returns the natural logarithm of x; **log10** returns the base 10 logarithm.

double pow(x, y); double x, y;
Pow returns the value of x raised to the power y.

double sqrt(x) double x;
The square root of x is returned.

D.5. Miscellany

abort()
Abort is machine dependent. On the PDP-11 an IOT instruction is executed which causes a core dump. There are better methods of debugging available ! (e.g. adb)

abs(x)
The absolute value of integer x is returned.

#include <assert.h>
assert(expression)
Assert is a macro which indicates that the expression should be true

(not zero) at this point in the program. If the the expression proves to be false (0) then an **exit** is caused with a diagnostic comment on the standard output. Assertion may be turned off by compiling with the **cc** option − **DNDEBUG**

double atof(ptr) char *ptr;
atoi(ptr) char *ptr;
long atol(ptr) char *ptr;
These functions convert a character string pointed to by 'ptr' to floating (**atof**), integer (**atoi**), and long integer (**atol**) representations. They ignore leading spaces and tabs and recognise an optional sign.

char *crypt(key, salt) char *key, *salt;
setkey(key) char *key;
encrypt(block, edflag) char *block;
Crypt is the encryption routine for passwords, it is based on the NBS Data Encryption Standard. 'Key' is the string to be encrypted and 'salt' is a two character string chosen from [a–zA–Z0–9./] which is used to perturb the encryption algorithm. A pointer to the encrypted string is returned. **Setkey** and **encrypt** provide direct access to the DES algorithm for users who wish to implement their own security scheme.

#**include** <**time.h**>
char *ctime(clock) long *clock;
struct tm *localtime(clock) long *clock;
struct tm *gmtime(clock) long *clock;
char *asctime(tm) struct tm *tm;
char *timezone(zone, dst)
Ctime converts a time pointed to by 'clock', such as returned from the system call **time** into ascii and returns a pointer to a zero terminated string of the form

   Mon Mar 8 18:33:58 GMT 1982\n

All the fields have constant width; so to print out just the month and date the following C statements may be used

  long clock;

  time(&clock); printf('%.6s\n', &ctime(&clock)[4]);

Localtime and **gmtime** return pointers to structures containing the broken-down time, and **localtime** corrects for the time zone; **gmtime** converts directly to GMT, which is the time UNIX uses. **Asctime** converts a broken-down time, as produced by **localtime** or **gmtime**

and returns a pointer to a zero terminated string of the same form as produced by **ctime**. **Timezone** returns a pointer to a string containing the name of the time zone associated with 'zone'.

#include <ctype.h>
isalpha(c), isupper(c), islower(c), isdigit(c), isalnum(c), isspace(c), ispunct(c), isprint(c), iscntrl(c), isascii(c)
These are macros to perform character tests; each returns non-zero if the test is true and zero if false.

isalpha(c)   − true if c is a letter
isupper(c)   − true if c is an upper case letter
islower(c)   − true if c is a lower case letter
isdigit(c)   − true if c is a digit (0–9)
isalnum(c)   − true if c is an alphanumeric character (letter or digit)
isspace(c)   − true if c is a space, tab, carriage return, newline or formfeed
ispunct(c)   − true if c is a punctuation character (not control or alphanumeric)
isprint(c)   − true if c is a printing character (in the range 040 thru 0176)
iscntrl(c)   − true if c is a control character or delete (0–037 and 0177)
isascii(c)   − true if c is an ASCII character (less than 0200)

char *ecvt(value, ndigit, decpt, sign)
char *fcvt(value, ndigit, decpt, sign)
char *gcvt(value, ndigit, buf)
     double value; int ndigit *decpt, *sign; char *buf;
These routines convert numererical values to zero terminated strings of characters. **Ecvt** is the simplest of the routines, it returns the position of the decimal within the string via 'decpt'. The sign of the converted string is indicated by the value of the integer pointed to by 'sign', a negative result gives non-zero, zero for positive. **Fcvt** is identical to **ecvt** except that the output is to FORTRAN F-format. **Gcvt** places the converted string in 'buf' and returns a pointer to 'buf'. FORTAN F-format is produced if possible, E-format otherwise.

extern end;
extern etext;
extern edata;
The above names do not refer to functions, they are fixed locations within a compiled program. **Etext** is the first address above the program text, **edata** above the initialised data region, and **end** above the uninitialised

data region. When execution begins, the program break (the top of memory available to the program) coincides with **end** but many functions reset this. The current value of the program break is returned by 'sbrk(0);'.

double frexp(num, eptr) double num; int *eptr;
double ldexp(num, exp) double num;
double modf(num, iptr) double num, *iptr;
These functions are used for splitting floating format numbers into mantissa and exponent. **Frexp** returns the mantissa of num as a double quantity of magnitude less than 1, and the exponent via pointer 'eptr'. **Ldexp** returns the value 'num * 2**exp'. **Modf** returns the fractional part of num and stores the integer part via 'iptr'.

char *getenv(name) char *name;
A process environment description consists of strings of the form 'name=value' (see environ(5)) . **Getenv** searches for a string of the above form such that the name part matches 'name' and returns a pointer to a zero terminated string containing its value. If no match can be found NULL is returned.

#**include** <**grp.h**>
struct group *getgrent()
struct group *getgrgid(gid) int gid;
struct group *getgrnam(name) char *name;
setgrent()
endgrent()
These functions are used for manipulating the entries in the group file '/etc/group'. The pointer NULL is returned on error.

char *getlogin()
Getlogin returns a pointer to the login name of the user who owns the process. If the process has no typewriter attached then NULL is returned.

char *getpass(prompt) char *prompt;
Getpass reads a line from the standard input after printing the zero terminated string 'prompt' and turning off echoing. A pointer to a zero terminated string of at most 8 characters is returned.

getpw(uid, buf) char *buf;
Getpw searches the password file '/etc/passwd' for the numerical uid. If successful it fills in the character array pointed to by 'buf' with the corresponding zero terminated line and returns zero, otherwise non-zero is returned to indicate failure.

#include <pwd.h>
struct passwd *getpwent()
struct passwd *getpwuid(uid)
struct passwd *getpwnam(name) char *name;
setpwent()
endpwent()
These functions are used for manipulating entries in the password file
'/etc/passwd'. The pointer NULL is returned on error.

l3tol(lp, cp, n) long *lp; char *cp;
ltol3(cp, lp, n) char *cp; long *lp;
L3tol converts a list of n three byte integers pointed to by 'cp' into a list
of long integers pointed to by 'lp'. **Ltol3** performs the reverse conversion.
These functions are used by programs that manipulate the file-system;
e.g. **icheck** and **dcheck**

char *malloc(size) unsigned size;
free(ptr) char *ptr;
char *realloc(ptr, size) char *ptr; unsigned size;
char *calloc(nelem, elsize) unsigned nelem, elsize;
These functions provide a simple memory allocation system. **Malloc**
returns a pointer to a block of memory of at least 'size' bytes, aligned to a
word boundary. When no longer needed this block should be released
using **free**. **Realloc** may be used to change the size of a block previously
allocated by **malloc**. **Calloc** returns a pointer to enough memory to hold
nelem object of size elsize, or the NULL pointer if the request cannot be
satisfied. The usual use of this function is

        ptr = calloc(n, sizeof(object));

char *mktemp(template) char *template;
Mktemp uses the string pointed to by 'template' to construct a unique
filename using the current process id. Template should be a zero
terminated string with six trailing X's, e.g.

        char *acp;
        acp = mktemp('/tmp/andyxxxxxx');

monitor(lowpc, highpc, buffer, bufsize, nfunc)
        int (*lowpc)(), (*highpc)(); short buffer[];
Monitor is used to generate an execution profile of C programs. The
'−p' flag to **cc** automatically creates calls to **monitor** with default
parameters.

#include <a.out.h>
nlist(filename, nl) char *filename; struct nlist nl[];
Nlist extracts symbol table information from the name list of the executable file 'filename'. 'nl' consists of an array of structures containing names, types and values, terminated by a null name. If name is found , its type and value are inserted into the appropriate fields of nl.

perror(s) char *s;
int sys__nerr;
char *sys__errlist[];
Perror first prints on the standard error file (stderr) the zero terminated string 's' and then a message describing the last error that occurred during a system call. The message is determined by indexing into the array of character pointers, **sys__errlist**, using the external variable 'errno'. **Sys__errno** contains the number of messages provided in the table.

qsort(base, nel, width, compar) char *base; int (*compar)();
Qsort is an implementation of the quicker-sort algorithm. The user must provide a comparison function, 'compar', to be called with two arguments which are pointers to the elements being considered. Compar should return an integer value less than, equal to, or greater than zero according to whether the first argument is to be considered less than, equal to, or greater than the second.

rand()
srand(seed)
Rand returns a psedo-random number in the range 0 to 28158. The generator is initialised to a random starting point by calling **srand** with whatever you like.

#include <setjmp.h>
setjmp(env) jmp__buf env;
longjmp(env) jmp__buf env;
These functions are used for performing non-local jumps in C programs; they are useful for dealing with errors which occur in a deeply nested function. **Setjmp** saves its stack environment in 'env' for later use by **longjmp**, which returns in such a way that it appears if **setjmp** has just returned the value 'val' to the function that invoked **setjmp**. **Setjmp** itself returns zero.

sleep(seconds) unsigned seconds;
The current process is suspended from execution for the integer number of seconds specified by 'seconds'.

String handling functions

```
char *strcat(s1, s2)
char *strncat(s1, s2, n)
strcmp(s1, s2)
strncmp(s1, s2, n)
*strcpy(s1, s2)
char *strncpy(s1, s2, n)
strlen(s)
char *index(s, c)
char *rindex(s, c)
     char c, *s, *s1, *s2;
```

These functions operate on zero terminated strings; they do NOT check for overflow when creating or appending to strings. It is up to the user to check that there is enough space available in the receiving array. **Strcat** appends the string pointed to by 's1' onto the end of the string pointed to by 's2'; **strncat** copies only n characters of string s2. Both functions return a pointer to the new string. **Strcmp** compares the two strings s1, s2 and returns an integer value greater than, equal to, or less than zero depending on whether the string s1 was lexically less than, equal to, or greater than the string s2. **Strncmp** compares at most n characters from the strings. **Strcpy** copies the string pointed to by s2 to the place pointed at by s1; **strncpy** copies at most only n characters of string s2 truncating or null padding as appropriate. Both functions return a pointer to s1. **Strlen** returns the number of characters in string 's'. **Index** returns a pointer to the first occurence of character 'c' in string s; **rindex** returns a pointer to the last occurence. Both return the value zero if character c does not occur in the string.

swab(from, to, nbytes) char *from, *to;
This function is useful when transferring binary data between two machines with different byte order. **Nbytes** are copied from location 'from' to location 'to' swapping adjacent even and odd bytes.

system(cmd_string) char *cmd_string;
System executes the command line contained in the zero terminated string 'cmd_string'. When the command line finishes execution **system** returns to the calling process with the value of the command's exit status. The command executes as if it had been typed in response to a shell prompt; a returned value of 127 indicates the command couldn't be executed.

```
char *ttyname(fildes)
isatty(fildes)
ttyslot()
```
These functions are used for determining the existence of a controlling
terminal for the current process. **Ttyname** returns a pointer to a zero
terminated string containing the path name of the terminal device
associated with file descriptor fildes, otherwise the pointer NULL. **Isatty**
returns non-zero if a terminal is associated with fildes, 0 otherwise.
Ttyslot returns the entry number in the ttys file '/etc/ttys' for the
controlling terminal of the current process, 0 if none can be found.

D.6 Special Libraries

D.6.1. Multiple Precision Arithmetic

Routines from this library can perform arithmetic on integers of
arbitrary length.

```
Loader flag : -lmp
Functions :
typedef struct { int len; short *val; } mint;
madd(a, b, c)
msub(a, b, c)
mult(a, b, c)
mdiv(a, b, q, r)
min(a)
mout(a)
pow(a, b, m, c)
gcd(a, b, c)
rpow(a, b, c)
msqrt(a, b, r)          mint *a, *b, *c, *m, *q, *r;
sdiv(a, n, q, r)        mint *a, *q; short *r;
mint *itom(n)
```
Integers to be used with these functions should be stored using the type
mint; pointers to **mint** may be initialised using **itom** which sets the
initial value to n. **Madd**, **msub** and **mult** assign to their third argument,
c, the sum, difference and product, respectively, of their first two
arguments a and b. **Mdiv** assigns the quotient and remainder to q and r.
Sdiv is like **mdiv** except that the divisor, n, is an ordinary integer. **Msqrt**
produces the square root and remainder of a. **Rpow** calculates a raised to
the power b; **pow** calculates the reduced modulo m. (Whatever that is?)
Min and **mout** do decimal input and output.

D.6.2. Graphics Interface Routines

Functions from this library generate graphical output in a device independent fashion. The **plot** filter may be used to transform the output from a program using these functions and draw on a particular device.

Functions :
openpl()
This function must be called before any other to open the device for writing.

erase()
Another frame, or page, of output is started.

label(s) char *s;
The string 's' is written so that its first character falls on the current point. The string is terminated by either newline or zero.

line(x1, y1, x2, y2)
Draw a line from x1,y1 to x2,y2.

circle(x, y, r)
Draw a circle with centre x,y and radius r.

arc(x, y, x0, y1, x1, y1)
Draw an arc of a circle with centre x,y, starting point x1,y2, and end point x2,y2. The arc is drawn counter-clockwise.

move(x, y)
The current plotting point is moved to x,y.

cont(x, y)
A continuous line is drawn from the current point to x,y.

point(x, y)
Plot a point at x,y.

linemod(s) char *s;
The zero terminated string **s** is used as a style for plotting subsequent lines. The possible styles are **dotted, solid, longdashed, shortdashed** and **dotdashed**. **Linemod** will only have effect if the hardware is capable of plotting non-continuous lines.

space(x0, y0, x1, y1)
Define an area for plotting; x0,y0 gives the lower left hand corner, and
x1,y1 gives the upper right hand corner. The plot produced is scaled to fit
the actual plotting device as closely as possible; the area is always taken
to be square.

closepl()
used to flush the output.

Loader flags :

−**lplot**	device-independent commands output to **stdout** for **plot**(l)
−**l300**	output for GSI 300 terminal.
−**l300s**	output for GSI 300S terminal.
−**l450**	output for DASI terminal.
−**l4014**	output for Tektronix 4014 or compatible devices

System Calls

For reference we now provide a list of important system calls and their uses. The descriptions will contain things like this:

    long lseek(fildes,offset,whence)
    long offset;

which means that **lseek** is a function returning a **long** value, and that the **offset** parameter is also a **long** whilst all the others are **int** in type. Arguments defined as **char ∗xxx;** can be replaced with strings – many users don't realise this. Look at **open** and compare its definition with its use earlier. Some definitions mention #**include** <**xxx.h**>, this means that a header file containing useful definitions should be included in programs using this call.

These are not full descriptions of the calls, neither are all the calls described – ones likely to be regarded as 'curiosities' have been left out. You will *not* learn enough from these descriptions to be able to use the calls; they're meant for people who want a quick crib – if in doubt you'll have to look in the proper manual.

UNIX system calls

access(name,mode)char ∗name;
Check file named for access w.r.t. real uid & gid. Mode 4 for read, 2 for write, 1 for execute – these may be ORed for combinations. Mode 0 checks pathname. Returns 0 for success −1 for failure.

acct(file)char ∗file;
Turn on accounting; info goes to file. Argument of zero turns it off. Super user only.

alarm(seconds)unsigned seconds;
Causes the alarm signal to be sent to this process in the specified number of seconds. Returns number of seconds left in previous timer.

char *brk(addr)
char *sbrk(incr)
Gets more memory; up to addr for brk or adds incr to the break if using sbrk. Returns 0 for success, −1 for failure.

chdir(dirname)char *dirname;
Changes current directory to dirname. Returns 0 for success, −1 for failure.

chmod(name,mode)char *name;
Change the mode of a file − see filestore details for what the modes may be. Only the owner or the super user may change a file's mode. Returns 0 for success, −1 for failure.

chown(name,owner,group)char *name;
Change ownership & group of a file. Super user only. Returns 0 for success, −1 for failure.

close(fildes)
Close the file whose descriptor is fildes. Returns 0 for success, −1 for failure.

creat(name,mode)char *name;
Create the named file with mode specified. Returns a file descriptor if successful (for writing), −1 on failure.

dup(old)
dup2(old,new)
Returns a new file descriptor which is a duplicate of old. Dup returns the first free one, dup2 the one specified by the new argument. returned. If new was open it's closed first. Returns −1 on error.

execle(name,arg0,arg1,.....,0,envp)char *name,*arg1,... *envp[];
execve(name,argv,envp)char *name,*argv[],*envp[];
Execute named file.Depending on which version used, you supply a list of character pointers or an array of them. Both versions are terminated by a null pointer. The environment list is always an array of character pointers, terminated by a null one. Look this call up in the manual. Returns −1 on error, does not return if successful.

exit(arg)
Exit from the program. Cleans up certain things like the standard i/o buffers. Calling __exit prevents any cleanup. Low 8 bits of arg available for parent. Does not ever return.

fork()
Split into two. Parent is returned pid of child, child is returned zero. -1 returned if fork not possible.

getpid()
Returns pid of current process.

getuid()
getgid()
geteuid()
getegid()
Return uid, gid, or the effective uid, gid.

#include <sgtty.h>
ioctl(fildes,request,argp)struct sgtty *argp;
Used in multifarious ways. See manual. Returns -1 on failure, 0 for success.

kill(pid,sig)
Sends the signal sig to process number pid. Sender and target must have same effective uid, unless sender is super user. If pid is zero, all process in this process group get the signal. If pid is -1 and sender is super user, signal is sent to all processes except 0 and 1. Returns 0 for success, -1 for failure.

link(name1,name2)char *name1,*name2;
Make a link called name2 to file name1. Return 0 for success, -1 for failure.

long lseek(fildes,offset,whence)long offset;
Move r/w pointer of file descriptor fildes, pointer moved to offset if whence 0, current location plus offset if whence 1, size of file plus offset if whence 2. Returns previous position or -1 if error.

mknod(name,mode,addr)char *name;
Super user only. Creates a new file with given name and mode, mode may contain directory bits, special file etc. The addr argument is used to specify which special file – normally zero unless special file. Returns 0 for success, -1 on failure.

mount(special,name,rwflag)char *special,*name;
Mounts special file at filestore node named. If rwflag nonzero, no writing will be done on this volume. Returns 0 for success, -1 for failure.

nice(incr)
Set scheduling priority of this process to current plus incr, in range $+20$ to -20, out of range values are truncated to within range. Positive is lower priority. Only super user may give negative increments.

open(name,mode)char *name;
Open named file. Mode 0 for read, 1 for write, 2 for both. Returns a file descriptor or -1 on error.

pause()
Process is stopped until it gets a signal.

pipe(fildes)int fildes[2];
This creates a pipe. Two file descriptors are returned, in fildes[0] you get the read one, fildes[1] is for writing on. Writing to a pipe without a reading process causes a signal. Returns 0 for success, -1 for failure.

profil(...)
Used to get execution profile of your process. Details depend on implementation.

#include <signal.h>
ptrace(request,pid,addr,data)int *addr;
Used whilst tracing/debugging running processes. Details depend on implementation.

read(fildes,buf,bytes)char *buffer;
The number of bytes is read from the file defined by fildes into buf. Bytes is the maximum length of the read and may not be completely fulfilled, particularly from teletypes. Returns 0 for end of file, -1 for error, otherwise number of bytes actually read.

setuid(uid)
setgid(gid)
Set user/group id. Sets both real and effective. You may only supply your real uid/gid unless you are super user. Returns 0 for success, -1 for failure.

#include <signal.h>
(*signal(sig,func)()(*func)();
That lot means a function returning a pointer to a function. The func argument is also a function pointer. After the call, when signal sig is received, function func is called with the signal number as the argument.

See your manual. Returns the previous value of func for that signal, −1 if no such signal known.

#**include** <**sys/types.h**>
#**include** <**sys/stat.h**>
stat(name,buf)char *name;struct stat buf;
fstat(fildes,buf)struct stat *buf;
Copies all sorts of information about an i-node into buf. The two versions allow you to give either a name or a file descriptor as the argument. See your manual. Returns 0 on success, −1 on failure.

stime(tp)long *tp;
Sets the system's time from wherever tp points; this represents seconds since 0hrs GMT Jan 1 1970. Must be super user. Returns 0 on success, −1 on failure.

sync( )
Causes operating system buffers to be flushed and written to disc. Ordinary users may ignore this.

long time(tloc)long *tloc;
#**include** <**sys/types.h**>
#**include** <**sys/timeb.h**>
ftime(tp)struct timeb *tp;
These are used to get the system's idea of the time, as set by 'stime'. Time returns a long integer containing the value, also if tloc is a nonzero value, the same result is stored where tloc points. Ftime fills in a structure defined in the timeb.h header file − see the manual.

times(buffer)struct tbuffer *buffer;
Used to find time accounting information. The place where buffer points contains 4 long integers: proc__user__time, proc__system__time, child__user__time, child__system__time.

umask(mask)
The mask shows which bits must be zero in the mode of any files created after this call. Returns the previous value of the mask.

unlink(name)char *name;
Unlinks a directory entry. If this was the last link, the file is destroyed when the last process which has it open closes it. Returns 0 for success, −1 on failure. Only super user may unlink directories; bits of the filestore become detached if non-empty directories are unlinked.

#include <sys/types.h>
utime(file,timep)char *file; time_t timep[2];
Set the 'accessed' and 'updated' times (in that order) from timep. You must own the file or be super user. Returns 0 for success, −1 for failure, we think.

wait(status)int *status;
Find out about children terminated. Pid of child is returned, *status set to returned status; high byte is value returned by child, low byte is system status. Low byte contains signal number causing termination if any; ORed with 0200 if a core image was produced. Returns −1 if no children.

write(fildes,buffer,nbytes)char *buffer;
Just like read but writes. Normally all nbytes will be written. Returns −1 on error.

Errors

Here follows a very brief list of possible errors from system calls, together with their standard names, which are defined in <errno.h>. The error number is set in the external variable 'errno' for use after the error.

ERROR	NAME	MEANING
0	none	nothing
1	EPERM	you don't have permission
2	ENOENT	can't find the file
3	ESRCH	no such process
4	EINTR	system call interrupted by signal
5	EIO	i/o error
6	ENXIO	no such i/o device
7	E2BIG	too many arguments to 'exec'
8	ENOEXEC	wrong format for executable file
9	EBADF	bad file descriptor
10	ECHILD	no children
11	EAGAIN	can't fork
12	ENOMEM	too little memory available
13	EACCESS	you can't do this to this file
14	EFAULT	bad memory address supplied
15	ENOTBLK	wrong sort of device
16	EBUSY	device already in use
17	EEXIST	the file already exists
18	EXDEV	you can't link across devices
19	ENODEV	silly access to this device

20	ENOTDIR	directory name expected
21	EISDIR	directory name not expected
22	EINVAL	invalid argument (obscure)
23	ENFILE	system out of file table space
24	EMFILE	you want too many file descriptors
25	ENOTTY	not a teletype
26	ETXTBSY	file busy – you can't write/execute it
27	EFBIG	file became too big
28	ENOSPC	disc out of space
29	ESPIPE	seek on a pipe
30	EROFS	read only filesystem
31	EMLINK	too many links to a file
32	EPIPE	write on a broken pipe
33	EDOM	out of domain
34	ERANGE	result too large/small to be held

The last two are not errors from system calls, but set by the library maths routines if errors occur. You might as well have them to complete the table.

Signals

A list of signals and their usual names; this list is for PDP11 UNIX systems. On non-PDP11 systems there may be some changes, especially to SIGIOT and SIGEMT which are caused by execution of certain PDP11 instructions. The include file <signal.h> contains the names of these signals and the definitions needed to use the **signal** library function.

signal	name	caused by
1	SIGHUP	hanging up a dial-in line
2	SIGINT	pressing the INTERRUPT key
3	SIGQUIT	sending the signal from elsewhere
4	SIGILL	illegal instruction
5	SIGTRAP	trace trap
6	SIGIOT	iot instruction
7	SIGEMT	emt instruction
8	SIGFPE	floating point exception
9	SIGKILL	like SIGQUIT, perhaps sent from 'kill' sys. call
10	SIGBUS	addressing error (bus error)
11	SIGSEGV	segmentation violation (bad address)
12	SIGSYS	bad argument to system call
13	SIGPIPE	write on pipe, no reader
14	SIGALRM	alarm clock signal

You must re-apply to catch all but signals 4 and 5 every time they are received. Signals 3,4,5,6,7,8,10,11 and 12 will cause a core image to be taken if they are received by a process which is not catching or ignoring them. Signal 9 can't be caught or ignored and is the one guaranteed way of killing a process you want to be rid of – send it signal 9 and that's the end of it.

The number of signals is restricted to sixteen for reasons to do with the way that signals are implemented inside the operating system, but there's no philosophical restriction to prevent more being implemented.